READINGS
ON
DRUG EDUCATION

Prepared by

American Foundation for Continuing Education
at Syracuse University

Michael V. Reagen

Editor

The Scarecrow Press, Inc.

Metuchen, N.J.   1972

Library of Congress Cataloging in Publication Data

Reagen, Michael V   comp.
  Readings on drug education.

  1. Drug abuse--United States--Addresses, essays, lec-
tures. 2. Drug abuse--Treatment--United States--Ad-
dresses, essays, lectures. I. American Foundation for
Continuing Education. II. Title.
HV5825.R4   362.2'93   72-7237
ISBN 0-8108-0548-0

A NOTE ON THE AMERICAN FOUNDATION
FOR CONTINUING EDUCATION

The AFCE is a not-for-profit educational organization, currently based at Syracuse University, devoted to the development of reading material in many fields. We should be happy to have your comments and criticism on <u>Readings on Drug Education,</u> as such evaluations will help determine the direction of public policy programs adopted by our Board of Directors.

Alexander N. Charters
President, AFCE

Address all correspondence to:
Doris S. Chertow, Editor
American Foundation for Continuing Education
105 Roney Lane
Syracuse, New York 13210

ACKNOWLEDGEMENTS

This book and all of the other educational materials developed by the staff of the Continuing Education Center for the Public Service at Syracuse University for the Institute for Drug Education were produced under the auspices of the Onondaga County Department of Mental Health with funds from the New York State Narcotics Addiction Control Commission and the assistance of the Board of Cooperative Educational Services of Onondaga County.

Many individuals played important "behind the scenes" roles in the development of this volume. Several public officials who indirectly facilitated its production deserve recognition: The Honorable John Mulroy, County Executive for Onondaga County; Dr. Harold Rankin, Superintendent of Schools for Jamesville-Dewitt School System; New York State Senator Tarky Lombardi; and, Rayburn Hess of the New York State Narcotics Addiction Control Commission.

Five men at Syracuse University were especially helpful. Thomas Briggs, Associate Professor of Social Work, first suggested the idea of a volume of this type a year ago. Lee Smith, Assistant Dean of University College, provided warm encouragement and support throughout the book's development; Jere Hallenbeck, a guest lecturer at the Continuing Education Center; Sol Gordon, Professor of Family Life and Child Development; and William Alsever, Professor of Preventative Medicine, served as editorial consultants.

Special mention must be made of two women: Wanda Hoffman, a Ph.D. candidate at the Maxwell School for Citizenship and Public Affairs, and Dr. Doris Chertow of the American Foundation for Continuing Education. Mrs. Hoffman prepared the original manuscript and Dr. Chertow provided the editor with invaluable assistance.

Without the cooperation of generous authors and publishers, inclusion of much of the material in this volume would not have been possible.

Syracuse University   Michael V. Reagen, Ph.D.
Research Corporation
July, 1972

INTRODUCTION

The substances we refer to as "drugs" have been used--in one form or another--by people since the start of recorded history. But the rampant misuse of drugs appears to be primarily a twentieth century, American phenomenon.

The fact that millions of our citizens-- representing all walks of life and all age groups--are abusing a wide variety of substances for, apparently, many different reasons should perplex all thoughtful Americans.

Our current "drug problem" has obvious cultural and pathological implications which threaten to recast the basic fabric of our society. We have several theories about why we have a drug problem and many notions about preventing and treating it. But we do not have any real answers.

In fact, as a society, we are expending more energy publicizing drug abuse than we are in trying to understand it. We are spending more funds to cope with it than we are in researching basic questions about it. Only recently have we begun to seriously and systematically attempt to study drug abuse.

American history is rich with examples of the development of solutions to societal problems before the problems themselves were clearly defined. We are an impulsive people who have a tendency to act swiftly more than wisely.

This book of readings was not designed to be a definitive work; rather, it merely represents an attempt to provide its reader with a brief, descriptive overview of some of the complexities of the drug abuse problem.

Although the intended audience for this volume are teachers in our nation's schools, this book should be a valuable reference for parents, clergy and others concerned about our nation's well-being.

Our purpose in producing this book is to stimulate all its readers to learn more about the drug abuse dilemma. Unless every responsible American commits himself to continuing his education, we can never hope to humanely and practically deal with the complex problems of our dynamic society.

iii

CONTENTS

STUDENT DRUG USE
by
Helen H. Nowlis*

Student drug use is a highly emotionally
charged topic for virtually everyone. For an increasing number of people "student" arouses be-
wilderment, frustration, even anger, and "drug"
adds a measure of panic, fear, revulsion, and
indignation. Together they hardly provide a
climate which is conducive to clear thinking and
to constructive action.

What I would like to do this afternoon is
to share with you some of the experiences I have
had during the past three years as a psychologist,
an educator, and an erstwhile psychopharmacologist
who has been concerned with all aspects of this
complex problem. I have managed to become involved with students who use a wide variety of
drugs in a variety of ways and for a variety of
reasons, with students who do not use drugs, with
scientists from biochemists to sociologists, with
professionals from medicine and education to various aspects of the mass media, with legislators
who make laws and with enforcement personnel who
are charged with enforcing those laws, as well as
with diverse segments of the general public.

I hope that many of you will not be dis-
appointed that we will be discussing only incidentally the prevalence of student drug use, the
kinds of drugs they use, and the outcomes of drug
use. There are others who can do this better
than I. In this connection I would strongly
recommend that anyone who is concerned with any
aspect of student drug use become thoroughly familiar with both the methodology and the conclusion
of Blum and his associates in his two important
recently published volumes, Society and Drugs and
Students and Drugs. My own role has been that of
psychologist analyzing the problem, interpreting
the research of others, assessing the current
state of our knowledge and relating it to what is
considered by many to be one of society's major

---

*Helen H. Nowlis, Ph.D., "Student Drug Use," in
F. F. Korten (ed.), Psychology and the Problems
of Society (Washington, D.C.: American Psychological Association, 1972), pp. 408-419.

problems. At least bills related to drug use and
abuse have been introduced in the current session
of Congress.

Although I shall be discussing one particular problem, I would like to suggest that it
is a prototype for many other problems which
involve individuals and groups of individuals,
society's response to some of the things they do,
and psychology's role in contributing to the understanding of these problems and, hopefully, to
their solution. I would also suggest that without being aware of it or without intending to do
so, many of us actually contribute to these
problems simply by the way we report our research.
Once was the time when we could talk only to each
other, and we developed a special elliptical dis-
course which, in most instances, communicated
effectively and efficiently. We no longer talk
only to each other, and our discourse--jargon for
others--with all of its implicit assumptions is
getting us into trouble. Our so-called conclusions are spread abroad by and to people who do
not understand sampling and correlation and experimental controls and significance of difference and the prevalence of error, who do not read
or understand our operational definitions, our
null hypotheses, of the limited validity and
reliability or our measures. They surround
every word we use with their own apperceptive
mass. The current "drug problem" is an excellent example of what can happen. One scientist
reports chromosome breakage in a "significant"
number of white blood cells as a result of adding
LSD in a test tube, and the word spreads across
the nation and reverberates in the halls of Congress that LSD is threatening future generations.
I am not at all sure how we can cope with this
problem, but it might be helpful if each of us
reread his Summary and Conclusions as if he were
John Doe and perhaps added a "may" or an "in
some cases," hopefully specified. We may even
have to include a new final paragraph, "Cautions."
It may not enhance one's ego or one's pleasure
over significance at the P=.01 level of confidence, but it certainly would help in educating
non-scientists in the proper use of scientific
information.

"Student drug use" has been widely interpreted as the "spread of narcotic addiction from
the ghetto to our middle class and suburban
youth," a threat to the future of our society.

In the wake of this increasingly widely held
feeling, it is almost impossible to study student
drug use or to discuss it objectively. In the
face of society's decision to consider much of
this drug use criminal, it is difficult even to
study it. In estimating incidence of use, of
adverse effects, of any drug-related phenomenon
we have many numerators but virtually no reliable denominators. The challenges involved in
persuading students that their admission to having committed a felony will be confidential and,
indeed, being able to guarantee that confidentiality are sometimes great.

Within the limits of the time available,
I would like to discuss the nature and extent
of student drug use, its meaning and significance, society's response to it, and some of
the problems resulting from efforts to control
it. But before we do this we must define some
terms lest we add to, rather than reduce, the
confusion and controversy which exists.

The first term we must define is "drug."
In our society there are two widely accepted
definitions of "drug," and both of these contain many implicit assumptions. One defines
drug as a chemical useful in the art and practice of medicine; the other defines drug as a
"narcotic" with narcotic defined as a socially
disapproved substance or an otherwise approved
substance used for socially disapproved reasons.
Many problems result from definitions based on
the purposes for which a drug is used. For
example, there is the fact that one and the
same substance may be a medicine under one cir-
cumstance and a "narcotic" under another or not
even a drug under still another. Secondly,
there is a great temptation to study one type
of drug or drug use out of the context of all
drugs. Third, there is a tendency to assume
that the use of all drugs which fall under one
definition has the same significance and the
same effects. This has led to complete confusion in surveys of student drug use. One investigator will ask if the individual has used
any drugs without the advice or supervision of
a physician, another will ask if the individual
has used specific socially disapproved drugs
(with the list varying from survey to survey),
and at least one has surveyed a wide span of
drugs, including social drugs such as alcohol
and tobacco, home remedies, painkillers,

prescription drugs, over-the-counter drugs, as well as exotic and illicit drugs. Only the latter is in any real sense a survey of student drug use. You will note that I have carefully avoided the word abuse. We will come to that later.

What is needed is a definition of drug which is objective and descriptive and does not have within it a variety of implicit value judgments which are the source of much of the confusion and controversy which abounds in discussions of drugs and drug use. The basic pharmacological definition of drug as any substance which by its chemical nature affects the structure or function of the living organism is about as descriptive and objective as one can be. This definition includes a wide range of substances. It includes both medicines and socially disapproved substances, and it also includes a wide range of substances which we do not call drugs ordinarily, such as beverage alcohol and caffeine, nicotine, agricultural, industrial, and household chemicals, pollutants, even food. For many purposes this is too broad a definition, but it forms a base from which we can select groups of drugs, and it forces us to make explicit the basis on which we make a given classification. Hopefully it reminds us that a drug is a drug, and the principles by which it interacts with the living organism are the same whether we call it a medicine, a "narcotic," or by some other name.

The other term which we must define is "use." Again, there are certain advantages in starting from a descriptive and objective base. Use is often defined in terms of frequency as ever having tried, occasional, regular, or excessive. But even these terms leave plenty of room for value judgments. It is necessary to specify each in terms of actual frequency of use over specified time. Whatever one's definition of excessive, it is then at least explicit.

This is perhaps the point at which we should consider abuse and to recognize that, as currently used, both socially and legally, it has little correspondence to use as I have defined it. In other contexts and even for our national drug, alcohol, abuse is defined as a pattern of use which interferes with the psychological, social, academic or vocational functioning of a given individual. As far as many other drugs

are involved, if we call them drugs, abuse is
legally defined as <u>any</u> use of a non-medically
approved drug or of a medically approved drug
for a non-medically approved purpose. Our efforts to justify and support this as abuse in
terms of "effects" of drugs so used are among
the main factors in the current controversy over
drugs. When research indicating that monosodium
glutamate injected peritoneally into pregnant
mice produces offspring with neural damage,
ataxia, obesity, and sterility, eminent experts
testify that this is irrelevant because people
do not inject MSG and, as commonly used, MSG
produces the temporary and relatively minor
symptoms of Chinese restaurant syndrome in only
a few individuals. When the same type of evidence is presented for LSD, it is used as at
least partial grounds for labelling it society's
most dangerous drug, placing it in a category
with heroin, and singling it out for the severest
criminal penalties. I am not making a case for
LSD. I am merely pointing out that we are invit-
ing controversy and charges of hypocrisy.

    With all of these qualifications and
with the recognition that we have absolutely no
research from which we can confidently generalize
to all students, what can we say about student
drug use? Most students use drugs. In Blum's
1967 survey of a random sample of approximately
200 students from each of five differing west
coast colleges, from 68% to 81% had used tobacco
one or more times, from 89% to 97% had used alcohol, from 11% to 32% had used amphetamines,
from 18% to 31% had used sedatives, from 11% to
28% had used tranquilizers, from 10% to 33% had
used marijuana, from 2% to 9% had used any of a
variety of hallucinogens, and from 1% to 2% had
used narcotics. Lest you forget, let me remind
you that these percentages represent reports of
having been used one or more times. A follow-
up survey in 1968 on marijuana use in the school
which had shown 21% marijuana use in the initial
survey showed 57% marijuana use. Reports of
regular use had increased from 6% to perhaps as
high as 17%. Opium use (not heroin) was estimated to have increased from 1% to 10%. Again,
a word of caution. We know on the basis of a
variety of surveys of institutions around the
country that use of illicit drugs varies from
institution to institution and from area to area.
We also know that the west coast tends to be a
relatively high use area. Even here, it is a

small minority of students who are involved in
regular use, with regular use defined as more
than once a week but less than daily.

There are two surveys in the planning
stage which should provide us with more adequate
data on which to base generalizations. One will
involve 200 colleges of varying sizes and loca-
tions, hopefully with a follow-up after two years.
The other will involve a sample of high schools
together with their feeder junior high schools
in a four-year longitudinal study.

Estimates currently made by Dr. Stanley
Yolles, Director of the National Institute of
Mental Health, on the basis of results of a
majority of studies which have been done throughout the country, are that from 20% to 40% of
high school and college students have tried
marihuana at least once. Of these about 65% are
experimenting (one to ten times and then discon-
tinuing use), 25% are social users, smoking on
occasion when it is available, and 10% of those
who have tried at least once use regularly, with
regular defined as devoting a significant portion
of their time to obtaining and using the drug.
This would mean that somewhere between two and
four per cent of students are regular users. This
would seem to bear little relationship to statements by prominent people headlined in the news
media that one out of ten students is "hooked"
on marihuana.

NIMH also estimates that the use of LSD,
even in relatively high use areas is low, with
probably not more than five per cent ever having
tried, and an even smaller percentage country-
wide.

There can be little doubt that use of
illicit drugs is increasing and that use is
spreading both up and down the age scale. In
recent years it has begun to appear at the
junior high and elementary school levels. Large
numbers of middle-class adults are believed to
be using marihuana. We do not have and probably
will not have hard data on this group (or any
group) as long as possession of marihuana is a
felony. In all cases it is the spread of marihuana use which is predominant. The fact that
there is increasing use of a mood-changing drug
should not surprise us. Mood-changing drugs
are the largest single type of drugs used, even

in prescriptions. The thing which is significant
is that marihuana is a drug which carries the
heaviest criminal penalties and a degree of
social disapproval equivalent to that of heroin
to most people.

The reasons for non-medical drug use are
predominantly the same reasons for which man has
used drugs throughout the ages: to relieve pain,
to allay anxiety, to produce euphoria, and to
modify experience, perception and thought. It
is tempting to speculate that modern man's increased use of mood and mind-altering substances
is at least in part an indication that modern
man has more pain, more anxiety, less euphoria,
and less satisfying experiences, but this is the
kind of speculation that has gotten us into
trouble. Many of the reasons that young people
use drugs are in large measure the reasons that
adults use drugs: for fun, to facilitate social
interaction, to feel better, to relieve boredom,
to escape from problems, even to protest a little.
The main difference is that most adults get their
stimulants and sedatives and tranquilizers from
physicians and their social drug, alcohol, is
legal. Their tension, anxiety, fatigue, and
depression are judged to be legitimate consequences of their full participation in pursuit
of socially approved social and economic goals
or values. That the outcomes of their drug use
are not always good is attested to by the fact
that an increasing number of hospital admissions
are directly attributable to drug related illness
and that we have from six to nine million alco-
holics, depending on how one defines alcoholic.

Please note my use of outcomes of drug
use rather than drug effects. The concept of
drug effect is an example of a term which may be
used to communicate effectively among scientists who understand how drugs act and that they
do not have within them the power to produce a
specifiable and reliable effect. The average
layman with his "magic-potion-notion" of drug
does not understand that we are really involved
in a numbers game. For example, the effective
dose (ED50) of any drug is that dosage level or
amount of the drug by which, not at which, fifty
per cent of a given population show whatever
effect is desired. The official toxic dose is
TD50 and depends on how one defines toxic. Even
the lethal dose (LD50) is that dosage level by
which fifty per cent of a group of animals die

under specified conditions. The lethal dose may
vary with the temperature under which the animals
are kept or whether they are housed singly or in
large groups. The reason for this numbers game
is that the "effect" of many drugs is largely a
function of non-drug factors.

"The effect" of any drug is a myth. All
drugs are chemicals which are absorbed into the
blood stream and interact with the complex,
delicately balanced biochemical system that is
the living organism. It is a system which varies
from individual to individual and from time to
time in the same individual. It varies with
age. It varies with sex. It varies in sickness
and health. One needs only to read the counter-
indications and the list of idiosyncratic and
side effects and diseases, and of medical progress in the advertisement of drugs in medical
and scientific journals to be aware of the com-
plexity of factors influencing the effects of a
drug. Effects also vary with psychological
characteristics of the individual, with his expectations, and with the setting in which the
drug is taken or administered. Outcomes of or
reactions to use of a drug at least put the
organism, physiologically and psychologically
defined, into the picture and leave room for
discrimination among patterns of use.

Whether outcome or reactions are good or
bad is a value judgment. The widely hailed outcome of treating mentally disturbed patients with
the major tranquilizers, i.e., "emptying our
mental hospitals," is considered by at least one
prominent psychiatrist to be the equivalent of
putting the patient in a chemical straight-
jacket and depriving him of his right to attempt
to solve his problems. The methadone treatment
for heroin addiction is regarded by many, including some addicts, as a bright hope and by
others as no treatment at all and as outright
immoral because it substitutes dependency on
one drug for dependency on another. It is just
a matter of values, to be dependent or to be
free of supporting one's habit on the black
market.

Somewhat guardedly, Blum concludes from
his data, "It is clear. . . that a variety of
unpleasant outcomes can occur, but one gets the
impression that very few suffer anything damaging over the long run. Thus, one can conclude,

as we do, that anything but acute toxic ill
effects are unlikely and that illicit-exotic
drugs when used as students are now doing, for
the most part, do not seem to pose serious hazards to school performance or to health." He
hastens to point out that his sample did not
include any information on students who had
dropped out of school, and that those who remained and were studied were a select group.
He also points out that his data give no indication of the possible outcomes of long-term,
low-dosage use.

Yolles reports from NIMH that the incidence of serious adverse reaction to marihuana
use appears to be low but also points out that
as the total number of users increases, the
number experiencing adverse reaction will increase, that the effects of the drug on judgment
and perception might very well be a factor in
automobile accidents, and that users with significant psychiatric problems might avoid psychiatric treatment as a result of this form of
"self medication."

Both of these statements function as pro-
jective tests. Those who, because of their personal beliefs, attitudes, and values, believe
that illicit drugs are by definition "bad" and
that illicit drug use can bring nothing but harm
to the individual and to society will dismiss the
data and dismiss the questions. Those who attempt to be objective will advise caution until
we have more data based on research. The irony
is that more research will probably leave us
with essentially the same dilemma.

I cannot conceive of a research design
that could provide definitive answers. The
number of and interactions among independent
variables involved in the driving performance of
individuals who have used marihuana is staggering. Administering marihuana of known composition in known amounts in a double blind situation
in the laboratory to naive subjects of equivalent
driving skill as measured on a simulator will
tell us very little about the driving performance
of individuals who, for a variety of reasons,
have chosen to use an illegal drug of unknown
strength and purity, who have expectations and
varying amounts of experience as to the "effects"
of that drug, who choose to drive cars of varying type and condition under varying road

conditions, and who have had varying degrees of experience in coping with whatever reactions they as individuals experience when they use "marihuana."

We do need laboratory research on all drugs. We need to know the ways in which they modify the biochemical and neurochemical organism. But beyond this we need to know how these changes are related to changes in behavior. This is the greater challenge. In the meantime, differences "significantly greater than chance" in situations where as many important independent variables have been controlled will not provide us with the answers to social problems, especially when they are used inappropriately by people grasping at anything that will support what they believe about drugs which, for a variety of historical and cultural reasons, have been labeled bad, dangerous, or evil.

The use of virtually all drugs involves adverse reactions or bad outcomes, including death and in some cases life imprisonment, at some dosage level in some people under some circumstances. This includes aspirin, smallpox vaccine, penicillin, alcohol, nicotine, barbiturates, amphetamines, as well as heroin, LSD, and marihuana. In this regard it is of interest that, to my knowledge, there are no known deaths directly attributable to either LSD or marihuana as pharmacological agents except Jolly West's elephant.

As we turn to the meaning and significance of student drug use, society's response to it, and efforts to control it, I want to make it very clear that I am speaking as one psychologist who is acutely aware of the fact that her background, training, and experience, her own beliefs, attitudes, and values, even her basic beliefs about the nature of man, are important factors in her analysis and assessment of these phenomena. One always hopes that awareness inspires caution. My only special qualifications to comment on this social problem are that, because of commitments entered into almost adventitiously, I have been forced to look at student drug use from almost every possible point of view and have had the privilege of interacting with many representatives of disciplines and professions who espouse these points of view, including students of all shades of opinion and involvement.

If one wants to understand drug effect
and drug use one must look, not solely at the
pharmacological agent, but at the person who
chooses to use drugs and at what he expects,
wants, or believes will result from that use.
We are learning to our dismay that to try to
control drug use by limiting the supply of the
particular drug used does not decrease drug use.
Users merely turn to another substance which may
involve even more risk. And in our society drugs
are everywhere: legal drugs, illegal drugs, and
substances which we do not call drugs.

In addition, we have mounted a gigantic
campaign to persuade the public that there is a
drug for every ill or misery--anxiety, depression, tension, and the physical symptoms associated with these, irritability, fatigue, lack of
success in business, in social life, in the family. This has rocketed the pharmaceutical industry to the number one profit making industry
in the country, passing the automobile industry
in 1967. All of this, of course, has to do with
the promotion of legal drugs, both prescription
and over-the-counter drugs, obtained through
legal means. But I seem to remember learning in
introductory psychology about a principle known
as generalization. It should not surprise us
that young people do not understand why we are
so excited about their use of drugs for their
miseries and ills and problems. It is also
relevant to note that there has also been an
almost equally vigorous campaign in behalf of
their drugs via the news reporting of the drug
scene. Just because most of us who are over
thirty do not seek adventure, new experience,
insight into one's self, independence, and have
either found or given up looking for new insights, meaningful social relationships, creative
expression, even a dash of rebellion against the
restrictions that apparently go with living in a
modern technological society, and a pinch of fun,
we should not underestimate the appeal of anything which promises any or all of these, regardless of whether those promises can be ful-
filled. This particular characteristic of many
drugs does not seem to deter many of us from
seeking what is promised. In addition, we have
learned that many drugs are much more effective
if we believe that they will be and that "sugar
pills" have cured great ills and produced profound negative effects. One physician has been
reported to have said facetiously, "Whenever a

new drug comes on the market, rush to your physician while both he and you still believe in its powers."

It is almost trite to point out to an audience of psychologists that drug use serves different functions for different individuals. Despite this, "Escape to Nowhere" has become the banner for numerous efforts to dissuade all from the use of certain drugs. It is astounding to note how often mere use of illicit drugs is taken as an indication that the user needs psychiatric treatment. This would seem to be, in part, the result of our concept of drug abuse as a disease and our definition of any use of illegal drugs as abuse. We seem to assume both that drugs are to cure illness and that if one takes drugs he is ill. There is no doubt that some young people use drugs to escape from pressure, from anxiety, from impulses which threaten them, from the stresses and strains of growing up. There is also no doubt that some people who are ill use drugs. But unless one defines doing anything that is not socially approved as illness, the great majority of young people who use drugs illegally are not ill or in need of psychiatric treatment. Many use them because they think it is fun. Many try them out of curiosity. Many use marihuana much as we use alcohol to facilitate social interaction. Some use them as occasional respite from the pressures of increasing academic demands.

Fun, curiosity, social interaction, change of pace are all rather normal motivations. There are many ways to satisfy them. The important question is why increasing numbers of students are choosing to risk severe legal penalties by choosing to use illegal drugs. It could have something to do with society's response to their use of drugs or, perhaps more important, society's response to young people.

The very small minority of students who use illegal drugs regularly and who devote a considerable portion of their time to obtaining drugs, to using them, and to talking about their drug experiences are also a varied group. Many of them are bright enough and well enough put together to manage their drug use and still fulfill their academic obligations. Others are not. Some are convinced that drugs will solve any of a variety of problems, some developmental

and some pathological. Some are sick. Again, we
should ask the question, "Why illegal drugs?"

        Society's undiscriminating response to
all student drug use has been emotional and extremely punitive. It is outraged at many of the
things some young people are doing and saying
these days. There are those who would pass laws
against them and even some who would shoot a few
in the belief that that would serve as a deterrent. If one watches the faces of those who
suggest the latter one gets the feeling that it
might also serve to reduce their anger and frustration. But there are calmer voices to be
heard and as yet the more violent reactions have
been held in check in most cases. But the drug
issue is different. For a great variety of
historical and cultural reasons we have carefully
nurtured attitudes, beliefs, and stereotypes
about all drugs which are outside of medicine or
used for non-medical reasons. Beginning with
the Harrison Narcotic Act we have forged a system
of criminal penalties, including mandatory jail
sentences, denial of probation and parole, for
possession and "sale" (sell is legally defined
as sell, give or otherwise dispose) of "narcotics" which would suggest that these were greater
than any crime other than treason or first degree
murder. I would suggest the hypothesis that the
drug issue may represent a rallying point for
frustration, resentment, and anger generated by
many things that young people are saying and doing and that the drug laws are a rough and
ready weapon for retaliation. Many are quick to
blame drugs for everything from dropping out,
criticizing, and protesting to violence. His-
torically non-medical drug use has been associated primarily with minority groups and, with
the persistent "magic-potion-notion" of drugs,
drug use has been a convenient scapegoat and a
ready target for aggression against these
groups. Students are a fast growing minority.

        Estimates of the number of persons in
the United States who have used marijuana vary
from 8 million to 20 million. NIMH considers
that 8 million is a conservative estimate and
that there may be 12 million. All of these
people are criminals since they have committed a
felony. They possessed marihuana. Psychology
has something to say about the effects of label-
ing. Psychology and common sense certainly have

14

something to say about punishment as a deterrent when the chances of being punished are somewhere near one in five-hundred. But it either is not being said or is not being heard.

Because of the nature of the law enforcement approach to the control of drug use and because of the persistent attitudes and beliefs which support that approach, the drug issue has also become a target and a rallying point for many young peoples' frustration, resentment, and charges of hypocrisy against a society which promotes the use of alcohol, is unwilling even to require registration of guns, and seems unwilling to regulate much behavior which results in thousands of deaths and injuries.

The other major approach to control of illegal drug use is that of education. I use the word reluctantly because most so-called drug education until very recently has consisted of preaching and of attempts to scare with information which was inaccurate or patently false. Much of it still is. It seems to be designed to preserve and justify our attitudes and beliefs and our laws. It obviously has not prevented illegal drug use. Some of it may have instigated use.

Drug education is desperately needed. Students need it. Parents need it. Legislators need it. Physicians need it. The general public needs it. We are living in an increasingly chemically dominated environment. Drugs are an important part of that chemical environment. One of our most urgent social problems is to learn to live wisely in it, but we cannot do this as long as we do not understand what drugs are and how they act, what risks are involved in all drug use and how they can be minimized. We also need to expand our concept of drug to include the many substances which by their chemical nature affect the structure and function of the living organism.

To do honest and sound and effective drug education, we will need all of our skills in communication and persuasion. We will have to change long held beliefs and attitudes about drugs. We will have to separate the problem of drugs as pharmacological agents from the problem of people who make value judgments about drugs, about "drug effects," about the reasons for using drugs, and about people who use drugs. The people problem will be the more difficult to solve, but the solution to the drug problem should make it easier.

THE DRUG CHALLENGE
by
Michael V. Reagen*

The use and misuse of drugs is extensive in America. All indications suggest that in every age in our society the extent of psychological and physiological dependence on drugs is so widespread that it is having a profound impact on our national life style.

Consider just five statistics:

1. A number of published estimates by credible sources indicate that at least twenty million Americans (almost ten per cent of our total population--half of which is under the age of twenty-six) reportedly use marijuana on a routine basis.

2. The National Institute of Mental Health estimates that 200,000 Americans are addicted to hard drugs.

3. The U.S. pharmaceutical houses report through their national associations that they annually manufacture more than 350 tons of barbiturates--an amount sufficient to put the entire population of the United States to sleep every night for three weeks.

4. The N.Y. Chamber of Commerce reported in a recent study on the incidence of drug abuse in business and industry in New York State that an estimated 500,000 Americans illegally use prescription drugs.

5. According to the New York State Narcotic Addiction Control Commission, more than 30,000 known heroin addicts with individual habits ranging in cost from $7,000 to $15,000 per year live in N. Y. State.

Statements on drug use and misuse abound in a bewildering array. Close scrutiny of these

---

*Michael V. Reagen, Ph.D., is Associate Director of the Urban Studies Center of the Policy Institute of the Syracuse University Research Corporation.

statements, however, yield three facts: First, data are admittedly incomplete and inaccurate (but more Americans than is normally suspected regularly use and misuse drugs in one form or another); second, the incidence of drug usage among the young is growing at an alarming rate; and third, the heart of the drug problem exists not in our schools but in our society.

It is important to realize that this last statement rests on the broad definition of drugs as substances which act on the central nervous system to produce unusual drowsiness, dullness, perceptional distortion, sleep, insensibility, pain reduction and/or euphoria.

Included under this definition are a number of familiar drugs: morphine, codeine, amphetamines, barbiturates, heroin, opium, hashish, cocaine, marijuana, and hallucinogens. Also included under this definition are a few we do not normally consider: volatiles, tobacco, coffee, tea and alcohol.

Social and behavioral scientists using this definition suggest more adults than youngsters regularly drug themselves; however, during the past decade the emphasis has been on drug use and abuse by children. Often, it is easier for adults to focus on the behavior of children than upon an examination of their own behavior.

Children, on the other hand, not only observe and evaluate their own behavior but also that of adults. They may imitate their peers but they also model their behavior on what "daddy says" and on what "daddy does." Adults lose credibility when they react to the fast pace of modern life by smoking, drinking and taking pills while at the same time criticizing comparable behavior in children. Children soon become aware of adult dependence on these drugs and not infrequently interpret criticism as hypocritical.

During the past ten years American adults have spent millions of dollars on highly-publicized programs designed to sell the negative aspects of drug abuse and addiction to children-- in the same way soap powder is sold to adults. If the objective of these programs has been to reduce the incidence of drug usage by children, then the programs have clearly not sold themselves. More youngsters drug themselves today than they did ten years ago. Why have programs failed? No one can be sure but research indicates seven significant flaws:

1. The programs do not "tell it like it is." They stress the negative aspects of drug abuse without mentioning the pleasurable aspects. They present information which the youngsters (either from personal experience or from shared experiences with peers) can easily deny. For example, programs often either state or imply that marijuana smoking automatically leads to using hard drugs. Even if it were true that every heroin addict smoked marijuana at one time in his life, it is not true that every marijuana smoker goes on to use physiologically addictive narcotics.

2. Programs have not addressed themselves to the differing viewpoints adults and youngsters have on the drug problem. While there is general agreement between both generations that hard drugs are harmful (especially with respect to the opiates), there is a wide divergence of opinion among both youngsters and adults about the possible harmful effects of soft drugs such as marijuana. Some youngsters see marijuana as a safe alternative to the use of alcohol, except for the possibility that they may be caught for illegally possessing and using it. Medical evidence only clouds the picture because at this writing the data are inconclusive as to whether or not recreational use of marijuana and some other soft drugs--in their pure form--is inherently damaging either psychologically or physiologically.

3. Programs reach children at too late an age. Physicians and police report an increase in narcotics use by elementary and junior high school students in our metropolitan area during the past two years.

By the time youngsters reach high school they have already been exposed to a drug culture, if not through

personal experience then surely through
their observations of adult behavior and
through the artifacts of their culture:
music, films, magazines, and the mass
media. Dr. William Alsever of Syracuse
University's Student Health Service
believes many students who use drugs
in college brought their drug habits
with them from home. He also suggests
that the acknowledged drug problem in
the Armed Forces may represent a similar
phenomenon.

5. <u>Youngsters are rarely involved in planning the programs</u>. As a result, they
usually "tune out" on drug prevention
programs. They do not immediately perceive any relevance to their personal
knowledge, experience or situations or
see any compelling reason why they
should force themselves to find any
relevance.

6. <u>The programs often fail to positively
reinforce one another</u>. This flaw is
very evident in our metropolitan area.
Here in Syracuse at least fifteen individuals or organizations offer narcotics education programs--individually
and collectively each provides a genuine
public service that results in a minimal
impact on the drug problem. Because of
intense competition to gain recognition
for their specific efforts to alleviate
the drug problem, little cooperation
and coordination has developed for an
overall strategy which could maximize
possibilities for making <u>all</u> programs
successful in their impact.

7. <u>Programs often use inappropriate techniques and strategies</u>. One of the most
inappropriate techniques or strategies
for dealing with the drug problem in
schools is for a school to deny any
knowledge of drug use within its school
population. It is most unlikely that
the population of students in any one
school is so unique a sample of the
total population of students in the
United States that it has completely
isolated itself from drug problems.

Some schools deal with the issue in
a superficial manner, e.g., handing out
pamphlets or providing an hour's lecture
in health education classes. Still
others lump "hard" and "soft" drugs together, use the shock technique of showing a "horror" film depicting the evil
consequences of hard drug addiction or
have a former addict speak about heroin.

These attempts, while influencing
some impressionable youngsters, usually
"turn off" the majority of students,
who may be merely curious about marijuana.
As a result, these techniques and strategies are skeptically viewed by youngsters as just more attempts by adults to
control, falsify, intimidate and to
otherwise deny youngsters free expression
and the opportunity to "do their own
thing." While these techniques and
strategies are conceived with good intentions, good intentions do not necessarily lead to good results.

However, through the cooperation of interested
citizens and federal, state and local government
officials, efforts are now being made to correct
the weaknesses of previous programs and to launch
a coordinated attack on the drug problem in our
metropolitan area.

The first step to this coordinated attack was
in the spring of 1970 with the establishment of
the Mayor's Temporary Commission on Narcotics
Abuse Addiction in Syracuse. Through the invitation of Mayor Lee Alexander, twenty-one citizens representing various supportive services
met throughout the summer of 1970 to study com-
prehensively the drug problem in the Syracuse
metropolitan area.

The Commission proved to be a genuine working force. Shared with the Commission was information obtained from a fifty-seven item ques-
tionnaire completed by more than 15,000 students
in grades 7 through 12 in both private and public
schools in the City of Syracuse. The students
reported that 12.7% of them had smoked marijuana; 3.5% of them had tried speed; 1.6% of
them had tried heroin; 4.6% had tried acid or
LSD; 8.3% had tried pep pills and 11.8 had
sniffed glue or other volatile substances.

Throughout the summer of 1970 the Commission, chaired by the author, met with a variety of individuals knowledgeable about the drug problem in the Syracuse Metropolitan area. As a result of the Commission's hearings and investigations a report calling for a three-pronged attack to curb drug use and drug pushing in the Syracuse metropolitan area was begun on October 17, 1970.

The Temporary Commission's report called for: first, establishment of a comprehensive school drug education program to be conducted throughout Onondaga County; second, establishment of a City-County Drug Abuse Commission to coordinate all the efforts in the areas of education, law enforcement, treatment and rehabilitation to combat drug abuse in our community; and third, formation of a Central Narcotics Squad involving City-County police agencies to enforce laws that relate to drug abuse and drug pushing.

With the submission of its final report to the Mayor, the Temporary Commission no longer met. In its final comments, the Commission took note of the apathetic attitude of the general public toward the drug abuse problem. The Commission observed that there was in our metropolitan area an apparent lack of concern about drugs, not only by the general public but also by social and political institutions. Only occasional shortsighted, hysterical public utterances and reactions had broken an otherwise long seige of malaise.

The impact drugs are having on our young people and on our culture is phenomenal. Scientists working with our government in casting alternative futures for our society are alarmed. Some see millions of future Americans "turning on" with drugs as a normal recreational pasttime that will be legally and morally blessed by a society so affluent that only a few will work while a majority play. All, however, see the immediate personal horror for millions of individuals in the general societal discord unless our society as a whole addresses itself to the drug problem.

During the latter part of the summer of August, 1970, Syracuse University (through its continuing education arm--University College), contracted with the New York State Education Department to develop and field a year-long drug program for six school districts in major cities

in New York State outside of New York City to be
under the direction of Professor Thomas Briggs
of Syracuse University, School of Social Work.
Target districts included Yonkers, Albany, Utica,
Syracuse, Rochester, and Buffalo.

Each city was invited to select a number of
teams consisting of a school administrator, a
guidance counselor, a community leader and two
students. These teams (a total of 85 persons)
were involved in a week-long workshop at the University's Sagamore Conference Center and, then,
were offered consultation for a period of two
months.

There were four objectives behind the "Sagamore Experiment" as it has now come to be called:

1. To provide the participants in the experiment with basic, factual and up-to-
date data concerning drug use and abuse.

2. To provide the participants with the
opportunity to discuss and become involved with effective new techniques
of dealing with drug education at the
school level.

3. To enable each participating team to
develop its own community action plan
to attack the drug problem in its
city.

4. To provide intensive leadership and
planning training for student members
of the teams.

The results of the Sagamore Experiment were
mixed. In several cities, the teams were quite
successful in implementing new and unique approaches to the drug abuse problem and, at this
writing, seem to be bearing fruit. In two
cities the experiment achieved only modest results and in the remaining city, it was obviously
a failure.

The key variable underscoring the success or
failure of the Sagamore Experiment seemed to be
the degree of interest and dedication of the
participants. The Sagamore Experiment has,
however, provided us with a useful model for
launching a comprehensive preventive drug abuse

education program in this metropolitan area.

Throughout 1970 and the spring of 1971, City and County officials studied the recommendations of the Mayor's Temporary Commission. In May 1971, the City and County legislatures established the first City-County Drug Abuse Commission. The enabling legislation establishes the Commission and gives it five functions:

1. To act as a review board for drug abuse programs serving the City of Syracuse and Onondaga County.

2. To act as a coordinating agency for all drug abuse programs in Syracuse and Onondaga County.

3. To act as a clearing house for information about drug abuse programs and services available to the residences of Syracuse and Onondaga County.

4. To act as a sounding board for all future drug abuse programs in Syracuse and Onondaga County.

5. To act as a stimulus for new approaches in dealing with the drug dilemma in the City and County.

The City-County Drug Abuse Commission has broad recommendatory and investigatory powers and reports directly to the County Executive and the Mayor. It has four subcommittees--one each on Treatment and Rehabilitation, Law Enforcement, Education, and Priorities.

At this writing the Commission is in the process of organizing itself, meeting with representatives of the various public and private agencies in the City and County and taking steps to provide itself with a staff to carry out the functions given to it by the County Legislature and the Syracuse Common Council.

During the winter of 1970-1971, superintendents of the twenty-one school districts in Onondaga County met regularly to discuss ways in which they might work more cooperatively to combat drug abuse among the children of the metropolitan area. A task force was formed under the leadership of Dr. Harold Ranken, Superintendent

of Schools in the Jamesville-DeWitt school dis-
trict. The task force, with the assistance of
Dr. Donald Boudreau, Commissioner of Mental
Hygiene for Onondaga County, applied for funds
through the New York Narcotics Addiction Control
Commission (NACC) to implement the recommendations
on the comprehensive education program made by the
Mayor's Temporary Commission.

The result of the Superintendent's task force
was that NACC granted all the school districts of
Onondaga County 1.8 million dollars. A small
portion of that grant provided for the establishment of the Institute for Drug Education at Syracuse (IDEAS).

The Institute will train over 550 school personnel, formed into teams, representing every
school building in Onondaga County. These teams
are expected to return to their school and to
conduct inservice training for other teachers,
students and parents. They will also work with
appropriate school officials in developing and
coordinating preventive drug abuse education programs in the school curriculum for each district.
The solution to any community problem demands the
cooperation and interest of all the members of
that community. The degree to which the community solves its problems is the degree to which
each segment of that community cooperates in
finding the solutions.

RECOGNITION OF THE DRUG USER FOR ENFORCEMENT
AGENTS, TEACHERS AND OTHERS
by
William D. Alsever*

Alcohol: The Alcoholic and the Problem Drinker

Not all of these signals will be seen in an affected person. The occurrence of several should suggest the possibility of uncontrolled drinking. The diagnosis should be made by the physician on your referral to him. This is important for both the safety and well-being of the individual involved and for the image of the department concerned. Mistakes are made in both directions. A stuporous head injury case may simulate the drunk. The diabetic coma (or pre-coma stage) has been mislabelled as a juice-head. Also acute alcoholism may mask the presence of severe disease discernible only to a trained doctor, but only if he is requested to examine the patient. Leave diagnosing to the doctor--it's his bag, not yours.

The profile of the average alcoholic reveals that he is 30-50 old, a good worker, has a good record of long company service and often is a key person. He is also a rationalizer, manipulator and a con-artist as is the junkie. In addition he surrounds himself with a wall of denial as far as his drinking habits go. The following apply to both the young student and the adult who is working.

(A) Drinking Habits--On the job drinking, hangovers, gulps drinks rapidly, and resents any reference to his drinking.

1. Escape Drinking--To avoid tension or frustration or to release anger.

2. Signal Drinking--Seems to drink on signal being motivated to drink by certain circumstances which may or may not be ritualistic, i.e., with lunch, before dinner, before retiring at night, to celebrate, to commiserate, etc.

*Dr. Alsever is a physician at the Student Health Service, Syracuse University, Syracuse, N. Y. (September 1971).

3. Fun Drinking--Becomes necessary to drink in order to enjoy oneself at ordinary activities as party, cards, bowling, golf, fishing, football games, watching television, etc.

(B) Physical Appearance--Red eyes, flushed face, nervous, shaky, tremors, etc.

(C) Absenteeism--Fridays, Mondays, day after pay day and working day prior to following holiday. Prolonged lunch hour. Leaves work early. Habitual tardiness. Unscheduled vacation time taken if possible.

(D) Productivity--Not up to customary standards in school or on the job. Homework either late, not done or poorly completed. Work on the job is diminished quantitatively and/or qualitatively. Tends to be spasmodic without a steady output as before.

(E) Accuracy--Mistakes and errors in school-work or job increase in frequency. Impaired manual dexterity. Poor judgment and unrealistic decisions.

(F) Attitudes and Habits--Changing and labile. Volatile personality who blows off readily. Intolerant and suspicious of others. Avoids boss and colleagues.

(G) Safety Record--Poor. More accidents and near misses in the shop. Disproportionate number auto accidents and home accidents compared with non-alcoholic.

(H) Blackouts--Temporary amnesia for an event even though did not pass out.

(I) Finances--Repetitive borrowing from friends. Company loans and garnishments, etc.

Drugs: User of Illicit Drugs and Misuser of Legal Drugs

Not all of these signs will be noted in any one individual. The presence of several of the general manifestations should raise the question

of either drug use or abnormal drinking. The
general signs listed in (A) below are quite similar to those of alcoholism and are in no way
specific for drug abuse. They only suggest a
problem which could be drugs or alcohol. The
definitive signs tabulated in (B) below many times
will pinpoint drug abuse rather than alcohol abuse.
Again the diagnosis is up to the doctor--not you!
Sometimes even the physician will have his problems in establishing a correct verdict. At present there is no telltale profile of the addict
or the drug dependent person--much less of the
occasional episodic user of drugs. He demonstrates
the same talent for manipulation, rationalization
and conning that the alcoholic does.

In general there are four major differences
that may be helpful sometimes in distinguishing
between the user of drugs and the user of alcohol:

1. The average drug user is under 30 years
   of age compared with the usual alcoholic
   who is over 30 years old.

2. The drug user's wall of denial may be
   harder to demolish than that of the
   juicehead since drugs are not socially
   acceptable as is liquor.

3. The drug taker speaks in a special jargon all his own which is characteristic
   of both the youth counter culture and
   the drug subculture (see the Glossary
   for details). The alcoholic converses
   in the customary square or straight
   idiom of the adult world unless he
   happens to be a young person. Use of
   this atypical vocabulary obviously does
   not prove that the person is a drug
   user. It only indicates that he is
   part of the current scene.

4. The individual who has been drinking
   excessively will always show signs of
   this though they may be minimal if his
   tolerance and experience are great.
   On the other hand the drug user may or
   may not demonstrate stigmata of contact
   with drugs. Somebody may be stoned out
   of his head without your being able to
   recognize it since some users possess
   the rare ability to suppress manifestations

of drugs especially when they realize
they are under observation. Others
fail to get high on grass or acid but
then of course they will not be a
problem to you.

To further compound your difficulties there
are no pathognomic signs of tripping that are in-
fallible and incontrovertible to the average
doctor. They are certainly strongly suggestive
but not proof positive in a tough case. For
example, some of the things listed for acid and
speed are seen in acute psychoses which are not
drug induced at all; dilated pupils may be present on a nervous or psychological basis completely free of any drug orientation and an insulin reaction in a diabetic may present the
picture of somebody who is freaking out. Accordingly one must be extremely cautious and circum-
spect before accepting unequivocally the diagnosis
of being under the influence of or intoxicated
from a drug. Charges must be made with care!
Remember that everybody who freaks out is not
always an acidhead, meth monster, frost freak,
etc. He may have a bad head from non-drug causes.

Recognition of the Drug User

(A) General Signs: Note the resemblance
given for alcoholism.

1. Physical Appearance: Normal or may
adopt hippy look. This may be mis-
leading as not all hippy-type young
people are into drugs by any means.

2. Absenteeism: Increased and unexplained.
Tardy; leaves school or work early;
prolonged lunch hour or coffee break,
leaving school or work for short un-
accounted for reasons, etc.

3. Friends: May discard old acquaintances
for new ones. Often secretive and
furtive about them; will not discuss
them or bring them home.

4. Productivity and Achievement: Deterioration in academic work and lessened
productivity on the job. Qualitative
and/or quantitative lessening of both.
Intermittent or spree type effort
rather than steady output.

5. Mistakes and Errors: Increased. Homework poor or missing. Less manual
dexterity. Decline of decision making and judgment skill.

6. Attitudes and Habits: Alteration in
habits, personality and attitudes.
Personality reversal--from shy and
quiet to gregarious and noisy; from
friendly to hostile, etc. Volatile
and labile. Indifference, amotiva-
tion, apathy and goal reversal.

7. Safety Record: More auto accidents.
Increase in home accidents and shop
accidents.

8. Language: New alien vocabulary which
you do not dig. Again, the use of
this new mode of expression does not
imply that one is behind drugs at
all! It merely means that he is a
member of the current youth culture
and may or may not be doing drugs.
See the Glossary for explanation of
many of the words.

9. Finances: Surreptitious disappearance
of money from the home or articles
to be pawned. May steal or borrow
from classmates or fellow workers
things necessary to support a drug
habit.

(B) Signs of Specific Drugs: Not all present
in one person. Not necessarily diagnostic, but may be suggestive. Remember
that certain diseases can produce all of
these signs! This listing is not complete since it has been prepared for
non-medical personnel.

1. Marijuana--Pot, grass, etc.

Physical - Negligible effects. Red
eyes, dry cough and possibly slight
tremor and incoordination. Pupils
usually normal and not dilated contrary to popular opinion. Urinary
frequency. Hunger for sweets.

Mental - Happy and mildly high.
Talkative at first--later may be

quiet and withdrawn. Laughs and
giggles easily. Contented and
happy. Thoughts may be incoherent
and immediate memory faulty in some.
After initial high and elation may
become sleepy. Placid and inactive
and rarely aggressive and antisocial. A few may develop feelings
of fear, anxiety, panic, paranoia or
depression.

Some will not get any effect from
blowing grass at all. A certain
number of potheads will be able to
suppress the effects of their being
stoned so that the diagnosis cannot
be made. This is especially true if
they know they are under surveillance.

Possible physical evidence:

Marijuana--May have odor of hay and
odor of burning rope when being
smoked. Greener than tobacco.
Usually cut with inert substances as
oregano, alfalfa, hay, tobacco, catnip, etc. If it has not been manicured you will see seeds and bits
of stems mixed in with the ground-
up leaves. Sticks or joints are
typically smaller than conventional
cigarettes (a few are fatter) with
both ends twisted or tucked in and
may be rolled in two pieces of paper
(or one) which is frequently white,
tan and more recently colored or
figured. Pipes are of all designs
and there is nothing diagnostic about
them due to the infinite variation
seen. A pipe with a small piece of
mesh or metal screen in the bottom
is a pot or hash pipe. However,
roaches (butts) may be found. Likewise a crutch is often present--a
holder for smoking the roach without
burning the fingers. These also
vary according to locality and preference and may be bobby pin, paper
clip, split paper match and all sorts
of metal devices. Incense commonly
present but this is also burned by
non-drug using students as well.

2. <u>LSD</u>--Acid, etc.

Physical - Negligible effects. Most
characteristic is dilated pupils.
Dark glasses (shades) commonly worn
although this does not prove drug
use. May show slight tremor, incoordination and somewhat rapid pulse.
Nausea and vomiting. Sensitivity of
eyes to bright light.

Mental - Effects often bizarre and
unpredictable. Vary with dose,
presence of other drugs with the
acid, personality and expectations
of the user, conditions under which
the drug is taken, etc. Disturbances
of Perception - Magnification time
and space. Cerebration--May talk
about increased insight, awareness,
etc. May be incoherent or out of
contact with reality. Poor judgment.
Illusions (false response to sensory
stimulus)--walls move, etc. Hallucinations (perception of external
object when no such thing present)--
may be false in nature in that that
person realizes what he is seeing
is not for real. Visual commonest.
May be auditory, olfactory, tactile.
Religious Orientation--May be mentioned by the patient. Includes
the transcendal visionary experience
reported by many and also the epi-
phanies or visions with religious
content (Christ, Virgin Mary, heaven,
etc.). Depersonalization or Alteration of Body Image--body image distorted grossly or grotesquely and
loss of sense of ownership of parts
of body. Derealization or Reality
Loss: delusion that one is invul-
nerable to the hostile things in the
external environment so that one can
fly, walk on water or stop cars with
outstretched hands, etc. Responsible
for a few accidental suicides. Mood--
primarily euphoria and elation followed later in the trip by depression
or "blessed repose."

Typical acidhead is quiet, not argu-
mentative, withdrawn and not physically

aggressive. A few become psychotic
and assaultive, some develop cate-
tonia, others may show delusions of
grandeur and omnipotence and a rare
individual may become truly hyper-
ative, physically.

Possible physical evidence:

LSD now comes in all sizes, shapes
and colors so there is nothing characteristic about the material. May
be liquid, pill, tablet, capsule,
impregnated paper, sugar cube, gum
drop, licorice, tooth picks, stamps,
blotting paper, tiny piece of gelatin, etc. Must be analyzed by the
laboratory.

2. Heroin--Junk, scag, smack, horse, etc.

Physical - Constricted or pinned
pupils. May be malnourished. Pocks--
Oval depressed scars from skin popping. On legs and arms. Nasal
membrane lining inside of the nose
may be reddened, moist with secretions
or may show residual white powder
flecks. Septum which divides the
inside of the nose may be infected
or perforated. All these manifestations are from use by snorting.

Tracks--Needle marks, scars from areas
of infected hits and scars overlying
thrombosed (clotted) veins. Commonest sites--the ditch or valley (inside of elbow), forearms, legs, top
of hands and feet, between toes and
fingers. Less well known and less
frequently used areas include side
of the neck (jugular vein), floor
of the mouth (lingual veins along-
side attachment tongue to floor of
mouth) and rarely the penis (large
dorsal vein on top of the shaft of
the organ).

Mental--Initially a euphoria from the
rush or flash after the hit. This
then gives way to sleepiness to the
point of sleeping (on the nod or
nodding), and lethargy with inaction.

Will offer all sorts of reasons and
rationalizations for his addiction
with promises to go straight and
kick the habit. Blames everybody
else for his problem--never himself.

May wear long sleeves to hide tracks.
May dress unseasonably warm as addicts often tend to feel chilly.
May show craving for sweets, i.e.,
soda pop, etc.

Possible physical evidence:

Heroin--White or brown powder with
bitter taste in various containers
such as glassene envelopes, foil
packets, toy balloons, capsules,
folded paper decks, etc. See the
Glossary.

Equipment--The works or artillery.
See the Glossary for breakdown of
the various components one may find
as evidence of popping or shooting.

Overdose--The OD. Typical case is
comatose (or soon will be), cold,
sweaty, having trouble breathing
(slow infrequent respirations) and
may have tenacious froth at nose and
mouth resembling shaving cream.
Death is common! Get to the hospital
as soon as possible--a true medical
emergency.

Withdrawal Illness--Abstinence
Syndrome:

Generally resembles a mild case of
the flu. Not severe now due to heavy
cutting of junk. Not fatal as is
the case with overdoses! Runny nose,
sweating, watery eyes, yawning, goose
flesh, abdominal and muscular cramps,
nausea, vomiting, chills, diarrhea,
sneezing, twitching of feet, etc.
As one advances into withdrawal the
previously constricted pupils become
normal but then dilate.

Methadone--Remember that this drug
can be diverted to the street and

can produce true physical addiction,
withdrawal syndrome and overdose
with death. Same clinical manifestations as with heroin.

4. Depressants--Sedatives and tranquilizers. Goofballs, downers, etc.

Three classes--Barbiturates (amytal,
seconal, tuinal, nembutal, phenobarbital) non-barbiturate sedatives
(doriden, placidyl, quaalude) and
minor tranquilizers (miltown, librium, valium, valmid, noludar, etc.).
All produce physical addiction, withdrawal, illness and acute intoxication (overdose).

Acute Intoxication (Overdose)--drunk
without the odor of booze being
present. Pupils normal size, flick-
ering movements of eyes, staggering,
slurred speech, confusion, subnormal
temperature, shock, depressed slow
respirations, sleepy, eventual coma
and death. Medical emergency--will
die if not treated promptly!

Withdrawal Illness (Abstinence
Syndrome)--unlike withdrawal from
heroin 10-15% of these patients will
die! Another medical emergency!
Pupils normal size, anxiety, rest-
lessness, insomnia, agitation, sweating, nausea, vomiting, fever, delerium, tremors and muscular twitchings
which progress on if untreated to
generalized convulsions, shock, collapse and death. Some pillheads will
also be on heroin, alcohol or stimulants (up and downs).

5. Stimulants--Amphetamines and related
drugs (not amphetamines Speed, meth,
crank, uppers, etc.).

Two classes--True amphetamines as
benzedrine, dexedrine, methamphetamine, desoxyn, etc., and stimulants
that are not actually amphetamines
strictly speaking (but do the same
things) such as preludin, tepanil,
tenuate, ephedrine, antihistamines,

35

etc. Some are obesity pills, cold pills, allergy pills and a few are for other legitimate medical purposes.

Physical--Restless, agitated, continual repetitious activities, perpetual motion, sweating, malnutrition and weight loss, dilated pupils, dry mouth with licking of lips, lack of appetite, compulsive actions, aggressive, itching skin due to imaginary bugs with scratching and skin infections, tremors, fast pulse, occasionally convulsions and rarely death.

Mental--All psyched up or speeded up. Clear or confused. Insomnia. Continuous rapid talking which does not make much sense unless you happen to be a speed freak yourself (oral diarrhea with constipation of thought). Hallucinations, delerium, paranoia and maybe psychotic. Post-spree depression may occur after crashing (suicidal tendency occasionally). The speed freak (meth monster, speeder) may be very dangerous due to his tendency to be assaultive, aggressive, paranoid and sometimes psychotic. Therefore, he must be approached with caution because of possibility of physical danger to yourself unlike the typical kid who is tripping out on acid, mescaline, hashish, etc. In areas of high concentration of speeders guns and knives are often carried to protect themselves from being burned or ripped off and they may travel in gangs known as meth marauders or crank commandos in certain localities. The underground slogan "Speed kills" or "Meth is Death" is an exaggeration as not many speed freaks die. They tend rather to end up in jail, in a hospital or are forced to kick their habit. A few are murdered or killed in accidents.

6. Cocaine--Snow, Charlie, happy powder, etc.

The original "dope fiend" of years
ago. Cocaine is the "rich man's
speed" and all that has been pointed
out above about amphetamines is generally true of cocaine. On attempted
apprehension the snow bird may be the
same dangerous character that the
speed freak is.

It is claimed by addicts that cocaine
is the most pleasurable drug of all
at the gut level with its tremendous
rush, flash or jolt. It is likewise the most expensive habit of all
as to remain high one must hit every
2-3 hours due to its short action,
unlike heroin.

7. Volatile Solvents--deleriants.

Airplane glue, turpentine, acetone,
gasoline oven cleaners, toilet bowl
deodorizers, freon, spray deodorizers, aerosols, foot powder, motor
tune-up fluid, cleaning fluid, kero-
sene, paint and lacquer thinner,
tire-patch cement, lighter fluid,
Carbona, nail-polish remover, etc.

The huffer or flasher does his thing
straight from the can or bottle, by
inhaling from a rag soaked with the
fluid or by sniffing under a paper
or plastic bag.

High or intoxicated for 30-45 minutes
(nothing characteristic about the
high) followed by sleeping it off
for 1-2 hours. The only suggestive
findings exclusive of catching him
in the act include in some chronic
users red watery eyes, watery discharge from the nose which appears
red and inflamed on the inside,
peculiar odor to the breath, and
irritation and excoriation of the
skin of the upper lip.

Unlike most other drugs of abuse the
xylene, benzene, toluene, etc., contained in these substances can cause
demonstrable physical damage to organs
such as the liver, brain, kidneys and

bone marrow. A particularly dangerous type is the inhalation of
various aerosols, and sprays. These
all contain the propellant and refrigerant freon. Freon can displace
air from the lungs and provide heart
irregularities with death. Use of a
bag further enhances a fatal outcome.
Such cases die suddenly during or
after inhaling and are known as the
S.S.D. Syndrom (Sudden sniffing death
syndrom).

8. <u>Belladonna Alkaloids</u>--Witches brew,
green dragon, horror drugs, etc.

Includes legitimate medical drugs
such as atropine, homatropine, belladonna, strammonium, hyocyamus, scopa-
lamine (twilight sleep), etc.

Besides stealing these drugs from
medical sources varying amounts of
them are found in certain over-the-
counter items obtained without a
prescription such as Contact Cold
Capsules, Sominex, Asthmador,
Sleepeze, Compoz, etc.

They are taken alone or may be added
to LSD to enhance or prolong its
effects (see Salads or Combinations
in the <u>Glossary</u>).

Produce a high wild trip like acid
but lasting longer--up to 2-4 days.
While the pupils are dilated its
effects are different than stimulants
and hallucinogens in that there is
an absence of sweating combined with
a flushed face, dry mouth (absence
of saliva) and fever Delerium and
psychoses occur.

9. <u>Miscellaneous Drugs</u>.

<u>Darvon</u>--This non-narcotic pain re-
liever is used by some to turn on.
It may also result in an overdose
which looks exactly like the OD in
the junky with the added feature of
convulsions. It also is fatal if
not treated early.

MDA--The love pill. A synthetic
amphetamine which is quite dangerous.
Might show some features of acid and
speed both with added possibility of
convulsions, coma, and death.

STP--Serenity, Tranquility and Peace.
Also known as the "death trip" and
"D.O.A." (dead on arrival). Synthetic amphetamine combining effects
of speed and acid. Some fatalities
have occurred. One of the most potent
drugs of all.

Sernyl--PCP, HOG, PEACE PILL, etc.
Animal tranquilizer deemed too dangerous for human use. Causes hallucinations and psychoses. Shows some
features of amphetamines, belladonna
and acid such as red face, dry mouth,
dilated pupils, hallucinations, tremors, vomiting, delerium, etc.

GLOSSARY OF THE YOUTH SUBCULTURE AND DRUG
SCENE FOR THE ESTABLISHMENT AND OTHER
UPTIGHT ADULTS
by
William D. Alsever*

To find a word or phrase, first look in the
index or key words on the left side of the page.
If it is not located there, then look through
the capitalized words after the definitions as
these are synonyms for the index word. Most of
these synonyms are not included in the index words
to avoid making the dictionary unnecessarily cum-
bersome.

The language is constantly changing and also
varies markedly with geographical location. Much
of this will be somewhat out of date the day it
is printed.

Special acknowledgment is due my daughter,
Alice, for her numerous suggestions regarding
the vocabulary and for her assistance in typing
and arranging this glossary.

ACID: see LSD.

ACID ROCK: type of rock and roll music emphasiz-
ing electronically produced sounds and songs
with surrealistic imagery. Originated in
San Francisco and popularized by the Jefferson Airplane, the Grateful Dead, etc.

ACIDHEAD: chronic user of LSD. CUBEHEAD.

ACID TEST: costume party at which music and
lights combine to mimic or enhance LSD
experience.

ACTION: activity, excitement, what's going on.

ADDICTS AND ADDICTION (HEROIN): (Also see
sections on Heroin, Opium and Mainlining
elsewhere in glossary.)
JUNKIE: Heroin addict. JUNKY, DREAMER,
SLEEP WALKER, HYPE, HOPHEAD, SMACKHEAD,
A.D., NEEDLE MAN, POISON PEOPLE, STONER.
BEDBUGS: fellow addicts. CROWD: fat

---

*Dr. Alsever is a physician at the Student Health
Service, Syracuse University, Syracuse, N. Y.
13210. (August 1971).

addict. CREEP: one who scores by beg-
ging, loaning needle, etc., rather than
by hustling (GREASY JUNKIE). STONE AD-
DICT: one with very big or heavy habit.
LIFER: confirmed long-time addict
(CARPET WALKER). MEDICAL HYPE: one who
develops addiction inadvertently through
legitimate use of narcotics for medical
reasons.

HOOKED: physically addicted to morphine,
heroin or other opiates. CAUGHT, ON THE
NEEDLE, WIRED, MONKEY ON THE BACK, VUL-
TURE ON THE VEINS.

ARMY DISEASE: opiate addiction incurred
during Civil War when injection of morphine for pain was available for the
first time in treating wounded. On
return home some of the casualties kept
their habit, some passed their habit on
to civilians and others kicked their
habit.

BURNED OUT: addict who has kicked the habit,
one whose veins are all scarred up
(LOUSED UP) or one who no longer obtains
the desired effects from his drug.

CHAMP: addict who will not reveal source
of his drugs regardless of heat from the
authorities.

HABIT: amount of heroin used daily and
equated with its cost. See CHIPPING.

CHASING THE BAG: hustling heroin.

SYSTEM: degree of addict's tolerance for
the drug.

FIX: injection of junk (HIT, SHOT, JOB).
WAKEUP: initial fix of the day.

PANIC: temporary scarcity of drug when
supply has been cut off. FAMINE, HARD
TIMES.

NODDING: falling asleep after initial rush
following fix. ON THE NOD, COASTING.

PING THE PILL: removal of tiny amount of
heroin from each bag, deck, balloon or
cap, etc., so that eventually enough is
accumulated to provide a fix for emergency use when a panic occurs.

KICK THE HABIT: to get off heroin (break
the habit). Done with or without med-
ical assistance. BREAK THE NEEDLE, TAKE
A CURE, CLEAR UP, CLEAN UP, WITHDRAW,
WATER OFF, SNEEZE IT OUT, GET THE MONKEY
OFF YOUR BACK, GET THE VULTURE OFF YOUR
VEINS, SHAKE THE HABIT, FOLDING UP,
MATURING. COLD TURKEY: kicking the

habit without medical help.

STRONG OUT: not feeling well due to lack
of a fix on schedule. SICK, FRANTIC,
WAY DOWN.

STRAIGHT: feeling well after a fix. WELL.

WITHDRAWAL ILLNESS: ABSTINENCE SYNDROME,
COP SICKNESS. TWISTED: in act of with-
drawing. AGONIES: withdrawal symptoms.
YENNING: going through withdrawal illness. YEN SLEEP: restless uneasy sleep
seen during withdrawal. WINGDING: faked
withdrawal illness to con doctor into
giving narcotic drugs. Also to simulate
symptoms of a very painful illness such
as renal colic to pressure physician to
administer opiates for relief of non-
existent pain.

COLD TURKEY: going through withdrawal without medical help. ON THE NATCH.

HANG TOUGH: sweat withdrawal out alone
without assistance or go cold turkey.

STRAIGHTEN OUT: to provide medical treatment during withdrawal to prevent development of severe symptoms.

AROUND THE TURN: completion of withdrawal
by whatever method.

DRY OUT: to detoxify or withdraw from
heroin, barbiturates, minor tranquilizers,
alcohol or any drug that produces physical
addiction. DETOX.

REVOLVING DOOR: phenomenon seen in majority of addicts treated in institutions
such as Lexington, etc. Following successful withdrawal and therapy the
patient is released. On release re-
entry into the drug scene occurs and the
patient is back on the street and scoring
within several hours of discharge. This
pattern is repeated endlessly in cyclic
fashion every time he is readmitted.
Such a patient is known as a WINDER and
the process he keeps repeating is the
REVOLVING DOOR.

OD (OVERDOSE): near death or death from
intravenous narcotism due either to
excessive dose, poisoning of his stuff
or more likely allergy or anaphylaxis
from a filler such as quinine. OVER-
JOLT, OVERAMPING, FLATTENED, JAMMED UP,
FALLING OUT, TAKING THE PIPE.

SALT SHOT: do-it-yourself home treatment
for an OD consisting of intravenous
injection of salt and water. Ineffective
and irrational therapy.

A-HEAD: regular user of amphetamines.   WATER-
    HEAD, SPEEDFREAK.

ALCOHOL: street names include JUICE, SAUCE,
    RIPPLES, GALLO, RED, GRAPES.   (Last four
    mean wine only.)

AMPHETAMINES: BENNIES, DEXES, CARTWHEELS, FOOT-
    BALLS, LID-PROPPERS, CO-PILOTS, SPLASH,
    HEARTS, THRILL-PILLS, PEP-PILLS, WHITES,
    BROWNIES, WAKE-UPS, SWEETIES, CROSSROADS,
    SPEED, FORWARDS, UPPERS, TRUCK-DRIVERS,WATER,
    PEACHES, CRYSTALS, BLACK BEAUTIES, CROSS-
    COUNTRIES, JOLLY BEANS, DOUBLE CROSS, DRIVERS,
    ROSES, BLUE ANGELS, PURPLE HEARTS, RED DEVILS,
    A.M.Y., CHALK, THRUSTERS, EYE OPENERS, LOS
    ANGELES TURNAROUNDS, CHRISTMAS TREE - Dexamyl,
    STRAWBERRY SHORTCAKE - Oberin.   B-29's.
    ZOOM THRUST, JELLY BEANS, DRIVER, CROSS TOPS,
    SPARKLE-PLENTY.   (Also see SPEED.)

AMYL NITRITE: PEARLS, POPPERS, SNAPPERS, AMYS,
    SNIFFERS, AMY JOY.

ANGEL DUST: Sernyl (PCP) on parsley or grass
    dusted with hash.   (Probably different in
    other areas.)

ANTIHISTAMINES: allergy drugs being abused by
    some in effort to get high; i.e., Drama-
    mine, Histadyl, etc.

ANTSY: anxious, agitated, restless.

APART: confused, bewildered, flustered.   Oppo-
    site of TOGETHER.

ASHRAM: a retreat for meditation.

BABY WOOD ROSE: seeds contain lysergic acid
    amide and are hallucinogenic (like morning
    glory seeds).   Also called HAWAIIAN WOOD
    ROSE.

BACKWARDS: tranquilizers.   DOWNERS.

BAD HEAD: mentally confused from taking drugs
    or may be unrelated to drugs.   (May or may
    not be psychotic.)   SCRAMBLED BRAIN.

BAD SCENE: situation likely to produce unpleasant
    experience due to drug or whatever.

43

BAG: small package of illegal drugs; one's particular interest or thing.

BALL: good time; a party.

BAM: mixture of stimulant and depressant. BLACK BOMBER.

BARBITURATES: (Names for specific Barbiturates)
AMYTAL: BLUES, BLUE HEAVENS, BLUE JACKETS-BIRDS-BULLETS-DEVILS-88's,-BANDS.
NEMBUTAL: YELLOW JACKETS, YELLOW BIRDS, YELLOW BULLETS-DEVILS-88's, NEMBEES, NEMMY, NIMBY, ABBOTS.
PHENOBARBITAL: PHENIES, PHENOS, WHITES, PURPLE HEARTS.
SECONAL: SEGGIES, REDS, RED JACKETS-BIRDS-BULLETS-DEVILS-88's, PINKS, RED LILLIES, MEXICAN REDS.
TUINAL: combination of seconal and amytal. RAINBOWS, DOUBLE TROUBLES, REDS AND BLUES, TUIES.
Other names: GOOFBALLS, BARBS, CANDY, PEANUTS, SLEEPERS, IDIOT PILLS, BLOCK BUSTERS, COURAGE PILLS, G.B., KING-KONG PILLS, GORILLA PILLS, DOLLS, STUMBLERS.

B-BOMB: benzedrine inhaler, wyamine inhaler.

BEAUTIFUL: great, awe-inspiring, exciting. Term of approval.

BEAUTIFUL PEOPLE: enlightened and aware citizens who know where things are at and understand the youth subculture. Also the jet set.

BEHIND: involved with something, i.e., behind acid means using acid INTO ACID.

BE-IN: a collection of people meeting for a specific purpose as a love-in, study-in, etc.

BELLADONNA ALKALOIDS: atropine, schopalamine, strammonium and hyocyamine. Drugs obtained from Deadly Nightshade, Henbane, Jimsonweed, Datura, etc., all of which are potent physiologically and produce bizarre mental effects. Added to acid to intensify and prolong effects or taken alone. This practice is dangerous since thorazine administered under such circumstances to bring a patient down might prove fatal. HORROR

DRUGS, WITCHES BREW, GREEN DRAGON, DEATH TRIP. (Also see COMBINATIONS.)

BENACTYZINE: tranquilizer in low doses and a potent hallucinogen in high doses. SOUND, D.M.Z., SAM, JB313.

BENDER: drug orgy or alcohol spree.

BENT: under the influence of a drug, upset, angry.

BEST PIECE: wife or girl friend. MAIN SQUEEZE.

BIKE: motorcycle. BIKE PACK: Motorcycle gang.

BIT: activity, type of behavior, an interest. BAG, THING.

BLUE VELVET: paregoric and pyribenzamine taken by vein. Also elixer terpine hydrate, codeine and pyribenzamine mainlined.

BLOW THE MIND: render out of contact with reality (psychotic); drastically alter the consciousness or overcome. Commonly from drugs but not always, i.e., may be overcome by a person.

BLOWING SNOW: nasal use of cocaine.

BLOW YOUR COOL: become angry, lose control. Opposite is KEEP YOUR COOL.

BLAST: a quick, strong effect from a drug. Also a good time or party (BEER BLAST). Deep drag on a joint.

BOMBITA: vial of amphetamine. Mixture of heroin, speed, and tuinal (barbiturate).

BOO-HOO: priest in Neo-American Church.

BOOK: The P.D.R. (Physician's Desk Reference) which specifies doses and reactions of legal drugs. BIBLE, P.D.R., THE BOOK.

BOOSTER: added dose taken to prolong trip.

BOPPER: young person in tune with times and hip.

BOSS: great, good. OUT OF SIGHT, GROOVY.

BOTTOM-OUT: to hit rock bottom before rebounding

and starting to improve or kick a habit (i.e., drugs, alcohol).

BREAD: money, GREEN STUFF, FOLDING STUFF, SCRATCH. See CRUMBS.

BRING DOWN: something that mutes a high as food or an unwelcome person (noun). To abort a trip with or without medication (verb).

BROAD: a woman. CHICK, BABE, BABY.

BROTHER: (SISTER): term used by black man (woman) to address a black man (woman).

BUFOTENINE: chemical isolated from skin of certain toads which raises blood pressure and produces hallucination. Also found in some plants and a few mushrooms but not in bananas as recently claimed.

BUG: pester, annoy.

BUGGY: crazy.

BULB: pellet containing an active chemical within the inert powder or filler in a capsule such as Darvon compound 65. Used to trip with.

BULL: small talk, lies, JIVE.

BUM TRIP: bad or upsetting drug experience, often characterized by fear, anxiety, panic, depression or paranoia. BUMMER, BUM BEND, DOWN TRIP, BAD TRIP.

BUTCH: lesbian who plays role of male.

BUZZ: early feelings at onset of marihuana high; pleasant high (without hallucinations) from any drug or alcohol. As verb to try to buy drugs.

CACTUS: peyote cactus. See PEYOTE.

CAMP: something regarded as old fashioned and so far out of date that suddenly it becomes stylish again due to its very oldness.

CARTOON: visual hallucination. TRAIL, PATTERN.

CASE: to look over a place, to scrutinize something.

CATNIP: scented herb used for cutting grass (stretcher or filler). Sometimes sold as pot to naive. Alleged to be slightly hallucinogenic for some susceptible individuals but if so it must produce only a low high.

CAT: any male; male who is cool or with it; a swinger.

CHECK OUT: see what is going on.

CHEMICAL PROMISCUITY: multiple drug use. MULTI-HABITUATION, PAN-ADDICTION.

CHICK: girl. FLIPPED-OUT CHICK is a crazy girl.

CHICKEN: cowardly; afraid.

CHICKEN OUT: not doing something for fear of consequences.

CHILL: to ignore or brush-off; refuse to sell drugs to suspected buyer.

CHIP: use drugs only now and then. JOY POPPING, DABBLING.

CHIPPING: infrequent use of heroin or other opiate. EXPERIMENTING, DABBLING, SMALL HABIT, WEEKEND HABIT, SUNDAY HABIT, MICKEY-MOUSE HABIT, ICE-CREAM HABIT, PEPSI COLA HABIT, JOY RIDING, TRIPPING.

CIBA: Doriden, nonbarbiturate sedative, made by Ciba Company. D., C.B.

CLEAN: no drugs on person when arrested; free of all drugs. Pot without seeds or stems (MANICURED).

COCAINE: COKE, SNOW, HAPPY-POWDER, CHARLIE, HAPPY-DUST, POGO-POGO, C-DUST, STARDUST, BOUNCING POWDER, GIN, BIG-C, CANDY, BERNICE, CHOLLY, GIRL, GOLD DUST. GOOFY-DUST--powdered cocaine for snorting.

CODEINE: POP, SCHOOLBOY, TURP.

COKED-UP: under the influence of cocaine.

COKE HEAD: user of cocaine (LEAPER).

COMBINATIONS: mixtures of two or more drugs. At

present the usual basic ingredient is LSD to which is added any of the following contaminants: speed, sernyl, heroin, opium, strychnine, cocaine, atropine, belladonna, strammonium, STP, DMT, mescaline, etc. Also called SALADS. Their composition is usually unknown and even street names don't indicate ingredients. Following are current street names of these mixtures (some may be pure acid but it is impossible to tell now). Pure ones are RIGHTEOUS and adulterated ones are DIRTY, SALADS, COMBINATIONS. Blue haze, blue cap, green swirl, purple tab, black flat, green dot, purple haze, black acid, yellow flat, brown dot, blue splash, orange sunshine, orange blossom, orange wedge, strawberry field, strawberry acid, red dimple, orange double dimple, blue smear, paper acid, love, love saves, white lightning, peace pill, LBJ stay away, product IV, cupcake, greendome, let sunshine do, purple ozoline, purple barrel, grape parfait, peppermint swirl, yellow (pink, orange, purple) wedge, yellow dimple, blue cheer, blue flat, blue doubledome, chocolate-chip, orange dome, orange double dome, double dimple, squirrel, quicksilver, Hawaiian sunshine, California sunshine, clear dot, purple microdot. See LSD.

COME DOWN: return to normal state after being high on a drug; lost effects of a drug. COME HOME, LAND, SOBER UP.

COME ON: start to get effects of a drug.

COMMUNE: group with similar philosophy and life style living together and supporting each other. ENCLAVE.

CON: to fool, deceive or swindle. BEAT, FLIM-FLAM.

CONTACT HIGH: turning on by coming in contact and interacting empathetically with someone already high on a drug; becoming high from being in a small unventilated room where pot is being smoked without actually smoking it.

COOL: smart, knowledgeable in ways of drug scene, etc.; safe. GROOVY.

COOL IT: stop what you are doing.

COP: acquire, take, buy, steal.

COP TO: admit to something. COP OUT TO.

COP OUT: give up, drop out of drug scene, society, etc., avoid a situation.

COP OUT ON: fail to do something.

COPE: handle self effectively while high on a drug or otherwise.

CORAL: chloral hydrate (non-barbituric sedative). JOY JUICE. Also see MICKEY FINN.

CRACK A BENNIE: crack open benzedrine inhaler (or other type) to get drug impregnated wick for use.

CRANK BUGS: imaginary insects on skin while speeding.

CRANKING: using speed (CRANK) repeatedly. SPEED-ING.

CRASH: enter somebody's apartment or pad to sleep; fall asleep; come down hard from a high.

CRASH PAD: facility run by non-professionals to treat bum trips by talking-down method. Street level operation to care for trippers right off the street without hassling them or informing authorities, either parental, academic, or police. A crisis center for the care of bummers.

CRAZY: enjoyable, exciting, great.

CROAKER: doctor who sells illegal drugs or writes prescriptions for them. HACK.

CRYSTAL PALACE: place where speed (amphetamine) is shot (injected).

CRYSTALS: speed in powder form.

CYCLAZOCINE: narcotic antagonist being tried for heroin addiction. CYC.

CRUMBS: money (small change).

CUFF: stand somebody up.

CURE: speed up maturing of plants which yield drugs by moistening with sugar water or wine and then slowly drying them.

D: Doriden (non-barbiturate sedative). CIBA.

DABBLE: to take small amounts of drugs on an irregular basis.

DARVON: non-opiate analgesic abused by some. PINKS, RED & GRAYS.

DEMOROL: synthetic opiate which has replaced morphine due to fewer side effects. Does not constrict the pupils. Favorite drug of addiction by doctors and nurses rather than heroin. MEPERIDINE, PETHIDINE.

DESTROY: ruin, smash.

D.E.T.: variant of D.M.T.

DHARMA: right to do; a proper way of life for an individual.

DIG: to enjoy, appreciate, understand.

DIGGERS: hippie group which gives aid to other hippies (i.e., providing food, etc.).

DILAUDID: opiate stronger than morphine with fewer side effects. Effective by mouth as well as by injection. DILLIES.

DILL: a plant of the parsley family alleged to produce mild stimulation and euphoria. See Z.N.A.

DIPPIE: former hippie who dropped out of movement and into straight society.

DITRAN: piperidyl benzilate. A potent hallucinogen producing catatonia, auditory hallucinations and psychoses. J.B.-239.

D.M.A.: a synthetic amphetamine.

D.M.D.A.: synthetic amphetamine.

D.M.T.: dimethyltryptamine. Very short acting (30') hallucinogenic drug related to LSD but milder. Easily synthesized and similar to psilocin. Parsley soaked in it and then eaten or smoked. Known as the BUSINESS-MAN'S PSYCHEDELIC MARTINI or BUSINESS MAN's TRIP. COMMUTING--taking D.M.T. See also D.E.T., D.P.T.

DOLLS: barbituates and amphetamines (from "Valley of the Dolls").

DOLLY: methadone, a synthetic opiate used in heroin withdrawal and addiction. DOLOPHINE, METHADONE. Synthesized in the Third Reich and named Dolophine after Adolph Hitler.

D.O.E.: synthetic amphetamine.

D.O.E.T.: synthetic amphetamine which is analog of S.T.P. and very potent.

DON'T SWEAT IT: don't fret, take it easy.

DON'T TREAD ON ME: don't lay your thing on me. Don't force me.

DOWNER: tranquilizer or barbiturate. BACKWARDS.

DO YOUR THING: doing what one enjoys; doing what one feels is right or necessary for one's happiness or peace of mind.

D.P.T.: variant of D.M.T.

DRAG: dull. A boring event, thing or person.

DROP IT: say it.

DROP OUT: withdraw from a disliked activity.

DRUG SCENE: the varied activities and actions related to drug users and their life style. STREET: the user's environment, his neighborhood or his milieu. Also referred to as NARCOLAND and LIVING ON THE BRICKS or LIVING ON THE STREET. (For specific drugs, consult appropriate headings in glossary.)

Marketing:

BIG MAN: top person in drug ring. SOURCE.
JOBBER: one who stores drugs in bulk for distribution.
PUSHER/DEALER: sometimes distinction made

that pusher deals only in hard drugs
and dealer in soft drugs. PEDDLER,
CANDY MAN, CONTACT, CONNECTION, ICE
CREAM MAN, PAPER BOY, MOTHER, SUPPLIER,
BAG MAN, TAMBOURINE MAN, BROKER, SOURCE,
TRAVEL AGENT, TRAFFICKER, JUNKER, SWING-
MAN, BIG MAN, COP MAN.

COYOTE: tricky or dishonest seller.

SNATCH-GRAB JUNKIE: unreliable small-time
pusher.

RUNNER: transporter of drugs from source
to pusher. MULE, CONDUCTOR ON TROLLEY.

MAKE A RUN: travel to another city to
obtain drugs.

GLOBETROTTER: one who contacts all local
pushers in effort to get the best stuff.

ARSENAL: pusher's supply of drugs. CARGO.

STASH: hidden supply of drugs. CACHE,
PLANT.

SQUIRREL: addict who stashes large amount
of drugs.

THOROUGHBRED: sells only pure drugs.
TAKE OFF ARTIST: steals from other
addicts or pushers.

Manufacture and Processing:

FACTORY: clandestine lab for making drugs.
BREWERY, MIDNIGHT LAB, KITCHEN LAB,
FEED STORE, LAB.

COOK: chemist who works in a clandestine
lab.

CAP: drug sold in gelatin capsule. CAP-
SULE, BEAN.

CAPPING: process of putting drug in
capsule. PUT UP.

DOTTING: dropping liquid drug as acid on
porous paper.

TABBING: placing liquid drug on tablet such
as vitamin C tablet.

TAB: tablet. PILL.

DUSTING: sprinkling powdered drug on
another substance as dusting PCP or HOG
on parsley or DMT on grass.

CUTTING: diluting down drug with another
substance which may be inert as milk,
sugar, talc, starch or active as quinine,
quinidine, procaine, histadyl. WACK UP.

STRETCHER: material used for cutting.
FILLER.

WEIGHT: amount of drug. HEAVY: large
amount. LIGHT: small amount.

ROLL: roll of tablets in foil or paper.
ROLL DECK.

BOTTLE: large number pills or tablets such
  as 1,000. JAR, JUG, BOTTLE or JAR
  DEALER.
KEG: very large number tablets, pills or
  capsules as 25,000.
FEED BAG: container for drugs.
BIZ: small amount of drug.
PIECE: unit of measurement of drugs. For
  various names see sections on heroin,
  speed and marihuana elsewhere in glossary.
PILLOW: sealed polyethylene bag of drugs.
TASTE: tiny amount of a drug offered as
  inducement to purchase as a sales promotion gimmick. PICK UP.
BAG, BINDLE, BALLOON, FOIL, SPOON, DECK,
  etc. (See under Heroin.)
WRAP: wrapping of paper, foil or plastic
  used to disguise package of drugs and
  to obliterate the odor.

Quality control (or lack of it):

RIGHTEOUS: pure, unadulterated drugs.
  HONEST, PURE.
COUNT: quality of purity of a drug.
BURNED: cheated in drug purchase, i.e.,
  drug not righteous due to additives or
  fillers or very weak due to excessive
  cutting.
BURN ARTIST: dishonest seller, i.e., poor
  quality as above or no delivery after
  payoff.
PUFF: to extol a drug as being better than
  it actually is, i.e., purer, stronger.
FRUIT SALAD: pooling of various drugs removed from home medicine chests. Participants then take them without any
  knowledge of what they are using. GRAB
  BAG, POT LUCK.
SALADS: combinations of drugs. See COM-
  BINATIONS elsewhere in glossary.

Drugs in general: (For specific drugs
refer to glossary.)

DOPE: any drug (originally referred to
  cocaine and opiates only). STUFF,
  GOODS, MERCHANDISE, CANDY, SUGAR;
  GOOD STUFF: high quality drugs.
STONEHEAD: person dependent on a drug.
  LEANING ON DRUGS.
DOPER: one who takes drugs of any sort.
  USER, DRUGGIE, PLAYER. (See also other

section on ADDICT/ADDICTION.)
DOING DRUGS: taking drugs. INTO, BEHIND,
USING, ON, GETTING ON.
DOPE FIEND: originally restricted to one
dependent on morphine or cocaine. Now
refers to user of any drug.
HEAD: chronic user of a drug, i.e., POTHEAD,
ACIDHEAD, PILLHEAD, etc.
MIND BLOWER: unusually pure drug. One that
is honest or righteous.
SMALL TIME: refers to drugs other than
heroin. SMALL STUFF, LIGHT STUFF.
BIG TIME: refers to heroin and cocaine.
HEAVY STUFF.
SOFT DRUGS: poor term referring to drugs
that do not cause physical addiction
(may produce psychological addiction,
however). Included are pot, speed, acid,
etc. LIGHT STUFF, HEAD DRUGS.
HARD DRUGS: equally undesirable term usually
thought to refer to drugs capable of resulting in true physical addiction.
Besides heroin and other opiates barbiturates and minor tranquilizers could be
included as they lead to physical addiction. Cocaine included in hard category
by some even though it produces psychological rather than physical addiction.
HEAVY STUFF, BODY DRUGS.
MIND BENDER: drug said to expand the consciousness or mind, i.e., hallucinogen
as LSD, etc.
TURN ON: to start somebody on drugs.

Methods of use and condition of users:

POP: take by mouth. DROP, PILL DROPPER,
PILL POPPER. PILLHEAD: chronic user
orally.
SNORT: use nasally like snuff. SNIFFING,
HUFFING, HORNING. MATCHHEAD: small
employed for.
MUSCLE: to inject intramuscularly.
SKIN POP: subcutaneous injection. POPPING,
SKINNING.
MAINLINE: inject intraveneously. LINING,
SHOOTING, FIXING.
TONGUE IT: to inject in floor of mouth at
base of tongue to escape detection.
SHOOTERS: mainliners.
SHOOT UP: a series of injections repeated
within short period of time as speed,
cocaine.

RUN: series of injections repeated over a
   period of several days without any
   respite as with speed, cocaine, etc.
   Longer duration than a shoot up. BINGE.
RUSH: initial pleasureable sensation follow-
   ing shooting heroin, speed, etc. FLASH,
   JOLT, ZING, TINGLE, THRILL, SPLASH,
   CHARGE, KICK.
SPREE: long period of steady use of drugs
   or alcohol.
BADS: post spree or post run depression.
   LIFE: respite from BADS.
STONED: under influence of drug or intoxi-
   cated from drug. CHARGED UP, RIPED,
   HIGH, LOADED, BLOCKED, LIT UP, BLASTED,
   TWISTED, FLYING, UP, BELTED, GROUND UP,
   TORN UP, COASTING, GOING UP, TAKING A
   TRIP, ZONKED, SPACED, SPACED OUT, FLOAT-
   ING, HOPPED UP, BLITZED, WIRED, LOADED,
   JACKED UP, BENT, BENT OUT OF SHAPE,
   BOMBED, BOXED, KNOCKED OUT, MESSED UP,
   MONOLITHIC, OUT OF ONE'S MIND, SPIKED,
   SINGING, SMASHED, BENDING AND BOWING.
WASTED: so deeply under influence of drug
   from repeated use that one no longer can
   function normally. DESTROYED, SPENT,
   WIPED OUT, WHIPPED, BEATEN. Exhausted
   physically and ruined psychologically.
STONEHEAD: one completely dependent on
   drugs. LEANING ON DRUGS.
WASHED UP: off drugs. WITHDRAWN, CLEAN,
   CLEARED UP, CLEAN HEAD, CLEANED UP,
   GOOD HEAD.
STRAIGHT: not intoxicated or under influence
   of drugs. Also means feeling well or
   not sick for lack of a fix.
LAUNCHING PAD: place where drugs are taken
   in a group. SHOOTING GALLERY, PAD, ACID
   PAD, FREAK HOUSE, FLASH HOUSE.

Buying drugs:

MEET: appointment for copping drugs.
   PICK UP: obtain drugs from somebody.
IN POWER: having drugs to sell. SLICE
   BREAD: make payoff.
SCORE: to buy drugs. COP, CONNECT, HIT,
   MAKE, MAKE BUY, MAKE THE MAN, MAKE STRIKE.
SHORT COUNT: small amount sold as a larger
   amount.
DEAL IN WEIGHT: sell large amounts. HEAVY
   DEALING. SCRATCHING: searching for
   drugs.

PUT OUT FIRST: pay in advance with
     delivery later. SPOT YOU.
HAND TO HAND: person to person delivery
     drugs with payment at the time.
BUY: evidential purchase by agent or by
     informer under supervision of agent.
BURNED: cheated in a purchase. BURN ARTIST:
     dealer who specializes in burning people.

DUDE: any male.

DUSTED: under influence of P.C.P.

DYKE: female homosexual, lesbian.

DYNAMITE: a great event, thing or happening.
     OUT OF SIGHT. Also potent, uncut heroin.

EGO GAMES: deprecatory term applied to social
     or business activities of the square world.

EGO TRIP: actions that bolster one's own ego
     irregardless of their possible harmful
     effects on others.

ELECTRIC: exciting, scintillating, mindblowing.
     Influenced by or containing a psychedelic
     drug as in electric kool-aid.

ELECTRIC KOOL-AID: punch containing LSD fre-
     quently served at Acid Tests.

ESTABLISHMENT: those of you who are over 30 years
     old and members of the decadent menopausal
     generation that is not to be trusted. Wel-
     come to the group! NEW ESTABLISHMENT:
     young adults just turning 30 and so just
     out of the youth and/or drug subculture.

EXPLORER'S CLUB: circle of acid users.

FAG: male homosexual. FAGGOT, GAY, FAIRY, FRUIT.

FAKE OUT: to fool.

FALL OUT: falling asleep. ON THE NOD, CRASH,
     FLAKE OUT.

FAR OUT: bizarre, unusual, avant-garde. WAY OUT.

FEED YOUR HEAD: take drugs.

FEED YOUR MONKEY: maintain a drug habit, especially
     heroin.

FEMME: lesbian who plays role of female.

FINK: one who gives information to the authorities or gives up to the establishment.

FINK OUT: to inform, fail to do something. RAT, SNITCH.

FIREPLACE RITUAL: verbal dressing down in presence of all residents. Synanon term.

FIX: injection of drug, usually heroin. JOLT, SHOT, JOB, GEEZE, CHARGE, WAKE-UP.

FLAKY: a little abnormal mentally or emotionally but not really psychotic.

FLAMING: adjective to intensify meaning of a noun, i.e., flaming chick. SCREAMING.

FLAP: fuss or commotion about something.

FLASHBACK: recurrence of drug reaction (acid, pot) weeks or months later without taking drug again. RECURRENCE, ECHO, FREE TRIP, RETURN TRIP.

FLIP: express unusually strong emotion; exhibit psychotic behavior; to become unduly excited or psyched up.

FLIP OUT: to have psychotic reaction to drug; lost control or develop anxiety. To have a mystical experience through drugs, yoga, meditation, etc. WIG OUT.

FLOWER CHILDREN (PEOPLE): youths who have dropped out of conventional society and practice free love, free drugs, free food, communal living, etc. They seek God, peace, love, nonmaterialism and noncompetitiveness. Not all of them necessarily use drugs.

FLOWER POWER: use of love rather than force to effect change in man and society.

FLUNK OUT: to start using stronger drugs than formerly. GRADUATE.

FLY AGARIC: hallucinogenic mushroom containing bufotenine.

FOURS: number 4 empirin compound (1 grain codeine).

FRACTURE: to shake up or disturb.

FRANTIC: nervous, jittery, desperate.

FREAK: one who uses a drug intensely (i.e., speed freak, acid freak, freon freak). Also one intensely interested in non-drug activity (i.e., car freak).

FREAK HOUSE: where speeders congregate to shoot. FLASH HOUSE.

FREAK OUT: lose contact with reality; wild or unusual behavior; have fun; change something radically, become temporarily deranged from a drug. Also to surprise or alarm (i.e., freak out my parents).

FREAKY: weird, strange.

FREON: a refrigerant. Also used as a propellant for many aerosols. Intoxicating and it may produce asphyxiation or cardiac irregularities when inhaled. Sometimes fatal--the S.S.D.S. (SUDDEN SNIFFING DEATH SYNDROME).

FREON FREAK: user of freon. FROST FREAK.

FRINGIES: non-students who hang around students or hippie groups without actually being part of the group.

FRISCO SPEEDBALL: cocaine, LSD, and heroin.

FRONT: false display of respectability (not genuine) as conventional clothing being worn by hippy for effect on the establishment. Also lending money for a purchase.

FROSTY: exceptionally knowledgeable and cool (almost to a point of being unapproachable). The acme of coolness. SUPERCOOL.

F.U.K.: hallucinogenic drug, possibly a form of S.T.P.

FLUNKY: distasteful and unattractive. Occasionally really neat or great depending on the attitude of the person.

GAME: conventional attitude or behavior; order of structured society; group therapy session (Daytop, Synanon, etc.).

GARBAGE HEAD: one who will take any drug offered without knowing or caring what it is.

GAS (GASSER): supreme or super experience; unusually pleasing thing.

GASSED-OUT: overcome by unusual experience be it amusing, beautiful, exciting, etc.

GERONIMO: drink of alcohol with barbiturates.

GET BEHIND IT: enjoy a high. Become completely involved in the action at hand.

GET IN THE WIND: ride a bike (motorcycle).

GET UP: to take drugs and notice an effect. GO UP, TAKE OFF, LIFT UP, GET OFF.

GIG: originally a performance by a musical group. Now a job, profession, or any activity.

GLOW: pleasant feelings from taking a drug.

GLUE-SNIFFING: inhalation of any volatile solvent that intoxicates as quickly drying glue, carbona, turpentine, gasoline, nail polish remover, freon, etc. (GASSING, HUFFING, BLOWING THE BAG, FLASHING). GLUEY: one who sniffs glue. (GLUEHEAD). WAD or GLAD RAG: cloth saturated with solvent and held to nose for sniffing. See FREON.

GETTING ON: taking drugs. USING. GOING-UP.

GOOD PEOPLE: a person who is all right; one who can be trusted with drugs or otherwise.

GOOF: make a mistake, take drugs.

GOOFED UP: under the influence of goofballs (barbiturates), originally; now includes pot, etc.

GOOFING: behavior in unusual or drunk fashion after taking goofballs; the playing of mind games when stoned.

GOOF-OFF: not to do a job; do something without a purpose.

GO STRAIGHT: get off drugs. To refrain from all illegal activities.

GRAB: to impress, appeal, suit (i.e., "How does that grab you?").

GRAVOL: hallucinogenic antihistamine used in Canada and England.

GREASER: formerly derogatory term for Mexican-Americans, Mexicans, etc. Now applied to one you don't like or respect regardless of color, race, etc.

GROSS: repulsive, crass, undesirable.

GROOVE: concentrate intensely on an object or activity with great pleasure (i.e., grooving on grass).

GROOVY: swinging, with it, great, extremely enjoyable. GASSEY, OUT OF SIGHT, WIGGY.

GROUNDMAN: one who remains straight during an acid party to care for the trippers. BABY SITTER, GUIDE, TOUR GUIDE, CO-PILOT, GROUND CONTROL.

GURU: Hindu teacher, hippie leader, one whose ideas or philosophies are greatly admired or esteemed.

GUT LEVEL: deep emotionally.

HACK IT: to tolerate something, to cope with a situation. CUT IT.

HAIRCUT: Daytop Village or Synanon term for severe verbal reprimand given to erring member of family by one of the older members. If offense is severe enough his head may be shaved in addition to the dressing-down.

HAIRY: difficult, rough.

HANG IN THERE: stay with it, keep strong. HANG TOUGH.

HANGUP: uncomfortable idea or habit, thing that is bugging one.

HANG LOOSE: stay calm and relaxed.

HAPPENING: the action at the moment; meaningful event.

HARMINE: hallucinogenic alkaloid from South
American vine. May be fatal.

HASHBURY: contraction of words HAIGHT-ASHBURY.

HASHISH: see marihuana. HASH.

HASSLE: argument; unpleasant situation. Verb
means to bother, annoy, argue.

HEAD: chronic user of drug, for example, acidhead (LSD), pothead (marihuana), A-head
(amphetamines).

HEAD SHOP: store specializing in items of interest to the drug subculture.

HEAD SHRINKER: psychiatrist. SHRINK, PSYCH.

HEAT: police pressure, administration pressure
(school) or pressure from any other source.

HEAVY: important, impressive, significant. A
strong drug, for example, heavy grass.
Doing a lot of something as heavy dealing
of drugs (HEAVY INTO DRUGS).

HEIFER DUST: baloney; b.s. JIVE, BULL.

HEROIN: MAINLINING, ADDICTS and ADDICTION,
OPIUM. (See also these headings elsewhere
in glossary.)

JUNK: heroin. H, HORSE, HARRY, SCAG,
SMACK, WHITE STUFF, GOODS, MERCHANDISE,
POISON. ANTIFREEZE, SCAT.
MAINLINING: intravenous injection. LINING.
POPPING: subcutaneous injection. SKIN
POPPING, SKINNING, POPPING.
SNORTING: nasal use like snuff. SNIFFING,
BLOWING, HORNING.
BREAKING IN: just commencing to use junk.
CADET: novice junkie.
HONEYMOON STAGE: period of early use
before addiction. VIRGIN STATE.
HEAVY, DYNAMITE, BOMB DYNO: strong heroin.
GARBAGE, LEMONADE, LIPTON TEA, FLEA POWDER,
CRAP: weak junk.
BLANK, TURKEY, DUMMY: alleged heroin but
none present in the powder.
HOT SHOT, RAT POISON: heroin purposely
poisoned with Ajax, rat poison, strych-
nine, etc.

CUTTING: diluting before sale by adding
    inert substances as milk sugar, starch,
    talc, and sometimes active ingredients
    as quinine, quinindine, histadyl, pro-
    caine.
STRETCHERS, FILLERS: substances as sugar,
    quinine, etc., used for cutting heroin.
BAD BUNDLE: package of heroin ruined by
    moisture or excessive cutting.

Quantities for sale:

DEUCE: $2 bag. TRES: $3 bag. NICKEL
    Bag: $5 worth.
DIME BAG: $10 worth. EIGHT: 1/8 ounce.
    QUARTER: 1/4 ounce.
PIECE: 1 ounce (CAN). HALF LOAD: 15 bags.
    BUNDLE: 25 bags.
KEY: 1 kilogram (2.2 pounds). CAP: cap-
    sule of heroin.
GRAM: 10 caps. BUNDLE, PACKET, DECK,
    PAPER: folder paper or glassene envel-
    opes of junk. FOIL: tinfoil packet of
    heroin. BIRD'S EYE: tiny amount.
    BALLOON: toy balloon containing heroin.
BROWN STUFF: heroin from Mexico, etc.,
    that is brown. BROWN.
CHINA WHITE: heroin from Europe, etc., that
    is white. WHITE.
RED CHICKEN: Chinese heroin.
RUMP: to be on junk. IN THE BIG TIME.

HIP: aware; in the know; informed; tuned-in.

HIPPIE: dropout from society who refuses to
    accept and adopt the values and mode of
    life of the Establishment.

HIT: arrest; rob; purchase drugs; find a vein;
    smoke a joint; one dose of a particular
    drug.

HIT THE MOON: achieve the highest point of a
    trip. PEAK, REACH FOR THE MOON.

HOLDING YOUR MUG: keeping a secret.

HOOKER: whore.

HORN: the telephone. Inhale drug through the
    nose (Snort, Sniff).

HORROR DRUG: one of the belladonna alkaloids.

HOT SEAT: chair in which member of Daytop Village or Synanon is seated during encounter therapy for infraction of rules.

HUNG UP: vacillating without being able to reach a decision. Involved with person or thing to exclusion of everything else.

HUSTLE: pursue women, money, drugs or fame. Work hard to accomplish something. To obtain money for drugs by thievery, prostitution (TURN A TRICK), PIMPING, etc.

HUSTLER: one who hustles; a go-getter.

HYDROCODONE: synthetic codeine. DIHYDROCODEINOWE, HYKE, HYCODAN.

IFIF: International Foundation, Foundation for Internal Freedom founded by Leary for experimenting with LSD, mescaline, etc.

IN: belonging to or accepted by a group.

INHALERS: glue and other volatile solvents (deliriants). Also nasal inhalers as wyamine. (See GLUE SNIFFING and FREON.)

INNER SPACE: one's innermost self; physical recesses of mind believed affected by drugs.

INTO: being involved in (i.e., "He is into acid now."). BEHIND.

IN TRANSIT: on an acid trip.

JAMMING: to blow your cool, at a loss for words.

JAZZ: small talk. JIVE.

JIVE: to lie or cheat. As noun--unimportant talk, lies, baloney (BULL), GARBAGE (JAZZ, ROUND AND ROUND).

JOHN: person who does not use drugs. Client of prostitutes.

JOINT: marihuana cigarette. STICK, REEFER.

JOY POPPING: intermittent use of heroin for kicks or tripping without being addicted.

JUICED: high on alcohol. JUICED UP, BOMBED,

SMASHED.

JUICEHEAD: alcoholic.

KARMA: alleged aura, radiations or vibrations given off by a person. May be good or bad. Also one's life as determined by fate.

KEEP THE FAITH BABY: phrase used when splitting.

KEEP THE LID ON: control or contain things.

KEEP IT ON ICE: to keep a secret.

KINK: a hang up, a particular habit or activity one has to indulge (i.e., a homosexual has to do his thing eventually).

LAY IT ON: attempt to force your thing or thinking on another; forceful arguing.

LAY IT ON ME: tell me all about it without holding back.

LAME: un-hip, not street-wise, subscribes to middle and upper-class morality. STRAIGHT, SQUARE.

LAND: come down easily from trip. COME HOME.

LEAN ON: to apply pressure (heat) of any kind.

L.B.J.: a piperdyl compound which is hallucinogenic. Not the same as L.B.J. Stay Away. J. B.-336 and T.W.A.

LEGAL HIGH: trip from over-the-counter item not requiring a prescription such as Amyl nitrite, Sominex, Contact, etc. (See NATCH TRIP.)

LEMAR: group advocating the legalization of marihuana.

LET IT ALL HANG OUT: level with somebody, speak freely hiding nothing.

LET IT SLIDE: to ignore something.

LIKE: filler word for pauses in conversation when hesitating.

LIPPIE: a hippie preoccupied with putting down straight society through debate, activism, etc.

LOOSE: relaxed.

LOOSE IN THE HEAD: disturbed mentally or emotionally. FLAKY.

LOSE ONE'S WIG: lose one's mind, become flaky.

LOSE YOUR COOKIES: vomit after taking drug. DUMP, FLASH, HEAVE.

LSD: League for Spiritual Discovery, a "religion" founded by Timothy Leary and using LSD, mescaline, etc., as sacrament.

LYSERGIC ACID: chemical precursor of LSD used in its manufacture. Not hallucinogenic itself. Illegal to buy now.

L.S.M.: chemical cogener of LSD.

LSD: ACID, CUBE, 25, BIG D, HAWK, CHIEF, BLUE, OWSLEY, GHOST, WHITE SANDOZ, CUBE, BEAST, CRACKER, COFFEE, etc.
Hallucinogenic derivative of lysergic acid, an alkaloid found in the rye fungus ergot (Claviceps purpura). Chemical name of LSD is d-lysergic acid diethylamide tartrate 25.
LSD--"love, security and devotion."
See COMBINATIONS for street names.
ONE WAY HIT: single tablet for one trip. SINGLE HIT.
TWO WAY HIT: single scored tablet with trip two people (i.e., double blue dome). DOUBLE HIT.
FOUR WAY HIT: tablet which is double scored so it can be broken into four parts. Micrograms sufficient so that four people can get off.
PAPER ACID: PAPER, LOVE SAVES, BLUE SPASH, BLUE DOT, RAGGEDY-ANNY, SKY-RIVER, GELATIN FLAKE ACID: WINDOW GLADD, CONTACT LENS, CLEAR LIGHT. (See Combinations for street names.)

M99: etorphine. Very potent opiate for animal use only.

MACE: spice derived from nutmeg and slightly
hallucinogenic due to mysticin (elemincin).
Also a repellent aerosol used as a defen-
sive weapon in law enforcement.

MADE IT: attained one's goal.

MAINLINING: (See also headings elsewhere in
glossary as HEROIN, SPEED, ADDICTS AND
ADDICTION.
Intravenous injection of junk. LINING,
BANGING, SHOOTING, JABBING, JOLTING,
SPLASHING, TAKING OFF, GETTING OFF,
GEEZING, DRILLING, HITTING.
DITCH, VALLEY: inside of elbow which is
favorite site for shooting. Other lo-
cations used include forearms, legs,
between toes and fingers, tops of hands
and feet, neck (external jugular vein),
floor of mouth at base of tongue (lingual
veins) and penis (dorsalis penis vein--
rarely used).
PIPE: large good vein for hitting. ROLLER:
large vein that rolls away from needle.
TRACKS: needle marks and scars from main-
lining. CRATERS, MARKS CORNS.
TRACKED UP: arms or legs covered with
TRACKS. LOUSED UP.
POCKS: depressed oval scars from skin
popping. POCK MARKS.
PAD, SHOOTING GALLERY, CRYSTAL PALACE:
place where junkies shoot in.
GIVE WINGS: teach one how to mainline.
CADET: Novice junkie.
WORKS: equipment for mainlining. KIT,
ARTILLERY, MACHINERY, TOOLS, GIMMICKS,
BIZ, LAYOUT.
SPIKE: needle (NAIL, POINT). GUN:
syringe or eyedropper (DRIPPER,
MACHINE).
SILVER BIKE: syringe with chrome fittings.
MOBY GRAPE: syringe or dropper with
rubber bulb from baby's pacifier.
COLLAR: tape or rubber band to improve
fit between hub of needle and end of
syringe or dropper. GASKET.
COOKER: spoon or bottle cap for heating
heroin and water.
COOK: dissolve heroin in water by heat-
ing (PAN UP). HOCUS: mixture ready
for shooting.
SATCH COTTON: cotton in spoon or bottle
cap for filtration before shooting up.

66

TIE: tourniquet (silk stocking, bow tie,
    belt, etc.). TIE UP: apply tourni-
    quet (DO UP).
HIT: to inject vein. BLOW: to miss vein
    (MISS).
REGISTER: aspirate to make certain in vein.
    BACK UP, BACKTRACK.
TAP: inject very slowly by tapping end of
    syringe or dropper with finger.
BOOTING: sequence of repeated aspirations
    followed by repeated injections to pro-
    long effects. JACKING.
SHOOTING GRAVEY: dissolving dried residue
    of heroin and blood in syringe or dropper
    by heating it. This can then be shot
    again.
COTTONHEAD: one who cooks up several satch
    cottons to obtain what little heroin is
    trapped in the fibers in order to get
    another fix. COTTON TOP.

MAINTAINING: keeping self at a certain level of
    drug effect and being able to function
    properly.

MAKE IT: achieve something; inject a drug; buy
    a drug; to be with it.

MAKES IT: something that is just good or merely
    acceptable but not out of sight or dynamite
    (i.e., "That song makes it but it's not out
    of sight.").

MAKE THE SCENE: go where the action is.

MAKE TRACKS: to split. To leave tracks on body
    from shooting.

MAN: general term for addressing a male in
    conversation; a narcotic agent.

MANDALA: Hindu mystic symbol (often worn around
    neck).

MANDREX: combination of pyribenzamine and
    quaalude shot in England.

MARATHON ENCOUNTER: Daytop Village term for pro-
    longed 14-48 hour encounter group therapy
    session held periodically.

MARIHUANA: POT, GRASS, TEA, HEMP, CANNABIS,
    ROPE, HAY, WEED, MARY JANE, GUAGE, MUGGIES,

GANGSTER, BUSH, TEXAS, TEA.
STICK: cigarette. JOINT, REEFER (old term),
    ROCKET, HAPPY CIGARETTE.
PIN: thin joint. BOMB: thick joint
    (THUMB). PANATELLA: large long joint.
COCKTAIL: conventional cigarette in end of
    which is deposited some grass or hash.
CANCELLED STICK: conventional cigarette
    emptied and refilled with marihuana.
ROLLING UP: making a joint.
SKIN: general term for paper used in making
    sticks. PAPER. Specific papers used
    include, among others, BAMBOO, ZIGZAG,
    TOP (pot backwards).
ROACH: butt of joint. SNIPE.
CRUTCH: holder for smoking roach so as not
    to burn fingers. BRIDGE, CLIP, AIRPLANE,
    JEFFERSON AIRPLANE.
BLOWING GRASS: smoking marihuana. SMOKING,
    GOOFING, TAKING UP, TOKING UP, FIRING
    UP, BLOWING A JOINT, BLASTING, GETTING
    ON, TAKING GIGGLE SMOKE, POKING, PICKING
    UP, LIGHTING UP, BLASTING A JOINT.
POTHEAD: regular smoker. TEAHEAD, GRASS-
    HOPPER, YOUNG BLOOD (Novice).
POT PARTY: group smoking. BLAST PARTY,
    TEA PARTY.
TUCK AND ROLL: fold ends of joint rather
    than twisting them.
SCARF A JOINT: swallow stick or roach to
    escape detection.
MUNCHIES: urge to eat (especially sweets)
    after smoking. HUNGRIES, PEPPERMINT
    CANDY JAG.
TOKE PIPE: marihuana pipe. HOOKAH, HUBBLY-
    BUBBLY: water pipes.
STEAMBOAT: joint stuck in hole cut in top
    of cardboard core of toilet paper roll.
ENLIGHTENED COOKING: use of marihuana in
    cooking. COOKING WITH GRASS INSTEAD OF
    GAS. POT LIKKER: beverage of conven-
    tional tea plus marihuana. GRASS BROWNIE
    (ALICE TOKLAS BROWNIE), GRASS MUFFINS,
    GRASS BREAD, GRASS SPAGHETTI SAUCE, APPLE
    TURN-ONS, CHILI POT, HOT POT FUDGE, GRASS
    SALAD, GRASS MEAT BALLS, etc.
SHOT GUN: holding lit end of joint in mouth
    and blowing smoke through it into mouth
    of another person.
BOGART A JOINT: letting stock dangle from
    lips in manner of late Humphrey Bogart;
    taking too long with joint before passing
    it to your neighbor. BOGART, HOG A JOINT.

Types of Marihuana:

Foreign: BHANG: weakest. GANJA, KIF, DAG-
GA: intermediate. HASHISH (HASH) and
CHARAS: most potent of all is made from
the resin and so is 5 to 8 times as
strong as ordinary street grass. BLACK
RUSSIAN: hashish. GOLD LEAF: general
term for foreign pot which is stronger
than native grass. Examples of foreign
marihuana include: CAMBODIAN RED, PANAMA
RED, AFRICAN BLACK, PANAMA GOLD, CANADIAN
BLACKY, TIAJUANA GREEN, ACAPULCO GOLD,
MIHOACAN, MEXICAN GREEN, BLUE DIRT.

Native: (American): MANHATTAN SILVER:
rumored to be grown in sewers without
sunshine and consequently pale in color
(probably a put-on). Current varieties
include ILLINOIS GREEN, CHICAGO GREEN,
BETHESDA GOLD, TENNESSEE BLUE, KENTUCKY
BLUE, etc., and are less potent than
foreign marihuana. O.J. (OPIUM JOINT):
stick to which opium has been added.
HEAVY GRASS: unusually strong pot (GOLD,
GOLD LEAF, SUPERPORT). TRIP GRASS: marihuana to which has been added speed, DMT,
opium, heroin, etc. (SALT AND PEPPER).
ICEBERG: marihuana added to iceberg
lettuce. ICE PACK: high quality grass
(ICE BAG). PURPLE SEEDLESS: specifi-
cations unknown but rumored to be heavy
grass.

Processing and Marketing:

DIRTY: contains seeds, stems and leaves.
UNMANICURED, ROUGH, ROUGH STUFF.
CLEAN: refined grass from which stems and
seeds have been removed. MANICURED.
SHORT: loosely packed. LONG: tightly
packed.
BRICK: a kilogram. KG, KEY. BALE: 50 to
100 pounds of compressed grass.
L.B.: pound. BAR: compressed block of
pot not as large as bale.
LID: one ounce. Originally Prince Albert
tobacco can was used. CAN.
BOX: about 1/5th of an ounce of lid (can).
Formerly the amount contained in old-
fashioned penny match box.
NICKLE BAG: $5 worth or about 1/4 of an ounce.

DIME BAG: $10 worth or approximately 1/2
    ounce.
SOLE: flat rectangular piece of hash.
STOCK: large number of joints.
T.H.C.:   tetrahydrocannabinol. Also called
    SYNTHETIC GRASS. One of the active
    ingredients of marihuana which can be
    extracted from the plant and more recently
    has been synthesized in the laboratory.
    Tablet and liquid preparations are avail-
    able. Since it is notoriously unstable,
    all the THC or SYNTHETIC GRASS sold on
    the street invariably is something other
    than THC--presently most of it appears
    to be P.C.P. It is produced legiti-
    mately for research. See PARAHEXYL.

MARK: one easily conned or tricked.

M.D.A.:   synthetic amphetamine; 3, 4-methylene-
    dioxyamphetamine which is a potent hallu-
    cinogen. LOVE PILL.

MEAN: exceptionally good, almost perfect.

MELLOW: happy. Pleasantly high--not too far up
    and not too far down.

MELLOW-YELLOW: dried banana fibers for smoking.
    Alleged to be hallucinogenic but a put-on.

MESCALINE: hallucinogenic alkaloid extracted
    from peyote cactus or synthesized in labor-
    atory. Stronger than pot but weaker than
    acid. Yields same effects as peyote but
    there is less nausea and vomiting. MESC.,
    PUMPKIN SEEDS, YELLOW FOOTBALLS, YELLOW
    SUBMARINES, STRAWBERRY MESC.

MESS AROUND: do something inconsequential for
    the hell of it. GOOFING.

MESS UP: make a mistake. FOUL UP, GOOF UP.

METHADONE: see DOLLY.

METHAPYRILINE (HISTADYL):   filler for cutting
    heroin. An antihistamine.

METOPON: opiate stronger than morphine and with
    fewer side effects.

MICKY FINN: knockout drops of alcohol and chloral
    hydrate.

MICKEY MOUSE: petty, chicken, phony. Small drug habit. Policeman.

MICROGRAM: a unit of dosage of some drugs as LSD, 1/1,000,000th of a gram or 1/1,000th of a milligram. MCG, MIKE.

MILLIGRAM: 1/1,000th of a gram. MG.

M.M.D.A.: synthetic amphetamine.

MOD SQUAD: biracial couple or group.

MONOAMINE OXIDASE: (M.A.O.) INHIBITORS: nervous system stimulants related to amphetamines and used as mood elevators (i.e., Nardil, Marplan, Niamil, Parnate, Eutonyl, etc.). Potent and unpredictable, so dangerous. Potentiates action of alcohol, amphetamines, narcotics, sedatives, depressants, antihist-amines, anesthetics and insulin. Deaths have resulted from its use with such drugs. Some get high and hallucinate on MAO and it is a very toxic drug (sometimes lethal).

MOOCH: to get or leach.

MORNING GLORY: seeds of blue and white species as Wedding Bells, Heavenly Blue, Flying Saucers, Pearly Gates, etc. contain a chemical related to LSD and so have hallu-cinogenic properties. Aztecs used such seeds and called them OLOLIUQUI or TLITLIT-ZEN. Stronger than grass but weaker than acid. ELSIE'S FRAPPE: milk, ice cream and seeds.

MORPHINE: one of the original opiates producing addiction. Now replaced by heroin. WHITE STUFF, HARD STUFF, MORPHO, M, MORPHIE, DREAMER, M.S., MORPH.

MOTHER'S DAY: day welfare check arrives. DAY THE EAGLE SCREAMS.

MOXIE: a loud mouth, wise guy, objectionable person. Also refers to having guts.

MUSHROOMS, SACRED: see PSILOCYBIN.

NALLINE: narcotic antagonist for treating an overdose of heroin.

NATCH TRIP: high produced by natural substances as mace, nutmeg, morning glory, peyote, mushrooms, grass, etc. See LEGAL HIGH.

NATIVE AMERICAN CHURCH: religious and healing rituals of some American Indian tribes in the west in which peyote is legally employed (i.e., Commanches, Kiowas, Omahas, Mescalero, Apaches, etc.).

NEEDLE-FREAK: a very needle happy person. SPIKE FREAK.

NEEDLE-HAPPY: not genuine confirmed addict. Intermittent craving for injections with needle but only a weekend user. Fascinated with paraphernalia and mystique of mainlining cult but not truly addicted. SPIKE-HAPPY.

NEO-AMERICAN CHURCH: "religion" pushed by Leary in the mid-1960's with drugs as sacraments.

NITTY-GRITTY: truth, basic or fundamental facts. Reality underlying what appears on surface.

NIRVANA: oblivion, paradise, final freeing of soul from all that enslaves it, supreme happiness with all hatred and delusions eliminated.

NOLUDAR: a piperidine. Non-barbituric sedative. ROCHE.

NON-USER OF DRUGS: SQUARE, JOHN, BROWN SHOES, DO-RIGHTER, APPLE.

NO SWEAT: no worry, no bother.

NO WAY: absolute refusal to do something.

NOWHERE: situation or person that is boring, meaningless or lacks status.

NURD: one lacking any social graces or savvy. JERK.

NUTMEG: dried seeds of East Indian evergreen tree used as spice. Can produce euphoria and high said to be similar to that from pot. Used by inmates of prisons and sailors. Active ingredient is MYRISTICIN (ELEMICIN).

OFF THE WALL: unusual, surprising.

OLD LADY: common-law wife in communal living.
   Involved male is OLD MAN.

ON THE ROAD: travelling around leading nomadic
   life. ON THE RUN.

OPIUM: dried juice from the opium poppy and the
   basic ingredient from which morphine and
   heroin are processed. Smoked by the Chinese
   for years and brought to this country in the
   19th Century. Formerly used in many patent
   medicines. Recently plain opium has become
   popular with some students for smoking. A
   true narcotic or opiate. Made into a ball,
   placed on screen or mesh in bottom of pipe
   and smoked. Also called POPPY, BLACK STAFF,
   TAR, PEN YEN, BROWN STUFF.
   COOKING: heating opium to form it into a
      ball for smoking or heating with water
      to shoot. (COOK UP A PILL)
   BLACK PILL: opium pellet in pipe.
   TOXY: small container of opium. YEN HOCK:
      opium pipe.
   YEN-SEE: opium ash. YEN-SEE SUEY: opium
      wine.
   O.J. or OPIUM JOINT: opium added to mari-
      huana. Cigarette.
   BROWN HASH: alleged to be a form of opium.
   GONG: opium pipe. GONG BEATER: opium
      smoker.
   CHASING THE DRAGON: method of inhaling
      opium fumes through paper tube (QUILL).
   PING PONG BALLS: small balls of opium for
      smoking.
   LAY DOWN: place where opium is smoked.
   ICE CREAM: opium.

OREGANO: herb resembling marihuana and used to
   cut pot. Inactive--an inert filler or
   stretcher.

ORIGINALS: clothing that has never been washed.

OUT FRONT: open, frank.

OUT OF IT: not part of drug scene; not in contact
   with things; not aware. OUT TO LUNCH.

OUT OF SIGHT: superb; too good to be believed;
   cannot be described by words. GROOVY:
   TOO MUCH.

OUT OF THE BODY: tripping and feeling outside one's own body. OUTSIDE MYSELF: OUT OF THIS WORLD.

OUT OF YOUR TREE: irrational, crazy.

OWSLEY: originally acid made by underground chemist August Stanley Owsley III and said to be pure and potent.

PAD: room, apartment or house (not necessarily associated with drugs).

PARAHEXYL: semisynthetic extract of cannabis plant prepared from oil or resin. More potent than street pot. Use in experimental work on marihuana in the 1930's and 1940's. PYRAHEXYL, SYNHEXYL.

PAREGORIC: liquid opiate sometimes used as a temporary replacement for junk during a panic. P.G., P.O. See BLUE VELVET. User: GEE-HEAD.

PARTNER: buddy; close friend.

PASS: collapse, pass out; transfer of drugs; receive immunity from police.

P.C.P.: see SERNYL.

PEACE: word of universal salutation when meeting or leaving.

PEANUT BUTTER: mainlined with mayonnaise. It is unknown at present whether there are any psychological effects. Several cases have shown serious and extensive hemorrhages in various organs which were fatal.

PEPPER: rotten green pepper said to be hallucinogenic. Apparently another hoax or put-on, like the banana bit. JACKSON ILLUSION PEPPER.

PERCODAN: synthetic opiate recently being abused. OXYCODONE.

PEYOTE: dwarf cactus which is hallucinogenic when eaten. Used by Western Indians in the Native American Church. Weaker than LSD and stronger than pot. Active ingredient is mescaline. TOP, CACTUS, BUTTON, ORGANIC or NATURAL MESCALINE. FULL MOON--slice of peyote cactus. Also see MESCALINE.

PICK UP ON: grasp; gain understanding of.

PIECE: pistol, revolver, unit of measurement of a drug.

PIMP: man who solicits for prostitute. STABLE: group of girls who work for a pimp.

PIN: identify a specific detail or characteristic about a person. PINPOINT.

PINNED: constricted pupils due to opiates (exception is demerol).

PIPERIDINE: piperidyl benzilates are psychotomimetic drugs. Effects resemble atropine and also cause hallucinations, euphoria and delerium. Called "J.B." compounds. See DITRAN, LBJ, BENACTAZINE.

PLACIDYL: non-barbiturate sedative.

PLANT YOUR SEED: spread your philosophy through love, talk, sharing, etc.

PLASTIC: part-time, flexible, phony, insecure, unreal.

PLASTIC HIPPIE: phony or pseudo-hippie who makes the scene weekends but is not serious drug user or really sympathetic with hippie philosophy.

POLICE AND ENFORCEMENT TERMS:
FUZZ: police. THE MAN, NARC, BULL, SAM, WHISKERS, UNCLE, FEDS, BULLS, SNOOPS, BIMS, G, BUSTER, T-MAN. HARNESS BULLS: uniformed officers. PIG and BLUE FASCIST derogatory terms.
BLACK AND WHITE: police car. SHORT: car (WHEELS, CAN). CRACK SHORT: steal a car.
RIP OFF: to rob or steal. BOOST, BEAT, TAKE OFF, BURN, STING, COP.
FINGER: to inform. BURN, DO IN, DROP A DIME, SNITCH, RAT, SPILL.
FINK: informer. STOOL PIGEON, STOOLY, PIGEON.
BURNED: recognition of identity of undercover agent. MADE.

FAKE A BLAST: undercover agent pretending
    to smoke a joint and get high.
DEADWOOD: undercover agent posing as drug
    user.
BUSTED: arrested. COLLARED, DROPPED,
    NICKED, BEEN HAD, BATTED OUT, HIT,
    GRABBED, CLIPPED, NAILED.
POPPED: picked up by police.
TOSS: to search. FRISK, SHAKE DOWN, RUMBLE.
FEDERAL BEEF: federal offense. JUG: to
    stab. HEIST: robbery.
SNUFF: to kill, eliminate.
HOT: wanted by police, stolen goods. RUN
    IT: transport stolen merchandise to
    fence.
THROW ROCKS: commit crime to support habit.
PAPER HANGING: supporting habit by forging
    checks.
JITTERBUGGING: gang fighting. RUMBLE:
    street fighting gangs.
VIOLATED: arrested for parole violation.
FLAT TIME: sentence without chance for
    parole.
BUM RAP: arrest or conviction when not
    guilty.
HACK: prison guard.
MASTER KEY: sledge hammer for breaking down
    door in raid.
BULL HORROR: the drug user's occupational
    disease, i.e., paranoia about being ob-
    served or busted. FUZZ FEAR.
CARRYING: possessing drugs on one's person
    when apprehended. DIRTY, HOLDING, HEELED.
CLEAN: not possessing drugs when appre-
    hended. SWEET.
PLANT: to frame someone by surreptitiously
    placing drugs on his person or in his pad
    to be used later as evidence. FRAME,
    SET UP.
COOLER: jail, JOINT, LOCK UP, CAN, IRON
    HOUSE.
ON ICE: in jail. BOXED, SLAMMED, IN THE
    HOLE, ON THE SHELF, LOCKED UP.
ON THE STREET: out of jail. SWEET, FRESH,
    FRESH AND SWEET, ON THE BRICKS.
DUKE IN: to expose an undercover agent.
FENCE: buyer of hot or stolen goods.

POLITICO: political activist, usually of the
    New Left.

POW WOW: meeting of kindred spirits.

PRESCRIPTION: PAPER READER, SCRIPT, PER.

PROBES: deep discussions in confrontation therapy as in Daytop Village.

PSILOCIN: substance psilocybin is changed into psilocin in body during metabolism.

PSILOCYBIN: hallucinogen from the magic or sacred mushroom of Mexico. Used by Indians of Mexico for centuries. Stronger than pot but weaker than LSD. GOD'S FLESH, TEONAN-ACTL, SIMPLE SIMON.

PSYCHEDELIC: mind manifesting, mind expanding, conscious expanding, mind altering or reality distorting. Applied to hallucinogenic drugs as acid, peyote, psilocybin, etc.

PSYCHEDELIC DELICATESSEN: shop specializing in equipment for psychedelic drug sessions.

PSYCH OUT: figure out. To disturb or disrupt.

PSYCHED OUT: irrational.

PSYCHED UP: emotionally excited.

PUT DOWN: criticize; discourage; knock something; deny. CUT UP, SHOOT DOWN.

PUT (LAY) ONE'S TRIP ON: attempt to persuade another that he should believe what you believe and think since that is more im-portant than what he happens to believe and think. Force your influence on some-body.

PUTTING ME ON: fooling me; deliberately deceiv-ing me.

PUT ON: a hoax. To fool or deceive.

QUILL: folded matchbox cover for snorting junk, speed or coke.

RACKED-UP: upset, distraught, bothered. UNGLUED, UNHINGED, FLAPPABLE.

RAM-ROD: foreman in Daytop, etc., who supervises a work detail.

RAP: communicate quietly and peacefully, discuss important matters, gossip, converse. RAPPING, CORTEX TAPPING, RIFFING, RASP.

READ: to understand, to dig (i.e., "I read you.").

RE-ENTRY: to return or come down from a trip (COME DOWN). To rejoin normal society after tour in treatment center.

RESIDENTIAL THERAPEUTIC COMMUNITY: facility run by ex-addicts to treat drug dependent individuals by group encounter therapy. Takes 12-18 months of residence and is voluntary. Examples: Synanon, Daytop Village, Argosy House, etc.

RIGHT: word used at end of phrase or sentence to check listener's attention. Implies an unasked question, i.e., "Are you listening?" "Do you dig me?"

RIGHT ON: in agreement or correct so continue on.

RITALIN: mild stimulant and anti-depressant which elevates the mood and overcomes fatigue. Use in some individuals may lead to psychotic behavior and psychic dependence (habituation). Used by some to turn on. Bigger on West Coast than in the East.

SALAD: see COMBINATIONS.

SAN FRANCISCO: alleged psychedelic capital of the world. TRIPSVILLE, PSYCHEDELPHIA.

SATORI: enlightenment; awakening to one's true inner self.

SCENE: place where the action is; where something is happening; where it is at--may be good or bad scene. Social pattern of drug use in a certain area.

SCREWED: been had, taken advantage of.

SCREW UP: to make mistakes. GOOF UP.

SCREWED UP: mixed up, confused, neurotic.

SEDATIVES: see BARBITURATES. Also included are non-barbiturates as DORIDEN, PLACIDYL and

GUAALUDE. Both groups are physically addicting.

SERNYL: animal tranquilizer (phencyclidine). Potent and dangerous hallucinogen. Used as a vehicle for acid sometimes and also marketed as T.H.C., P.C.P., HOG, K2, PEACE PILL, CYCLONES.

SET: mental state of person about to take a drug plus his underlying psychological tendencies. Combination of 2 downers and 1 upper.

SETTING: total environment in which user undergoes his drug experience; surroundings.

SET-UP: to frame or plant evidence for a bust; combination of speed and goofballs.

SEX JUICE: a put-on (oil of peppermint) and not an aphrodisiac. "68."

SHACK UP: live with opposite sex without being married.

SHADES: sun glasses. TEASHADES, SPECS.

SHAFT: to take advantage of. SHAFTED: GIVE THE SHAFT.

SHIM: one who from casual observation of hair, clothing, etc. could be either male or female (contraction of the words she and him). UNISEX, THE THIRD SEX.

SHINE: reject.

SHOOK UP: apprehensive, nervous, worried.

SHORT: to cheat; a car.

SHUCK: to deceive, lie or swindle. CON.

SHUCKS OFF: fails to do assigned work effectively as in Daytop, Synanon, etc.

SILK: white person.

SKIN HEAD: young working-class Englishmen who shave their heads to show contempt for longhairs (hippies) but who may use drugs themselves.

SLEIGH RIDE: to take cocaine.

SMASH: oil of cannabis with hashish for smoking.

SMOKE: wood alcohol.

SNAG: to catch.

SNOW JOB: insincere conversation and flattery in attempting to persuade someone.

SOCK IT TO ME: tell all the facts, speak plainly and honestly without reservation.

SPADE: a Negro. BLACK, BLOOD.

SPACED-OUT: in a daze or state of altered consciousness, usually from drug but not always. SPACED.

SPEED: types of amphetamine as DESOXYN, METHEDRINE, METHAMPHETAMINE. Popped, snorted or mainlined.
  SPOON: unit of measurement in which speed is packaged for sale (from 1/4 to 1 teaspoon). CRYSTAL SHIP: syringe of speed.
  DIME: square or rectangular piece of aluminum foil containing $10 worth of speed.
  Synonyms for speed: CRYSTALS, CHALK, CRANK, DICE, CRINK, CHRIS, CHRISTINE, CRISTINA, DYNAMITE STOCKS, GREENIES, PEPPERMINT STICK, CHRISTMAS TREES, STRAWBERRY SHORTCAKE, BLACK BEAUTIES.

SPEEDBALL: combination of heroin with either amphetamine or cocaine for mainlining. HOT AND COLD, H AND C.

SPEED FREAK: chronic user of speed. METH MONSTER, HYPER, SPEEDER. Groups of speed freaks hanging together known in some areas as CRANK COMMANDOS, METHEDRINE MARAUDERS, after famous World War II guerilla groups or special forces.

SPEEDING: under effects of speed. BEHIND SPEED, CRANKING.

SPLIT: to leave. CUT OUT, SLIDE.

SPOON: measure of drug to be injected.

SPRING: treat a person to a take or a joint. Free somebody from jail.

SQUARE: not with it; anti-hip; conforming and conventional; tobacco cigarette. One who does not use drugs. BROWN SHOES, LAMES, STRAIGHT.

SQUARE JOINT: tobacco cigarette.

SQUIRREL: addict who stashes large supply of drugs in a cache.

STIMULANTS: includes AMPHETAMINES, RITALIN, WYAMINE, T.M.A., T.M.M., M.D.A., M.M.D.A., D.O.E., D.O.E.T., D.M.A., D.M.D.A., EPHEDRINE, HUNGEX, PRELUDIN, TENUATE, RHINALGIN, PRIMATENE, TEPANIL, etc.

STONY: showing some features seen with drug users.

STRANGE: odd, weird, unique.

STRIP: area of street, sidewalk or grass on which hippies congregate (after Sunset Strip in Los Angeles). BEACH.

S.T.P.: dimethoxymethylamphetamine. "Serenity-Tranquility-Peace." Very potent and long-acting hallucinogen. Stronger and more dangerous than LSD. A megahallucinogen. Said to have been synthesized first by Dow Chemical Co. Rumored to be a secret nerve gas (it is not). Said to be named after the powerful motor additive "scientifically treated petroleum," hence S.T.P. Also called D.O.M., 72-HOUR BUMMER and D.O.A. (dead on arrival).

SUPER: groovy, great, fantastic.

SWEETIES: British term for Preludin, an amphetamine-like appetite suppressant, used like speed.

SWIFT: good, great.

SWING: actively participate in various activities such as drug subculture. To be free and uninhibited in general.

SWINGER: cat or check who really swings.

SWISH: effeminate looking and acting fag.

SYNTHETIC OPIATES: ALPHAPRODINE, LERITINE, PRI-WADOL, LEVODROMORAN, METOPON, NUMORPHAN, DEMEROL, PERCODAN, HYDROCODONE. Only last four are abused at present.

TAKE THE PIPE: commit suicide, kill one's self by overdose of drug.

TALL: good.

TALK DOWN: to bring a person down from a bum trip by rest, reassurance, sympathy, and support through rapping rather than by drug therapy.

TAR BEACH: rooftop used for sleeping or shooting.

TASTE OF HONEY: pleasurable experience (may or may not be through drugs).

TENNYBOPPER: pre-teenagers and early teenagers living at home who like to make the scene weekends and mingle with the college students. May or may not use drugs. LITTLE PEOPLE, BUBBLE GUMMERS, PIGTAILERS, and BAD NEWS.

TELL IT LIKE IT IS: tell entire truth without embellishment or withholding; be strictly factual.

T.H.C.: see MARIHUANA. TETRAHYDROCANNABINOL, SYNTHETIC GRASS.

THING: one's chief interest or preoccupation. DO YOUR THING: do what interests you or is best for you regardless of the consequences.

THIRD EYE: the inward-looking eye; the new vision into oneself said to be provided by psychedelic drugs.

THREADS: clothes. TWEEDS, VINES.

TICKED OFF: angry. TEED OFF.

T.M.A.: synthetic amphetamine.

TOGETHER: in control of the situation; state of

having a clean head after refraining from
drug use. Opposite of APART.

TOUGH: sharp; admirable; good.

TRANQUILIZERS: commonly abused ones are Librium,
Miltown, Valium, Valmid. DOWNERS, DOWNS,
BACKWARDS, TRANKS, TRANQS. These are minor
tranquilizers and produce physical addiction,
unlike the major tranquilizers such as
Thorazine, Stellazine, etc.

TRAVEL-AGENT: dealer in hallucinogenic drugs
such as LSD, etc.

TRICK: client of prostitute. TURN A TRICK:
solicit a customer.

TRIP: experience that goes beyond ordinary
thoughts, feelings and perceptions. Commonly
produced by drugs but may occur without re-
course to drugs. Classified as body or head
type depending on whether manifestations
are primarily physical (i.e., heroin) or
mental (i.e., acid). Verb: to take drug
and get high.

TRIP OUT: to get high on drugs.

TRIPPING-OUT: to go out of one's normal state
of mind or to go on a trip. Ordinarily due
to drugs, but may rarely be unrelated to
drugs.

TRIPPER: one who takes drugs to get high.

TUNE-IN: to become aware and perceptive of
things around one. Customarily drug
activated but does not have to be.

TUNE-OUT: ignore what is going on around one.

TURN-ABOUT: a change of mind. TURNAROUND.

TURN-OFF: to dispel interest in something, to
bore or to produce indifference by some
action.

TURN-ON: to come alive, to become excited or
affected by something or to become involved.
Done with or without drugs.

TURN ON TO: begin to show interest in something or somebody.

TURNED OFF: disinterested.

TURNED ON: under influence of drug.

TURP: cough syrup with high codeine content. Name originated from turpine hydrate with codeine.

UNCOOL: lack of self-control, inability to cope, unaware or ignorant.

UNDERGROUND: subculture of youth with its ritual, mystique, costume, jargon, etc. Usually alienated and against society and the establishment. May or may not be drug oriented.

UNFLAPPABLE: calm, unexcitable, imperturbable.

UNGLUED: fallen apart emotionally, being uncool, not remaining unflappable in face of pressure (heat). UNHINGED, RACKED-UP, FLAP-PABLE.

UP: euphoric, elated or high (with or without drugs).

UP TIGHT: nervous, anxious, worried or rigid.

USERS: addicts and students from various high schools, colleges and universities.

VIBES: (VIBS) perceptions, sensations, thought waves, atmosphere or spirit of a scene or happening. May be either good or bad vibes. VIBRATIONS.

VICE SQUAD: ones in group who are clean of drugs.

VOYAGEUR: person on hallucinogenic drug trip.

WAG TAIL: to conform.

WAY OUT: indescribable (good or bad). FAR OUT, FREAKY, KINKY.

WHERE IT'S AT: real or imagined place where action or event is taking place.

WHITE LIGHT: sudden complete comprehension of an idea or an ideology. Ultimate emotional experience behind a drug, especially acid or mescaline. Final discovery of one's inner self. Hallucination of blinding white light with a feeling of omniscience such as is said to occur sometimes from hallucinogenic drugs.

WIG: the mind.

WIGGED OUT: very excited, not in control emotionally. FLIPPED OUT.

WIG—OUT: blow one's mind, become psychotic. Usually due to drugs but may be other precipitating factors.

WILD GERONIMO: barbiturate in beer.

WOW: exclamation of amazement, surprise, admiration, excitement, etc.

WYAMINE: nasal inhaler containing stimulant related to amphetamine. SNIFFERS.

YIPPIE: different from traditional hippie in that he is more vocal and more of an activist politically and otherwise.

YOU KNOW: expression repeated frequently during talk but without any real meaning.

ZAP: to overwhelm, i.e., zap the fuzz with love. To strike back peacefully, i.e., zap the man with flower power. ZAPPED: destroyed, caught.

Z.N.A.: mixture of dill and monosodium glutinate smoked for alleged hallucinogenic effects. A put-on?

ZOO: psychiatric hospital. FUNNY FARM, GIGGLE HOUSE, LOONY BIN.

ZOOM: sernyl (PCP) on grass. ANGEL DUST, SUPER GRASS. Meaning of such street names varies with geographical location.

REFERENCES

Bloomquist, E. <u>Marihuana</u>, Glencoe Press. 1968. pb.

Brown, J. <u>The Hippies</u>, Time Inc. 1967. pb.

Geller, A. and Boas, M. <u>The Drug Beat</u>, Cowles Book Co. 1969. hb.

Gross, H. <u>The Flower People</u>, Ballantine Books. 1968. pb.

Horman and Fox, <u>Drug Awareness</u>, Avon Books. 1970. hb.

Landy, E. <u>The Underground Dictionary</u>, Simon and Schuster, 1971. pb.

Lingeman, R. <u>Drugs from A to Z: A Dictionary</u>, McGraw Hill Co. 1969. pb.

Louria, D. <u>The Drug Scene</u>, McGraw Hill. 1968. hb.

Rosevear, J. <u>Pot-Handbook of Marihuana</u>, University Books. 1967. hb.

Simmons, J. and Winograd, B. <u>It's Happening</u>, Marc Laird Co. pb.

Wolfe, B. <u>The Hippies</u>, Signet Books. 1968. pb.

DRUG ABUSE
PROBLEMS OF IDENTIFICATION

United States Department of Justice
Bureau of Narcotics and Dangerous Drugs*

It is important to recognize the symptoms and signs of drug abuse. The following outline was prepared by the Bureau of Narcotics and Dangerous Drugs based on the publication, Drug Abuse: Escape to Nowhere.

I. Common Symptoms of Drug Abuse

   A. Changes in school attendance, discipline and grades.
   B. Unusual flare-ups or outbreaks of temper.
   C. Poor physical appearance (often becomes slovenly).
   D. Furtive behavior regarding drugs (especially when in possession).
   E. Wearing of sunglasses at inappropriate times to hide dilated or constricted pupils.
   F. Long-sleeved shirts worn constantly to hide needle marks (if injecting drugs).
   G. Association with known drug abusers.
   H. Borrowing money from students to purchase drugs.
   I. Stealing small items from school or home.
   J. Finding the student in odd places during the day such as closets, storage rooms, etc., to take drugs.
   K. May attempt to appear inconspicuous in manner and appearance to mask drug usage.
   L. Withdrawal from responsibility.
   M. General change in overall attitude.

II. Manifestations of Specific Drugs

   A. The Glue Sniffer

      1. Odor of substance inhaled on breath and clothes.
      2. Excess nasal secretions, watering of the eyes.
      3. Poor muscular control, drowsiness or unconsciousness.
      4. Presence of plastic or paper bags or rags containing dry plastic cement.

*Government Printing Office 889-946 publication.

    5.   Usually becomes group oriented.

B. **The Depressant Abuser (barbiturates – "Goofballs" – "Downs")**

    1.   Symptoms of alcohol intoxication with one important exception, no odor of alcohol on the breath.
    2.   Staggering or stumbling in classroom or home.
    3.   May fall asleep in class or at home.
    4.   Lacks interest in school and family activities.
    5.   Is drowsy and may appear disoriented.

C. **The Stimulant Abuser (Amphetamine – "Bennies" – Speed)**

    1.   Cause excess activity--user is irritable, argumentative, nervous, and has difficulty sitting still in classrooms.
    2.   Pupils are dilated.
    3.   Mouth and nose are dry with bad breath, causing user to lick his lip frequently and rub and scratch his nose.
    4.   Chain smoking.
    5.   Goes long periods without eating or sleeping.

D. **The Narcotic Abuser (heroin, demerol, morphine)**

    1.   Inhaling heroin in powder form leaves traces of white powder around the nostrils, causing redness and rawness.
    2.   Injecting heroin leaves scars on the inner surface of the arms and elbows (mainlining). This causes the student to wear long-sleeved shirts most of the time. User may inject drugs in body where needle marks will not readily be seen.
    3.   Users often leave syringes, bent spoons, bottle caps, eyedroppers, cotton and needles in lockers and rooms--this is a telltale sign of an addict.
    4.   In the classroom the pupil is lethargic, drowsy. His pupils are constricted and fail to respond to light.

88

E. The Marihuana Abuser

(These individuals are difficult to recognize unless they are under the influence of the drug at the time they are being observed.)

1. In the early stages student may appear animated and hysterical with rapid, loud talking and burst of laughter.
2. In the later stages the student is sleepy or stuporous.
3. Depth perception is distorted, making driving dangerous.
4. Unable to define reality from unreality, e.g., will accept only their own point of view.
5. Affect on user varies from time to time, e.g., user may be docile most of the time but may become violent at other times.
6. Usually used in a group.

NOTE: Marihuana cigarettes are rolled in a double-thickness of brown or off-white cigarette paper. These cigarettes are smaller than a regular cigarette with the paper twisted or tucked in at both ends with tobacco that is greener in color than regular tobacco. The odor of burning marihuana resembles that of burning weeds or rope. Cigarettes are referred to as reefers, sticks, texas tea, pot, rope, Mary Jane, loco weed, jive, grass, hemp, hay. Many times is smoked in pipe (long stem, small bowl).

F. The Hallucinogen Abuser

(It is unlikely that students who use LSD will do so in a school setting since these drugs are usually used in a group situation under special conditions.)

1. Users sit or recline quietly in a dream or trance-like state.
2. Users may become fearful and experience a degree of terror which makes them attempt to escape from the group.

3. The drug affects the mind primarily as opposed to physical functions, producing changes in mood and behavior.

4. Perceptual changes involve senses of sight, hearing, touch, body-image and time.

NOTE: The drug is odorless, tasteless, and colorless and may be found in the form of impregnated sugar cubes, cookies, or crackers. LSD is usually taken orally, but may be injected. It is imported in ampules of clear blue liquid.

DRUGS AND NEW RELIGIOUS CULTS
by
C. Douglas Gunn*

Religious forms that are strange to most Americans are now emerging from the youth culture. Basic to most of these is a renewed interest in mysticism, in man's experience of transcendence, in the possibility of experiencing "extraordinary reality." American interest in mysticism and exotic forms of religion is not new--one can find, for example, such an interest in the Transcendentalism of Ralph Waldo Emerson--and an American concern with vital, experiential religion reaching back at least to the Great Awakening of the 1720's. Yet in modern times, the emergence of religious cults of experience seems novel to many. There _is_ novelty today--in the unique role played by psychedelic drugs in shaping the form of these new religious cults.

In the 1950's, the "Beat Generation" discovered Zen Buddhism, which became their adopted (and adapted) form of mysticism. However, there were more people who merely talked about Zen experience than who actually had it, since there were few qualified Zen masters in this country from whom to learn. Book-taught Zen mysticism was dubious mysticism and even more dubious Zen.

With the advent of psychedelic drugs, especially LSD, extraordinary experiences became easily available to all. It is hard to over-emphasize the importance of this availability on subsequent development of our culture. To many psychedelic users familiar with oriental religious terminology, it seemed that these new drugs offered mystical experience, enlightenment, _satori_, without the rigors of prolonged (and painful) meditation or asceticism. To some users, the new pills were a kind of Western yoga, a means by which years of religious questing could be condensed into hours.

Now, it is clear that many--probably most--people who take psychedelic drugs do not do so primarily for religious motives. They do it for "kicks." Nevertheless, it would seem that a large number of users move back and forth between the two poles of "casual usage" and "religious usage." It is difficult if not impossible to clearly distinguish between sacred or profane usage of psychedelics. Some users who allege

---

*C. Douglas Gunn is Assist. Prof. of Religion at College of Wooster in Ohio.

religious motives for drug-taking also enjoy casual tripping, while other users who initially approached the drugs for "kicks" alone later interpret their experiences in religious categories. With the present embargo on legal psychedelics, no one can say for certain how many people now associate these drugs with experiences they interpret as religious in nature.

The question of whether psychedelic experiences are "truly" religious or "authentically" mystic seems largely one of definition. This writer would wish to avoid the qualitative issue of the nature of these experiences: the data are insufficient and our tools neither well enough developed for interpreting it nor for giving us much assurance that we can claim validity in saying whether or not drug-induced experiences are mystical.

The real importance of psychedelic drugs for the growth of new religious cults in America lies less in the numbers who actually make a religion out of drug-taking than in the fact that the psychedelic experience has given to at least one generation their terminology to describe and evaluate experiences which they consider religious. In other words, the psychedelic experience and the language used to describe it have rapidly become normative in discussing not only drugs but in discussing other religious traditions and experiences as well. For example, the "high" of a chanter of the Hare Krishna mantra may be discussed and compared with that produced by pot; one may hear a "Jesus Freak" talking about "getting a better high with Jesus" than he did formerly with LSD; one may be "turned on" by various forms of meditation, and so on.

Thus the primary importance of the psychedelic experience for new religious cults in America is not that drug-taking underlies all of them. Far from it. Many of the most popular and growing cults, such as Transcendental Meditation and the Krishna Consciousness movement, disavow the use of drugs. Rather the importance of psychedelic drugs for such cults lies in the fact that the drugs provide a language framework in which religions are developing an articulated belief or theology. It is in the terms of psychedelic experience that religions--old or new--are being judged by America's youth culture.

Hence, discussion of religion in terms of
the psychedelic turn-on in these days need not
imply an actual drug experience on the part of
the speaker. By this time, the psychedelic
experience has been so widely publicized that
nearly all college or high-school-age youth are
familiar not only with its terminology but also
with its reported effects and sensations--whether
or not they have actually experienced them. The
centrality of the psychedelic experience as the
most powerful spiritual experience affecting
their generation provides the youth culture with
more than a religious terminology. It means that
they tend to judge other (non-drug) experiences,
including the rituals and activities of the religions of our society, in similar terms. Does
church or synagogue, Easter or Seder, sacrament
or sermon "turn on" anyone? Experience is central
to religion among youth. Extraordinary experience
is sought, and is judged in terms of the psychedelic categories.

Although the vocabulary of psychedelic drugs
remains normative, other techniques of mysticism
are becoming increasingly popular. Whether they
will become a major religious force in America
remains to be seen. Meditation, chanting and
various forms of yoga allegedly provide "safe"
and "natural" ways of achieving experiences anal-
agous to the psychedelic. The suppression of
drugs aids the growth of such cults, since cults
are legal and the drugs are not. Concern with
man's ineptitude in handling his own environment, as witnessed in such nutritional disasters
as mercury-polluted fish, has led some seekers
of the supra-normal to avoid man-made drugs
(like LSD) in favor of "natural" techniques of
transcendence such as meditation. On the other
hand, some people, despairing of the future of
the world as it rushes into ecological disaster,
show little concern for their own systems and
continue on drugs with little thought for the
morrow. Paths to experience are many, and
everyone decides for himself which, if any, he
will take.

For the immediate future, however, it would
seem that the ease with which the psychedelic
drugs produce a state of extraordinary reality,
and the fact that they have played such a large
role in the formation of a culture differentiated
from "establishment" society, makes it likely

that they will continue to be the norm by which
religion will be judged by the youth culture for
some time to come.

Suggestions for further reading:

A. On mystical and exotic religions in America:

    Hal Bridges. American Mysticism from
        William James to Zen. New York:
        Harper and Row, 1970.

    J. Stillson Judah. The History and Phil-
        osophy of the Metaphysical Movements
        in America. Philadelphia: Westminster
        Press, 1967.

    Charles S. Braden. These Also Believe: A
        Study of Modern American Cults and
        Minority Religious Movements. New
        York: Macmillan, 1949.

B. On drugs, religion and the youth culture:

    *William Braden. The Private Sea: LSD and
        the Search for God. Chicago: Quadrangle
        Books, 1967.

    *Timothy Leary. High Priest. New York:
        World Publishing Co., 1968.

    *Timothy Leary. The Politics of Ecstasy.
        New York: G. P. Putnam's Sons, 1968.

    *Walter Houston Clark. Chemical Ecstasy:
        Psychedelic Drugs and Religion. New
        York: Sheed and Ward, 1969.

    *Lewis Yablonsky. The Hippie Trip. New
        York: Western Publishing Co., 1968.

    *Jesse Kornbluth, ed. Notes from the New
        Underground. New York: Viking Press,
        1968.

    *Mitchell Goodman. The Movement Toward a
        New America. New York: Alfred Knopf/
        Pilgrim Press, 1970.

*Denotes books available also in paper editions.

*Nicholas von Hoffman. We Are the People Our
     Parents Warned Us Against. Chicago:
     Quadrangle Books, 1968.

*Jerry Hopkins, ed. The Hippie Papers. New
     York: New American Library (Signet
     paperback), 1968.

*Tom Wolfe. The Electric Kool-Aid Acid Test.
     New York: Farrar, Straus and Giroux,
     1968.

*Theodore Roszak. The Making of a Counter
     Culture. Garden City: Doubleday, 1969.

 Jacob Needleman. The New Religions. Garden
     City: Doubleday, 1970.

*Denotes books available also in paper editions.

THE DRUG PROBLEM IN CENTRAL NEW YORK
by
Greg Glassner*

Drug Fear Grows--562 CNY arrests in 1970

In New York City, drug abuse has replaced the automobile as the number one killer of 18 to 25 year olds. Many specialists close to the drug scene in Central New York fear that the problem--if unchecked--will also reach crisis proportions here.

They point to drugs as a relatively new social problem. Few arrests were made before 1965, rehabilitation facilities were virtually unknown here a year ago, and only recently have politicians taken up the issue.

Law enforcement officials point to an alarming spread of hard drugs into wealthy suburbs and rural areas, yet many parents and educators refuse to believe it.

Chief Investigator James R. McCaig of the State Police Narcotics Unit in Oneida, who covers a seven county area, flatly states "You can buy drugs in the corridors of any high school in the area."

Since McCaig's agents are responsible for Onondaga, Oswego, Madison, Oneida, Herkimer, Jefferson and Lewis Counties, his statements about the problem "bring it all back home."

Heroin--the killer--has long been associated as an inner city, or ghetto problem, but police and medical officials agree that the drug can be found "in DeWitt and Marcellus."

Law enforcement officials express alarm over the youthful flirtation with drugs, drug culture, and "acid-rock" music because it represents a growing trend among a whole generation.

---

*During June 1971 the Syracuse Herald Journal ran a series of articles written by Greg Glassner, one of its reporters, on the drug problem in Central New York, its magnitude, misconceptions, and solutions. We have been given permission by the Syracuse Herald Journal to reproduce this series.

"I don't see this thing leveling off for
another four or five years," McCaig said, adding
that law.enforcement alone cannot do the job
effectively.

True Problem

McCaig admits that his comments about the
size of the problem are greeted with a range of
emotions from indignation to flat denials, but
states adamantly, "I know it's true."

Drug Problem Growing

One educator who has studied the problem
locally said that arrest statistics reflect only
"top of the iceburg parameters" but increases in
both arrests and case loads are dramatic and
startling.

In Onondaga County alone, the State Police
arrested 140 persons on narcotic offenses in
1968, 203 in 1969 and 226 in 1970. Total arrests
in the seven county Central New York area were
562 in 1970.

Although the majority of the State Police
arrests are for selling marijuana and hashish,
McCaig pointed out that there were 12 arrests for
amphetamines and barbiturates, 26 for LSD and
other hallucinogens, and 37 for heroin in 1970.

Drug related arrests by the Syracuse Police
Department show a trend similar to the State
Police statistics. In 1964 there were 11 arrests;
in 1965, 22; in 1966, 24; 32 in 1967; 128 in
1968; 115 in 1969 and 150 in 1970.

Lt. Charles Delaney of the Onondaga County
Sheriff's Department said there really was no
drug problem five years ago. Although the department averages about 70 to 75 arrests a year
now, there were none prior to 1965.

Delaney, who also explains that his statements are greeted with disbelief and angry calls
from parents and educators, said that in a
typical suburban high school of 1,500 students,
perhaps 50 are in need of treatment for drug-
related problems and another 200 are using drugs
on a regular basis.

Although drugs such as opium and cocaine have been an urban ghetto problem since the 20's or 30's, it is the youthful user that accounts for most of the dramatic increase in the past five years, police officials agree.

They also fear the trend of marijuana and LSD users toward heroin. Although the scientific data is inconclusive, statistical evidence exists to show that the emotional problems that lead one to use "soft" drugs also lead to narcotic addiction.

Although the magnitude of any social problem is larger in areas of population concentration, law enforcement officials are in agreement that even rural communities are not immune to the drug threat.

McCaig points to a recent State Police raid in Camden, an Oneida County village of less than 3,000 people. Ten youths were arrested for sale and use of a dangerous drug.

A recent raid in Oneida and Herkimer counties netted $5,000 in marijuana and hashish. Of the 33 persons arrested, 20 of them were 18 or 19 years old, three younger. One of those charged with selling was 14 years old.

"I have seen 17-year-olds clearing $500 a week peddling drugs," McCaig said. "Pushers are generally 14 to 20 years old," he said, generally because that is the age group of their customers.

The arrest statistics point up another feature of drug abuse: Although it is by no means confined to youth, some of the worst, and most hypocritical offenders are adults who misuse prescribed drugs, it is the young offenders that officials are most concerned about.

The number of individuals receiving help under rehabilitation programs funded through the Onondaga County Mental Health Department supports the contentions of law enforcement officials that the drug problem is serious and growing.

Chris Gianapoulous of Mental Health reports that about 60 individuals are in active contact with Direction toward Education in Narcotics, an

agency that deals mostly with hard drug users on
the south side.

Argosy house, a therapeutic community that
deals with both "hard and soft" drug problems
has between 15 and 20 youngsters in residence and
is in active contact with another 50.

Aim at Pushers: Raids, arrests not sole solution to drug problem

Law enforcement officials are frank in admitting that raids and arrests are not the whole
solution to the drug problem in Central New York.

Lt. Charles Delaney, who heads the narcotics
squad of the Onondaga County Sheriff's Department says, with a shrug, "I don't even know if
arrests are really relevant to the problem."

Chief Investigator James R. McCaig of the
narcotics unit, State Police, Troop D in Oneida,
states flatly that the effects of raids are
blown out of proportion.

"We can cripple the traffic--two weeks later
it's back to normal. We can only hope that this
type of operation will force the fringe to drop
out," he added.

Both McCaig and Delaney point to a combination of education and enforcement, coupled with
a change in public attitude, as the ultimate
solution to drug abuse.

"Drugs are a symptom of another problem, not
the core itself," Delaney said. "It's like blaming the fever for the cold. An inner or outer
stimulus makes kids turn to drugs. It's a
psychological or social problem."

Both law officers point out that there are
common misconceptions about their roles. "We
have to look to the community to see what they
want," Delaney said.

"Three to four years ago we'd go out and
arrest anyone with a nickle bag, now we're
trying to get at the top, the pushers and suppliers," he added.

There are good reasons for concentrating on
selective raids, both officers point out. One is

that they don't have the personnel to blanket the
area and make mass arrests.

Delaney has three men including himself.
McCaig didn't divulge the strength of his unit--
responsible for a seven county area--but said if
pushers realized how few agents he did have "they
would be comforted."

Seek Source

"The raids are not for publicity," McCaig
added, "if we made single arrests an agent's cover
would soon be blown. We'd lose our chance at the
course. If pushers knew the heat was on they'd
leave town."

Another public misconception is the legal
definition of "selling." Anyone who gives, lends,
or takes money for even a small quantity of marijuana is technically guilty of "selling a dangerous drug."

There is a distinction between a "user-
dealer" and a "commercial dealer" in the eyes of
lawmen however. "If we knew there was a commercial dealer in town, we'd make an all-out effort
to get him, drop everything else," Delaney said.

The "selective raid," as McCaig calls it, is
designed to clear up a local drug ring, and if
possible, lead to the source. An arrest in
Central New York may result in series of arrests
around the country.

A state police investigation in Syracuse,
McCaig said, led to a raid on a lab in Boston,
the arrest of a chemist and two assistants, and
the seizure of $130,000 worth of Speed. Another
drug arrest led to a cache of counterfeit money
in Cleveland.

College campuses and high schools are often
blamed for the presence of drugs in a community.
Both officers said they would discourage such a
generalization.

McCaig said he has seen some campuses that
are a "haven," but not as a rule. He also
doesn't think of campuses as a clearing house for
a geographical area. In one investigation, a
local high school student was found to be

supplying the campus.

Critical Months Ahead

The community tends to forget about the drug problem when school lets out for the summer, Delaney said, yet these months may be the most critical.

"A college kid who's been blowing his mind regularly at school isn't going to come home cold. He will bring some stuff home with him or have a contact here," he said.

"If 'Joe' comes to town with a kilo of pot he bought for $25, by the time that stuff gets down to the high school students, 81 people will have touched it and $7,000 will have exchanged hands," he added.

Organized crime does not loom as large in the drug scene as some would believe, McCaig said. The fringe of crime is on heroin and cocaine, but marijuana and LSD are too unprofitable. "Every user is a potential pusher. It is too competitive."

The reasons for using drugs are many, according to Delaney. "The curious and malcontent experiment with drugs, those not at ease, running out of fear or trying to identify."

Peer pressure can also be an important motivation. The "cool man" on the pedestal for a 15-year-old girl of a decade ago was the athletic star or the guy with the convertible, Delaney added, today he may be the acid head or pusher.

"We have to realize that times have changed," he continued, "yet many youth cannot look beyond the pleasures to the pain."

The schools are not the only place for drug education, McCaig stressed, the family is important too. "If a child has trouble with school-work or friends, if he begins drinking and smoking, the average parent can draw upon experience to counsel him."

"With drugs, few parents have the knowledge necessary for counseling. Parents who become

frightened or hysterical make things worse. Some
regard the first puff on a marijuana cigarette
as addiction. This kind of attitude drives the
kid to a friend who claims he knows the score,"
McCaig added.

Both McCaig and Delaney were critical of
the "Professional panic" that has greeted the
drug problem. There are about 60 agencies in the
area dealing with some phase of drug abuse, according to Delaney, resulting in many uncoordin-
ated, though sincere efforts.

"This is a new ball of wax, that has grown
in the last four years. I haven't seen any responsible education yet," he concluded.

Doctor reports drug-related county deaths

In New York City there have been more than
400 deaths from acute reactions to heroin and
other drug-related causes since the beginning of
the year. Medical and governmental officials
fear that the trend will spread.

Heroin is the killer and should be the major
target of any programs to combat drug abuse, according to Dr. William D. Alsever of the Syracuse
University Health Service.

An assistant county medical examiner, Alsever said he gets "to see the other end of
this--the dead ones." Although nowhere near
New York's epidemic proportions, there have been
drug-related deaths in Onondaga County.

The local deaths are not publicized out of
deference to the families of the victims. "I am
often bothered by the decision not to draw attention to these incidents," Alsever said,
"perhaps we should."

The drug problem is a complicated one "full
of so many imponderables," Alsever continued.
There are many gaps in professional education on
dry drugs, just as there are many misconceptions
among the general public.

Although he has been tabbed many times as a
"local drug expert," he is quick to note that he
isn't. "There are few who can claim a complete
knowledge of drug abuse."

The heroin problem worries Alsever because of the dangers involved in its use and the difficulty of cutting off the supply. Customs officials are unable to prevent the inflow of the drug, he added.

"Heroin is the most profitable business I am aware of. Unless we can control the supply at the sources, Turkey, and the Orient, I don't see how we can stop it," Alsever said.

The threat of death from an overdose is only one of the medical dangers associated with heroin and other drugs that are injected. The occupational hazard of hepatitis, blood poisoning and tetanus accompanies use of a hypodermic needle under non-medical conditions.

Alsever said the "speed Kills" and "Meth is Death" claims generated by drug users themselves are somewhat overrated. Methadrine, a powerful amphetamine, carries nowhere near the dangers of heroin and other opiates.

"Heroin provides immediate and complete, albeit temporary relief from all pressures around you," he noted, making it attractive for those who want to escape from life.

Always a ghetto problem--the reasons for an impoverished black in an urban environment turning to heroin are apparent, and to a degree understandable--heroin has spread to the suburbs.

"Heroin is no longer an inner city problem," Alsever said. "You can now find it out in De-Witt or Marcellus," although many may find that hard to believe.

One misconception about heroin is that it has to be addictive. "Some people 'Joy pop' it--inject small doses irregularly--without becoming addicted," he pointed out.

High school and college kids may use heroin as a "downer" from bum trips on acid or from "Speeding," he added. In these applications it may or may not become addictive, although the users could easily become addicts.

Synthesized from morphine in 1896, heroin was quickly abandoned as a cure for morphine addiction when physicians discovered that they were simply substituting one addiction for another.

Many drugs in use today for non-medical purposes have, or had, legitimate medical uses,
Alsever pointed out.

Although youth is the apparent target of
anti-drug campaigns, many adults are just as
guilty of abusing prescribed drugs through overdoses.

Pressed for a medical definition of "drug
abuse," he said it would probably be "using drugs
for nonmedical purposes including intentionally
or unintentionally taking overdoses of any drug,
illegally or legally."

Alsever relates drug abuse to alcoholism.
Both are social problems, he said, and in terms
of human lives lost, alcoholism may be more de-
serving of attention than drug abuse.

"Some of the money being spent on the drug
problem may be better spent on the treatment of
drunks and keeping them off the roads," he added.

One misconception that needs to be cleared
up, Alsever said, is that every user of hard
drugs or hallucinogens is an addict. "Many are
dabblers, experimenters, or having a two to
three year flirtation" with the so-called drug
culture.

Some youthful drug users, he continued,
should be placed in the category of a social
drinker from a medical standpoint, according to
Alsever. Others are "hooked, have bad heads,
emotional problems, hangups."

Although some drug users are in need of
psychiatric help, just because a kid uses drugs
it doesn't necessarily mean he's a "scrambled
character."

"Many adults in this community have to re-
vise their attitudes about drugs--to be con-
versant with the facts and get rid of myths.
We have to update our information to be accurate
and credible," he said.

Theories vary on solution of local drug abuse problem

Almost everyone who deals with the local
drug problem decries the lack of education among

professionals and the public. But theories on how
to improve the situation vary.

Adults are targets for educational programs,
specialists say, because of many misconceptions
about drugs and drug addiction.

Junior High School and high school students
are another primary target of drug education, because arrest statistics and school surveys indicate that age group as a critical one.

A survey by the North Syracuse School district
a year ago and a more recent one in Syracuse city
schools documented a dramatic rise in drug use
and shocked a number of parents.

Michael Reagen, who chaired Mayor Lee Alexander's Temporary Commission on Narcotics Abuse
and Addiction that led to the City-County Drug
Advisory Committee, is critical of the work that
has been done.

Unconcern

"There is almost a malaise of unconcern by
all our social and political institutions and by
the general public that only recently, in this
election year, is being broken by a series of
short-sighted, hysterical public utterances and
reactions," he stated.

He added "much of the data we have had we
have distorted--we've lied." A great deal of
harm has been done by attributing false dangers
to drugs and losing credibility among youth, he
said.

One active force in drug education is the
State Narcotics Addiction Control Commission.
The Syracuse office is responsible for an eight
county area which includes Onondaga, Oswego,
Cortland, Cayuga, Tompkins, Schuyler, Madison and
Jefferson counties.

In addition to being a major supplier of
pamphlets, films and speakers for school or community drug prevention programs, the commission
funds local guidance councils and treatment
centers.

Walt Rosendale, community representative
for the commission admits it is poorly named. The

goals are prevention, research, and treatment, all accomplished through education, he said.

The commission concentrates on educating educators, law enforcement officials, school children and adult groups on the facts of drugs and drug addiction, Rosendale said.

The reaction to drug education is varied, according to Rosendale. Some school administrators would rather ignore or cover up a problem than face it, he said, but most are cooperative.

The community councils are, he added, only as good as the people in them. There are 340 community councils statewide, with another 150 in some stage of planning.

Gerald Maywright, director of the Syracuse NACC office said many people have misconstrued "drug information with drug education."

"You can reach a saturation point with drug facts; our schools should spend less time on academics and more time on emotional values," he added.

The goal, Maywright said, should be to "turn kids onto themselves," so they won't have to turn to drugs as an outlet for their emotional problems.

Councils may be started by villages, towns, cities, and other governmental units. The NACC has provided reimbursement for the first $2,000 spent each year, and additional funds on a full or half reimbursable basis for professional services such as psychiatric or medical help.

Rosendale said the NACC aims at a truthful approach, disdaining the "scare technique." The literature is thorough and objective--but there is no real gauge on how much effect it has. In any case, he notes, it provides an alternative to rumor and faulty advice.

NACC representatives have presented assemblies on drug abuse to children as young as third grade level. "We concentrate on values, role playing, and decision making," he said.

The youthful approach seems substantiated by the recent survey of students in Syracuse city

and parochial schools. The survey included
15,140 students in grades 7 to 12.

Of those, 12.1 per cent, or 1,843 indicated
that they had smoked marijuana, 6.5 per cent were
currently smoking it. Four per cent, or 613 said
they had used LSD and 3.1 per cent or 480 had
used Speed.

Perhaps most startling was the response from
1.1 per cent who indicated use of heroin, and
7.1 per cent, or 118 youngsters who admitted to
selling heroin.

The North Syracuse School District survey
of February 1970 revealed that 18 per cent of
the high school students and 6 per cent of the
middle school students said they "would like to
try marijuana if given the opportunity."

Many medical experts urge that youths be
given sound medical advice, dosage information,
and information on drug contamination to keep
the death toll down.

These suggestions have met with resistance
in many communities, since it would mean giving
out information useful to the drug user in
breaking the law, and could be construed as increasing interest in drugs.

Reagen, for one, is a fervent advocate of a
strong central body, such as the City County
committee, to control drug education, and to
coordinate law enforcement efforts in the community.

The Committee membership has been criticized
in some quarters because few of those named to
it are drug experts, and most are busy men.
Reagen justifies the choices on the grounds that
such men as Sheriff Patrick Corbett and Chief
Thomas J. Sardino are in positions of power, and
can be expected to act on the problem.

Drug Councils give out facts to interested persons

One way in which area residents are combating the misinformation associated with drugs, and
attempting to get at the causes of drug abuse,
is through community narcotics guidance councils.

A number of councils already are operating
in the Central New York area, with varying approaches to the problem and varying success.

Among the more established councils are
groups in Baldwinsville, Camillus and Town of
Salina. Although council chairmen get together
monthly, each has developed its own plan of action.

Raymond Clover, chairman of the Baldwinsville
council, sees his group's goal as preventive education and an attempt to provide counseling and
treatment facilities on a local level.

Clover said he doesn't believe a neighborhood
or small community should depend on an outside
agency or higher government to solve local problems.

This philosophy pretty much sums up the function of local councils--adults and youngsters
pitching in with their time and efforts to pass
around accurate information and lend a helping
hand.

One of the most successful programs in Baldwinsville has been the sponsorship of "coffee
hours" to disseminate information and discuss
problems in an informal "non-structured, environment."

A group of 10 or a dozen residents gather at
a host's home, and are joined by a few adults
and teen-agers from the guidance council.

Literature and drug identification kits are
available, but participants are urged to discuss
anything they want, Clover said. The intimate
atmosphere seems more conducive to frank questions
and discussion than a large group, he added.

"Fears, prejudices, and dogmatic views come
out in the open," he said, "but knowledgeable
people are there to argue with facts about drugs."
Several hundred Baldwinsville area residents
have already taken part in the coffee hour
technique.

In addition to sharing in the coffee hours,
youths are also used to staff the "hotline" on
Friday and Saturday evenings. Anyone with a
problem can call for counseling, referral, or
just a sympathetic ear, Clover added.

Volunteers who work with the Baldwinsville council are versed in drug facts, and counseling techniques, in addition to their desire to help. Most have trained through the continuing education department at Syracuse University.

The Camillus Narcotics Guidance Council was formed one year ago, drawing upon the experience of Baldwinsville and other established councils.

Jack Gardner, its chairman, said the response within the community has been excellent, but the council members feel that it has taken a year to build public confidence and it will be years before the drug problem is under control.

The council operates a youth center in the village of Camillus. Staffed by a young couple, "the Town Shop" is open five nights a week, providing a recreational facility as well as a source of information.

A "counseling line" is maintained, with an answering service on a 24-hour basis. Council members are willing to try to find an answer to any problem: sex, family, school, emotional, or drugs. Troubled individuals are referred to professional counseling or treatment.

Like Baldwinsville, and the successful treatment centers in the area, the Camillus council refuses to divulge information to the police. The problems of credibility are great enough, Gardner noted, without risking any link with law enforcement agencies.

The Camillus council concentrates in six areas: adult education, youth activities, school education, after school programs, a drug education booth, and counseling.

The drug education booth, located in a shopping center, is staffed by high school students, with a young person from Argosy House on hand Saturdays.

Mrs. Pat Doupe, a mother of three, is a member of the Town of Salina Narcotics Guidance Council because she believes "you should be willing to work if you are going to shoot your mouth off about something."

Salina operates a youth-oriented coffee house as one of its projects. Although Mrs. Doupe believes most of the youngsters who frequent the coffee house "are just looking for a place to go," she feels it an important project.

Former addict aids others' return to society through Argosy House

Tony Gangone made the trip from a $50-a-day heroin habit, through a therapeutic community, to a position as community representative of Syracuse's Argosy House--a hard row to hoe.

Candid about all aspects of the drug problem, Gangone admits that in a way he is glad he was hooked once, because the cure has given him insight into his own "emotional hangups" that he might never have attained under normal circumstances.

Gangone was the first graduate of Argosy House, which puts him in a unique position of seeing the therapeutic approach to drug rehabilitation and the problems of drug dependency "from the inside out."

Argosy House differs from other programs in the fact that drug dependency is attacked through its causes. The individual who undertakes the 12 to 18 month process is urged to progress through group dependency to confidence in himself.

According to Gangone and Harry Hulse, also an ex-addict, who acts as program director of the pioneer project, the basic cause of drug-dependency is fear and immaturity.

The fear, they added, can be of anything: failure, sexual inadequacy, the future, scholastic problems, loneliness, authority--all of the human fears and shortcomings that plague everyone to a degree.

Other people may take to alcohol, food, or daydreaming as an escape route from their personal "hang-ups," or may continue through life without even realizing they have any problems. The addict took to drugs as an answer.

"When you take drugs it's great, but when you come down off them you're worse off than before, so you want to take them again," Hulse said. "The perfect avenue of escape can lead to total dependency."

"Drug abuse exaggerates one's character defects out of proportion. It's like a crack in a wall that you keep hitting with a sledge hammer--nobody I know has become a better person through drugs," he added.

Physical addiction--a need stemming from chemical imbalance caused by constant drug use--is not the real problem according to Gangone. The mental and emotional dependence on drugs as a way out is the "real killer" he added.

Argosy House attempts to get an individual to cope without drugs. Talk therapy is interspaced with work therapy to instill a sense of responsibility, teach an individual his value as a person, and how to relate to other people, Hulse and Gangone said.

The process has a sound clinical basis, they added, and a psychiatrist is used on a consulting basis to diagnose problems too severe to respond to the treatment.

Not everyone has what it takes to complete the Argosy House course, Gangone explained. Because of limited space, applicants are screened for motivation before accepted.

Despite plans to expand, Gangone said, "Even 100 Argosy Houses are not going to do away with drug abuse; we can only hope to reduce the number of people involved."

Gangone and Hulse said they believe a lot can be done through the schools. Too much demand is being made on kids scholastically without helping them emotionally, they added.

"A teacher should be trained to spot the quiet kid in the back row who never says anything, the one with a family problem. Then they should be able to counsel him," Gangone concluded.

Two ex-addicts discover drug culture phony

The "drug culture" is a much publicized phenomenon that has sold records, clothing, books, magazines, making small or big fortunes for those quick to capitalize on it. It has also hooked a lot of kids on narcotics.

Charlie and Darryl see the psychedelic revo-
lution--drug culture bit--as "phony." They have
reason to know because they were once part of it.

"Kids want to believe a lot of things, like
'I saw God when I took acid.' Maybe they did,
but the chemical they took didn't do it for
them," Charlie said.

"The Peace-Love-Drugs thing is a farce,"
Darryl added. "Nobody really believed it, all
they wanted to do is get high. It would be nice
if it were true, but it isn't."

Charlie, now 21, got into drugs when he was
released from a 19-month term as a youthful offender. He travelled around and went through
the routine from pot to acid and speed, then
heroin. "I was a hippie, if you want to call it
that," he added with a shrug.

Darryl, 19, took another route to the same
place. He was brought up in one of Onondaga
County's wealthier suburbs, the son of a prominent family. In school he started with marijuana and glue, later got into pills.

"I was into pretty lightweight stuff," he
said, "but I was emotionally addicted. If I
ever needed something it was there but I was
still a pretty messed up individual."

Both Charlie and Darryl ended up at Argosy
House for therapeutic treatment. Charlie graduated from the storefront sessions, participating every day for a while, later a few times a
week. Darryl has been in the Argosy House
residence for 14 months and is about to graduate.

He said it's easy to look at the "drug culture" as a way of belonging, of finding friends.
"I was out west and thought I had to maintain a
'slick image' because I was from New York. When
somebody asked me if I wanted to try something,
I went along with it."

The "culture" revolves around loving everyone, he added, "But if you're shooting drugs
you're off by yourself. I wouldn't have admitted
it then, but I thought I was the loneliest person
in the world."

Outside images make you feel good about taking drugs, he added, "Like I'll take acid because of the war in Vietnam, it's nothing but an excuse."

Darryl tried marijuana while away at school. "Some friends offered it to me, I tried it, it gave me a good feeling, so I kept on trying things."

He said he can see things a lot more objectively now. "Society may create a lot of problems, but blaming it for drug abuse is an excuse, nothing more. It's still a kid's prerogative."

"The biggest thing with upper-middle class people is they don't think they're messed up," Darryl added. "Police, and parents in wealthy communities go out of their way to ignore the problem when there is one," he said.

"A friend and I were always getting into trouble," he noted. "We'd get picked up, taken to the police station, and let off. The police are always trying to coat something over where they should be involved. Whenever you have influential people, officials cater to them."

Darryl said he and his parents have been trying to get other kids from his area down to Argosy House. They have also tried to set up a store-front location in their village, but have encountered resistance. "They now regard my parents as radicals for trying to help," he added.

Both Darryl and Charlie encountered difficulty with their friends when they started going to Argosy House. "When they know you're clean and they're still on drugs they get uncomfortable, the scene never changes," Darryl noted.

Charlie thinks that the "drug culture" is getting to younger people. "The Peace thing is dying out, but drugs are expanding greatly. The kids we talk to that are 13 or 14 are impressionable. They've just got to experience something but they don't know where they are going."

"I was a dope fiend before I started using drugs," he noted. "I started robbing and switched to drugs. It was a substitute for

selfish reasons, there were no inner changes in
me."

Schools to start pilot plan for drug abuse education

A great deal has already been done to combat
the drug problem in Central New York. The effect
of this action is largely conjectural because the
problem is a new one and insufficient data is
available.

Of the six recommendations made by the
Mayor's Temporary Commission on Narcotics Abuse
and Addiction in Syracuse, specific progress has
been made in a few areas and attention given to
all of them.

State and local funds have been spent in the
area of prevention and education, with more ap-
propriated for new programs. Unfortunately,
according to Dr. Donald D. Boudreau, Commissioner
of Mental Health Onondaga County, "It's a gamble."

Boudreau is currently going ahead with plans
for a $4 million drug education program to be im-
plemented through the Board of Cooperative Educational Services (BOCES), with the cooperation
of the city, county and parochial school systems.

The pilot program--first in the upstate
area--will be funded half through state appropriations, and half locally with "in kind services." It will be concentrated over the 1971-
72 school year.

The funds were available some time ago,
Boudreau explained, but they would have had to
be used by September 15. To go ahead and spend
that amount this summer would have been "completely irresponsible," he added.

To encompass the entire spectrum of drug
education, the plan will include training of
teachers and students, providing counseling
services in the schools, and instituting adult
and community education through the school systems.

Although much planning has already been
done, and much more remains to be done in the
ensuing months, Boudreau admits, "We don't know

what effect it will have . . . we are kind of betting that it is a reasonable program."

Any efforts to retard the rapid spread of drug abuse, he noted, is hampered by the gaps in research and statistical information on the problem. Part of this is due to the fact that drug abuse on a massive scale is a relatively new phenomenon. Another is the fact that it is illegal.

There is no real evidence that the problem has actually grown, he explained. More people are using drugs, but the possibility exists that this may represent a switch from alcohol. "Public health needs statistics," he added, "but we cannot get them yet."

Drug abuse existed in the late 1800's, Dr. Boudreau said, but it was not recognized as a problem. Most patent medicines contained narcotics, but their users were not identified as addicts.

The drug education plan Boudreau described, was one of the recommendations of the temporary commission. Another that has shown progress over the past few months is the establishment of a city-county coordinating council.

The recently named 16-member City-County Drug Abuse Commission is designed to act as a "board of advocates" on the problem, according to Dr. Boudreau.

Its stated purpose is to review programs in existence, act as a coordinating agency for all programs, serve as a clearing house for information and services, and as a sounding board for future programs.

The board will also stimulate new approaches for dealing with the drug dilemma. Its powers, Boudreau said, will be recommendatory and investigatory.

He added that the commission will not have the power of approving programs, but it can be expected that legislative and enforcement bodies, as well as independent agencies will be guided by their recommendations.

With the exception of administrative costs
and the salary of staff members to serve the commission, the body should not add to the tax
burden of area residents, he said.

Other programs recommended by the temporary
commission which may reach fruition include speedy
processing of drug cases in the court system,
more response to treatment from the medical community and the mobilization of public concern.

Michael Reagen of the Syracuse University
continuing education department noted that a
final recommendation by the commission--the
creation of a central narcotics squad--could run
into a number of bureaucratic snags.

The only sane way for law enforcement officers to do their jobs, is to take the legal-
istic view, Reagen noted, but a central squad
could be empowered to go after heroin dealers
since that is the major source of death and criminal activity in the drug scene.

None of the commission's recommended programs
are designed to interfere with the work already
underway by public and privately funded agencies
in the area, Reagen explained, but to coordinate them and pass along information valuable to
them.

Direction in Education in Narcotics, DEN,
and Argosy House are funded through local and
state appropriations. DEN receives $60,000 a
year, half from the state, and half locally,
according to Dr. Boudreau.

Located on the South side, it identifies
hard drug users, refers them for treatment, and
provides counseling and supportive services before and after treatment, he explained.

Argosy House is budgeted at $172,000 for
1971, half the bill picked up by the state, and
another $67,000 by the county. Full time thera-
peutic treatment is offered hard and soft drug
users, as well as counseling services.

The Mental Health Department is also responsible for the Methadone Maintenance Clinic at
St. Joseph's Hospital, 100 per cent state funded
at $160,000 a year, and works closely with the
St. Mary's Detoxification unit.

116

Other services in the area, Boudreau noted,
include the 1012 crisis center, and the many
activities of individual schools and the community narcotics guidance councils.

More and more work is being put into finding
a solution to drug abuse, although there is a
variety of opinion on how to go about it. But
specialists agree that it is an uphill battle and
their efforts may go unrewarded for years.

PRESENTATION AND IMPLEMENTATION OF A DRUG ABUSE PREVENTION PROGRAM
by
Sol Gordon*

The critical need in a program to curb drug abuse is a strategy of communication: a way of getting young people to listen. This can be accomplished only if the presentation and implementation of the program is factual. And, to be effective, it must be presented in the language of the users and potential users.

It has been observed that most prevention campaigns fail because of outright lies, distortions of the facts and general confusion on the effects of drugs.

There is always some danger that publicity will stimulate interest in drug-use; on the other hand there is a definite need to clear up the confusion that has followed in the wake of the current hysteria about drugs.

However, scare propaganda is not the answer. It may appear to work sometimes with parents, but in the eyes of young people it does nothing for the credibility of the people putting out the information.

For instance, it is likely that overdoing the "dangers" of marijuana or hashish alienates young people very quickly. The fact is we don't know whether marijuana is in itself a harmful substance. We do know that occasional use by a socially adjusted youngster causes no apparent harmful side-effects and, as a matter of fact, its use may result in mild euphoria. Of course, adverse psychological reactions may occur in some people just because the drug is illegal. Many psychologists feel that the chief problem with marijuana is that it is illegal.

On the other hand, there are many drugs circulating through America's "drug culture" that are known to be dangerous. These include opium, LSD, heroin, barbiturates, amphetamines--to name a few.

---

*Professor of Family and Child Development, Syracuse University.

In all circles, there is confusion about these drugs.

For instance, a person is done no favor by being assured that he will become addicted on heroin after the first dose. Because he is being told something that is untrue 99 per cent of the time, authoritative credibility with him is damaged, particularly if he tries it and finds that he is not addicted.

He is done a favor if he is told that he risks infectious hepatitis due to unclean injection paraphernalia and that the more often he uses it the more likely he is to become addicted.

He could be helped if he could be convinced that there is no way these days to tell whether he is buying pure LSD, or some witch-doctor concoction, or insecticide. He is not helped if he is told all the lurid effects of LSD without acknowledging that many people have had pleasant experiences. It could be helpful if he is told that there is no way to tell whether the next drug-induced experience will be unpleasant. And perhaps most important, young people need to know that <u>treating their psychological problems with any drug, including alcohol, is risky business</u>. The usual effect is an initial period of euphoria after which <u>the anxiety and depression increases and the initial problem is magnified</u>--sometimes catastrophically.

Amphetamine-based drugs come in a wide variety of legal and illegal forms and with a wide variety of slang-terms associated with them. The detrimental effect of relying on <u>slogans</u> to communicate can be appreciated by considering a survey this writer made of 125 Upward Bound students: All had heard that "speed kills." Yet, not a single youngster knew what speed is, even though 20 per cent were using it under other names (including "blue-jackets" and diet pills).

Of course, these are only a few representative difficulties. A lot of work needs to be done in this area, including some considerably realistic research.

In a Syracuse-based community newspaper ("Priority One News," March 12, 1971) an editorial by a young man of this writer's acquaintance makes the following points:

119

In attempting to deal with its problems,
society often gets caught in the trap of
settling on cliched solutions. At present,
worry and concern about extensive drug use
and abuse has led people to "drug education"
as the great panacea for solving problems
with youth.

There is no doubt that the issue of drugs
is a serious one and that education is a
viable means of dealing with the problem.
Nevertheless, two things have kept drug
education programs from being as effective
as they might be. First is the mistaken
assumption that kids are ignorant about
drugs. To the contrary, most kids are
knowledgeable even though they may not always be factually correct. If the goal of
drug education is to inform the ignorant,
then a greater emphasis should be put on
adult education since most parents are less
familiar with drugs than are their children.

The second aspect which has kept drug education from being effective is the tendency
to moralize or tell half-truths. It is
very difficult to convince a person that
marijuana is bad when he has had good experiences with it. Likewise, to tell a
person that marijuana causes aggressive or
violent behavior when he knows both from
experience and research literature that
this is not the case, severely undercuts
the credibility of anything else that
agency or program may say.

This critique of drug education is not an
endorsement for drug use, but rather an
attempt to point out reasons why such
programs have not been successful in dealing with the situation.

When the public becomes concerned about a
problem, it demands quick and simple answers.
The danger with cliched solutions, however,
is that they often obscure their own value
by oversimplifying. The issue of drugs and
why people use them is not a simple one and
despite what the public may want to believe,
there are no simple answers. Drug education
will become effective only when this fact is
understood.

It is widely acknowledged that educational efforts made by high schools throughout the country to curb drug abuse have failed. As a matter of fact, very close observation of several high school programs leads this writer to believe that drug usage increases after such programs. The credibility gap as a factor when authority figures such as "narcs," physicians, and other experts talk to students has been discussed in a number of articles. What is not generally known is that widely heralded programs of youthful ex-drug addicts addressing assemblies also alienate students. These groups tend to make stereotyped presentations and invariably take a stronger position on marijuana than even "authority" figures. ("Let me put it to you straight man, I started on marijuana and look what happened to me," "We all started on marijuana..." and so forth.) It is also beginning to dawn on people that many ex-addicts have no other profession than being "ex-addicts"--not a very commendable model.

The apparent reduction of LSD seems to be unrelated to educational drug abuse programs, but does seem to be due to increasing actual experiences of youth with "bad trips" or witnessing such "trips" among close friends.

Another important consideration is that youth do not respect moralizing even by their heroes. Despite "Madison Ave." type advertising using pop singers, sports figures, and so forth, warning against drug use, individual behavior seems unaffected.

The _Miami Herald_ (September 7, 1970) contained the following not widely circulated UPI report (quoted in its entirety):

HEW ISSUES DRUG REPORT

Kick-the-habit drug abuse projects are doomed to failure if they set abstinence as a goal, a Health, Education and Welfare Department report says.
"It is safe to predict that despite anyone's efforts, drug use will not disappear in the foreseeable future," said the evaluation of nine HEW-supported drug abuse projects.

"Consequently, to set abstinence as a project goal is to foredoom the project to failure."

The report, released over the weekend, was issued with a disclaimer that HEW does not necessarily endorse its conclusions. The report was written by Richard Brotman and Frederick Suffet of New York Medical College.

They evaluated projects for drug users in Oakland, Calif., Denver and two in New York City, and five training and research programs.

Projects that set abstinence goals failed because many young drug users, especially marijuana smokers, do not share the belief that drug use is wrong and harmful, the authors said.

They cited an Oakland program where the directors reported failure because the young people rejected their arguments that drugs lead to poor health, broken homes and limited career opportunities.

Abstinence-directed projects also failed because they are too narrow, the authors said.

"If an occasional marijuana user experiences severe discord with his parents because they have discovered his marijuana use, then the first priority should be assigned to repairing the family relationships and not necessarily to obtaining from the youth a public declaration that he will refrain from smoking marijuana," they wrote.

The projects all were intended to reduce glue-sniffing, marijuana smoking and use of heroin and amphetamines. Their subjects were sometimes as young as 10 years old.

The New York Times (November 24, 1970) contained the following UPI news article (an excerpt):

ADS ARE BLAMED FOR PILL OVERUSE

Two doctors blamed Madison Avenue image makers today for enticing Americans to take pills for every imaginable purpose, including "sometimes utterly ridiculous reasons."

"In uncounted advertisements we are being told, persuaded and conditioned not to accept any minor discomfort," Dr. J. S. Gravenstein of Case Western University in

Cleveland testified before a Senate subcommittee.

"We are continuously bombarded to take
drugs for sometimes utterly ridiculous
reasons. We are cajoled to pop a couple of
pills into our mouth to get fast, fast
relief, freedom, pleasure, sleep, comfort,
relaxation and regularity.

"The consumer is continuously urged to
take drugs. Consequently, he demands drugs
also from his physician."

With such "pernicious, irresponsible,
advertising," Dr. Gravenstein said, "we
should not really be surprised when our
young people adopt this belief and seek their
own drugs to cure their own discomforts, imagined or real."

Dr. Gravenstein and Dr. Sidney Merlin of
the New York State Department of Mental Hygiene were critical of hard-sell tactics
used by drug companies.

An article in the March 14, 1971, issue of
The New York Times reemphasized the growing concern of the Federal government regarding the
media encouraging the use of "mind affecting"
drugs:

GROWING USE OF MIND-AFFECTING DRUGS
WORRIES F.D.A.

The mushrooming promotion, prescription
and use of mood and mind-affecting drugs--
stimulants, sedatives, tranquilizers and
the like--are drawing critical scrutiny
from the Federal Government and the medical
profession.

The Food and Drug Administration, a
spokesman said in an interview, began study-
ing the problem three months ago because it
was "thunderstruck" by the number of advertisements in medical journals that seemed
"to go way overboard."

He said the agency was concerned about
indiscriminate use of psychoactive drugs
without adequate knowledge of their long-
range effects...

I have in my possession a collection of
hundreds of pamphlets, books, and articles on
drug abuse published in the last two years. Only
two or three articles direct their attention to

the problem of communicating to youth in ways
that do not alienate them.

Among the most useful publications that I
have seen are distributed by the National Clear-
inghouse for Drug Abuse Information (Some of the
"Answers to the most frequently asked questions
about drug abuse" and "How to plan a drug abuse
education workshop for teachers"). Their pamphlets can be employed effectively providing that
we take seriously the most important reasons why
young people use drugs. The following list is
included in "Answers to the most frequently asked
questions about drug abuse":

1. The widespread belief that "medicines"
   can magically solve problems.

2. The numbers of young people who are
   dissatisfied or disillusioned, or who
   have lost faith in the prevailing social
   system.

3. The tendency of persons with psychological problems to seek easy solutions
   with chemicals.

4. The easy access to drugs of various sorts.

5. The development of an affluent society
   that can afford drugs.

6. The statements of proselytizers who
   proclaim the "goodness" of drugs.

As I see it the problem is at least, in part,
one of effective communication and new directions
in treatment.

There should be three main objectives in a
drug abuse program:

1. research

2. communication of the findings to both
   youngsters and professionals interested in prevention and in helping
   youngsters with drug problems.

3. with an enormous number of youth already
   heavily involved in drugs, we need also
   concern ourselves with the best therapeutic approaches for intervention, for

change, and for rehabilitation.

    <u>In my judgment no drug abuse program operating outside the context of improving conditions under which a drug culture will flourish will have significant impact</u>. Thus, students and teachers need to be able to broaden the scope of any "abuse" program to include improvement of the general climate of the school or community.

DRUG ADDICTION
by
Edwin M. Schur*

THE "DOPE FIEND" MYTH

In recent years there has been considerable repudiation of the once prevalent "dope fiend" myth[1]--which depicted the drug addict as a degenerate and vicious criminal much given to violent crimes and sex orgies. More and more people are coming to understand the nature of opiate drugs and the meaning of addiction. This discussion will be concerned primarily with that class of pain-killing and soothing drugs derived from or equivalent to opium. Morphine and heroin are the best known of these drugs; others include codeine, meperidine (Demerol), and methadone (Amidone, Dolophine). Such pain-killers are the drugs of choice of most persons who are fully addicted in the sense described below. This is an important point, because the continued use of these opiate-type drugs (to which the term narcotics may also be applied) produces characteristics and behavior quite at odds with stereotyped conceptions of the dope addict.

Effects of Opiates

Central to the various common misconceptions is the belief that the addict is dangerously "hopped up." Actually, opiates are depressants--that is, they produce a general lowering of the level of nervous and other bodily activity. The effects of these drugs have been summarized as follows:

> The depressant actions include analgesia (relief of pain), sedation (freedom from anxiety, muscular relaxation, decreased motor activity), hypnosis (drowsiness and lethargy), and euphoria (a sense of well-being and contentment).[2]

Although the relation between addiction

---

*Edwin M. Schur, Ph.D., Crimes Without Victims: Deviant Behavior and Public Policy, Abortion, Homosexuality, Drug Addiction (Englewood Cliffs, N. J.: Prentice-Hall, Inc., 1965), pp. 120-138. (c) 1965. Reprinted by permission of Prentice-Hall, Inc.

and criminality will be examined, there is nothing
about the operation of these drugs which would
incline a user to commit criminal offenses. In
fact, the specific effects of opiates serve to
decrease the likelihood of any violent antisocial behavior. Similarly, opiates produce a
marked diminishing of the sexual appetite--long-
term addiction producing impotence among most
male addicts; hence, concern about "dope fiend
sex orgies" is quite unfounded. Indeed, perhaps
the most striking characteristic of addicts is
their general inactivity--on the basis of which
they might be considered unproductive or withdrawn but hardly fearsome.[3]

It has also been widely believed that opiates
produce definite and extreme organic disturbance
and deterioration in the users. Yet, as an authoritative report recently emphasized, there are no
known organic diseases associated with chronic
opiate addiction--such as are produced by alcohol addiction, regular cigarette-smoking, and
even chronic over-eating. Although opiate use
does produce such effects as pupillary constric-
tion, constipation, and sexual impotence, none
of these conditions need be fully disabling, nor
are they permanent.[4] Similarly, many characteristics and ailments, such as unkempt appearance
and symptoms of malnutrition, which often are
exhibited by addicts in our society, are attributable to the difficulties they experience in
obtaining drugs rather than to the drugs' direct
effects.

There is also considerable misunderstanding
about the supposedly positive feelings the
addict receives from the drugs. As noted above,
a sense of well-being and contentment is often
produced by opiates. As a young female addict
has put it:

> You simply do not worry about things
> you worried about before. You look at
> them in a different way....Everything
> is always cool, everything is all right.
> It makes you not feel like fighting the
> world....I mean it's that sort of a
> thing, you know, when you're not
> hooked.[5]

Some discussions of addiction have exaggerated
the positive nature of these euphoric effects,
and this has led to the widespread belief that

addicts take drugs solely for "kicks." The
crucial misunderstanding is suggested by the
addict's express limitation of the above description of euphoria to <u>when you're</u> not <u>hooked</u>. In
most cases, positive feelings about the drug
are largely restricted to the early stages of
addiction. In the later stages, a reversal of
effects occurs, in which the drug is no longer
taken primarily to obtain positive pleasure but
rather to avoid the negative effects of withdrawal.[6] As the addict just quoted goes on to
say, the user's feeling about the drug changes
drastically once real dependence upon it is
reached: "Suddenly, the character of taking off
[injecting the drug] changes...all you're trying to do is keep from getting ill, really...."[7]
Indeed, the theory of "kicks" may be inadequate
even when applied to the early stages of addiction.
As one major research report has noted, the "kicks"
adolescent addicts seek may reflect their overwhelming general unhappiness. To the extent
that the drug combats this unhappiness, it primarily offers relief rather than positive
pleasure. The same report also refers to interesting laboratory findings of wide variation
in individual responses to an initial injection
of opiates. These data suggest that even if such
drugs tend to produce some euphoria, the nature
and extent of this feeling may be greatly affected
by the user's personality characteristics.[8]

The Addiction Process

The process of becoming addicted involves a
developing bondage to the drug. According to
a World Health Organization definition:

> Drug addiction is a state of periodic or
> chronic intoxication produced by the
> repeated consumption of a drug (natural
> or synthetic). Its characteristics in-
> clude: (1) an overpowering desire or
> need (compulsion) to continue taking the
> drug and to obtain it by any means; (2)
> a tendency to increase the dose; (3) a
> psychic (psychological) and generally a
> physical dependence on the effects of the
> drug; (4) an effect detrimental to the
> individual and to society.[9]

The term <u>intoxication</u> may not be the most appropriate to use in describing the effects of opiates,
and there is at least some dispute about the

nature and extent of detriment necessarily associated with addiction. However, the rest of the definition does highlight the crucial features of the addiction process. Tolerance and dependence are the characteristics which distinguish the confirmed addict from other drug users. Tolerance refers to the process through which the body adapts to the effects of a drug. Because of such adaptation, the dose must increase in size if the same effects are to be produced; likewise, with the growth of tolerance the drug user becomes able to safely take doses which might be dangerous or even fatal if taken by a nonuser. It is important to note that addiction exhibits a tendency to increase the dose. As will be seen, there is considerable dispute about whether this tendency is virtually unalterable or whether it is possible for some addicts to be maintained on a stabilized dose.

Once tolerance to opiates reaches a certain level, a distinct physiological (as well as psychological) dependence on the drug is produced. When this dependence has developed addiction is complete and the user is properly referred to as an addict (although the term addict sometimes has been used more broadly to cover regular use even of non-dependence-producing drugs). The user's bodily system now, in effect, requires the drug to function smoothly, and if it is withdrawn the addict experiences acute symptoms of distress, known as the "abstinence syndrome." This syndrome includes a variety of both somatic and psychological symptoms, the severity of which is directly related to "the nature of the narcotic, the daily dosage used and the intervals, the duration of the addiction, the rapidity with which the drug is withdrawn, and the intensity of psychic and somatic dependence. It is inversely related to the resistance, vigor, and well-being of the addict." As this same report notes, despite the likely variations just indicated, "all recent authorities agree that the withdrawal syndrome has an organic basis."[10] It also seems clear that withdrawal of the confirmed addict from drugs is always at least an extremely unpleasant experience. Although in some cases the physical symptoms (which reflect disturbances of the neuromuscular, gastrointestinal, and respiratory systems) may be no more severe than a bad case of the flu,[11] in other instances the addict may be acutely and violently ill. And

the psychological impact of the experience should
not be overlooked:

> I thought I would go mad. I was on the
> verge of insanity. I prayed for help,
> for relief, for death. My clothes must
> have been wet with sweat. I cursed the
> habit. If anyone could have seen me they
> would have thought I was a raving maniac.12

The phenomena of physical dependence and
withdrawal distress are important to an understanding of the addiction problem. However, it would
be a mistake to think that physical dependence
fully explains the confirmed addict's need for
drugs. Any individual administered opiates in
sufficient dosages over a long enough time will,
when administration is stopped, experience withdrawal distress. Thus many persons receiving
such drugs in the course of medical treatment
for the relief of pain become addicted to them.
Yet not all such individuals revert to drugs after
withdrawal. The term drug addict is ordinarily
applied to those persons who, over some period of
time, feel the "overpowering desire or need (compulsion)" mentioned in the WHO definition; a
recent study has employed the term craving in discussing this important aspect of addiction.13

At the same time, the fact that the long-
term addict has a physiological as well as psychological need for his drugs helps to put his
condition and his behavior in proper perspective.
Dependence also provides a basis for distinguishing truly addictive drugs from those which may
be said to be only habit-forming--or to which
users ordinarily develop merely a psychological
habituation or dependence. Tobacco and coffee
would be good examples of such habituating drugs.
Stimulants such as cocaine, marihuana, and
peyote (mescaline and LSD are similar) may produce striking effects on the users and sometimes
strong psychological habituation, but they are
not truly addicting. Amphetamines (such as
Benzedrine) also fall into this category. Barbiturate drugs can, in prolonged use, lead to
actual tolerance and physical dependence, but
despite the danger of such addiction the medical
use of barbiturates (primarily to treat insomnia)
is widespread and socially approved in our society.
Similarly, social approval of alcohol exists in
the face of the well-known dangers of excessive

drinking. Many experts insist that the condition of alcoholism is far more harmful to the individual than is opiate addiction. The unhappy lessons of the Prohibition experiment point up the key role negative social sanctions on drug use may play in creating secondary problems.

CAUSES OF ADDICTION

According to a large body of psychological and psychoanalytic literature, addiction is but a symptom of an underlying psychic disorder, and certain types of individuals are psychologically predisposed to drug addiction. Despite variations reflecting different schools of psychological theory, psychologists and psychiatrists seem to agree on one central point--that the personality type typically exhibited by addicts involves strong dependency needs and pronounced feelings of inadequacy.[14]

Sociologist Alfred Lindesmith, who highlighted the popular misconceptions embodied in the "dope fiend" myth, also provided a detailed critique of the psychiatric approach to addiction. He was especially disturbed by the prevalent diagnosis of the addict as a "psychopathic personality" or as a person with "psychopathic diathesis or predisposition. One early and influential report, for example, had found that 86 per cent of the addicts studied had been affected "with some forms of nervous instability before they became addicted"...the largest category comprising "care-free individuals, devoted to pleasure, seeking new excitements and sensations, and usually having some ill-defined instability of personality that often expresses itself in mild infractions of social customs."[15] Lindesmith insisted that an inordinate emphasis was being placed upon the gratification the addict supposedly received from drugs and insufficient attention paid to his need to avoid withdrawal distress. His basic criticism though, was that the psychiatric approach failed to develop a specific, self-consistent, and universally applicable theory of addiction. It evaded the problem of explaining how some psychologically "normal" persons (14 per cent in the study cited) become addicted. Nor did it explain cross-cultural and group variations in addiction rates. Early diagnostic studies, furthermore, made no use of control groups of non-addicts, so a finding

that 86 per cent of the addicts were psychologically disturbed could not really be evaluated.
Even the use of control groups, however, would
not remove the objection that the psychologists
used as subjects only those who were already
addicted--and in many cases, for many years. Such
studies do not distinguish those traits which were
the result of addiction from those which had
caused it. Finally, Lindesmith contended, the
very fact of addiction led the psychiatrist to
find some underlying psychic difficulty. He noted
the apparent tendency of psychiatrists to treat
almost any trait exhibited by an addict as a
possible indication of psychopathology. Thus
some cases of addiction were held to be caused by
lack of self-confidence; others by the pleasure-
seeking drive of carefree individuals. He concluded: "The addict is evidently judged in advance. He is damned if he is self-confident and
he is damned if he is not."16

On the basis of his own extensive inter-
views with addicts, Lindesmith developed what is
perhaps the only distinctly sociological theory
of addiction. He took as his goal an explanation
that would include all cases, on the assumption
that the only true causal explanation is one
that is applicable to all instances of the phenomenon being explained. (This approach is rather
different from that employed in most sociological
research, where association between variables
usually is stated in terms of probability--that
is, statements are made about the likelihood of
certain events, based on statistical outcomes
in past observation.) Lindesmith began his research with a working hypothesis, which he
revised to take account of negative cases wherever he encountered them. His final thesis, to
which no exceptions could be found, was that
"the knowledge or ignorance of the meaning of
withdrawal distress and the use of opiates
thereafter determines whether or not the individual becomes addicted."17 This refers to
the persistence of a craving for the drug after
withdrawal; continued use may result in physical
dependence, regardless of the presence of this
knowledge. Essentially what this explanation
provides is a retrospective description of the
learning process through which all addicts go.
A major criticism of the theory has been that
it does not afford a basis for predicting which
particular individuals will become addicted.
Although this criticism seems partly warranted,

Lindesmith's thesis has the merit of calling
attention to the important element of learning
involved in becoming an addict, and of suggesting that anyone could be susceptible to such a
learning experience. (As another writer notes,
in the current American drug situation this
learning process involves not only knowledge of
withdrawal and dependence but also important
changes in the individual's over-all self-concept, gradual preoccupation with the need to
obtain drug supplies, and likely involvement in
a drug-addict subculture.[18])   Howard S. Becker's
processual analysis of marihuana use has described the way in which, with that drug too, one
learns to become an habitual user.[19]

Another approach to the causes of addiction
lies in the extensive findings from research
into the nature, extent, and distribution (spatial
and social) of narcotics use in various large
metropolitan centers. These area studies derive,
in part, from the ecological approach developed
some years ago by the Chicago school of sociologists. Indeed, it had already been found by
Faris and Dunham in their classic study, Mental
Disorders in Urban Areas (1939),[20] that in Chicago
at that time addicts were highly concentrated in
the deteriorating and generally disorganized
"zone in transition" near the center of the city.
Recent studies in New York, Chicago, Detroit, and
other large cities show a persistent and clear
relationship between ecological structure and
the distribution of known addicts. Addiction is
invariably found to be concentrated in those
areas of the city that are most dilapidated and
overcrowded, inhabited by persons of low socioeconomic and minority-group status, and characterized by high rates of other types of social
pathology. One writer notes: "Such ecological
studies of drug-users known to courts and hospitals reveal a higher degree of concentration
of teen-age drug-users than is found for almost
any other type of psychological or social problem." [21] This type of research has also dis-
closed the emergence in the larger metropolitan
areas of a distinctive addict subculture.

A recent report has summarized the large
body of data obtained in a ten-year study of
juvenile drug use in New York, undertaken by the
Research Center for Human Relations at New York
University. This research, conducted under the
guidance of social psychologists, combined an

interest in the dynamic psychology of the individual deviant with an awareness of the importance
of the socioeconomic and even legal aspects of the
drug problem. The findings indicated that the
areas with the highest drug use were those that
were most overcrowded, had the highest poverty
rates, and were populated largely by minority
group members.[22] Not only was drug use found to
be correlated with significant socioeconomic
variables of that sort, but the New York researchers also concluded from an attitude survey that
the high-use neighborhoods were characterized by
a cultural climate conducive to experimentation
with drugs. (They found a pervasive outlook on
life which might be summarized as pessimistic
antisocial hedonism.[23])

A major theoretical problem for such studies
is posed by the fact that not all individuals in
the areas of addict concentration take up drugs
or even orient themselves to this dominant cultural climate. In seeking to explain the non-
users in high-use neighborhoods, Chein and his
associates revert in some degree to a psycho-
logical-predisposition approach. They note
certain functions the use of drugs may serve--
such as relieving various personal and interpersonal strains and in general "establishing
distance from the real-life demands of young
adulthood."[24] A comparison of the family back-
grounds of a group of addicts with those of a
group of nonaddicts suggested that such background might constitute the basis for suscepti-
bility to addiction. The unstable and dishar-
monious family milieux in which the addicts were
reared contributed, they felt, to "the development of weak ego functioning, defective super-
ego, inadequate masculine identification, lack
of realistic levels of aspiration with respect
to long-range goals, and a distrust of major
social institutions." They also found that the
fathers of the addicts had either been absent
much of the time or were themselves highly disturbed or deviant.[25]

Limits of the Causal Approach

These findings may suggest some of the
practical limitations of past and present studies of causes of addiction. It is not too difficult to summarize these findings in a very general
way. To begin with, it is now known that there
is no single "type" among addicts--the physician

who succumbs to addiction, for instance, is a
quite different type sociologically (and perhaps
psychologically) from the poverty-stricken minority-group member enmeshed in a delinquent and
addict subculture. However, individuals in
certain socioeconomic categories run a relatively
greater risk of encountering and using narcotics
than do those in other categories. Also, it
seems likely that of those individuals in the
high-risk categories it is the more troubled or
the more disadvantaged, situationally, who are
especially likely to take up drugs. (Although
in another sense they could be viewed simply as
those most fully socialized into the prevailing,
if deviant, pattern.) The specific policy implications stemming from conclusions of this sort are
not very clear. On the one hand it seems that
addiction is partly caused by other general social
disorders and that one way to deal with it is to
attack the various socioeconomic ills which constitute the breeding ground of drug use. Similarly, various types of family life are highlighted as being detrimental, and presumably
measures should be taken (assuming it could be
determined just how this might be done) to improve
the quality of interparent and parent-child relations. And if those individuals who do become
addicted have certain personality problems, some
kind of therapy or counselling should be aimed
at treating the addicts themselves.

It seems clear that pursuit of all these
types of treatment is desirable. At the same
time, in the absence of any theoretical or
therapeutic breakthrough that could be expected
to result in a high rate of prevention or "cure"
(the relapse rate in addiction cases is extremely
high), it may be useful to approach the question
of addiction in a somewhat different way. Whatever the causes of individual cases of addiction,
the broader dimensions of the addiction problem
may be amenable to improvement through variations
in public policy. As one expert has stated:

> The prevalence and consequences of
> addiction in any society depend as much
> upon the social and legal definitions
> placed upon the non-medical use of nar-
> cotics as upon the nature and effects of
> narcotics or the nature of the persons
> who become addicted.[26]

To some observers, attempted reforms of the legal
policies on addiction never reach the core of
the problem. Indeed most psychologically oriented
students of addiction maintain that, without individual treatment, persons succumbing to addiction would--even in the absence of drugs--be
involved in some kind of problematic behavior.
Yet few responsible students of the problem view
psychological treatment of susceptible individuals as offering a complete solution of the
addiction problem. Attention to narrowly defined
causes cannot lead to a full understanding of
addiction as a social problem. Such an understanding requires consideration of the legal policies
which define and seek to control that problem.

DRUG LAWS AND ENFORCEMENT

Narcotics Legislation

The practical effect of American narcotics
laws is to define the addict as a criminal offender.
This result has stemmed largely from the interpre-
tation given the Harrison Act passed by Congress
in 1914. This law requires registration of all
legitimate drug-handlers and payment of a special
tax on drug transactions. It thus establishes
a licensing system for the control of legitimate
domestic drug traffic. In this respect the Harrison Act has been extremely successful, and it
seems clear that originally the statute was intended merely to serve this function. It specifically provided that the restrictions would not
apply to dispensing of narcotics to a patient
by a physician "in the course of his professional
practice" and "for legitimate medical purposes."
As a recent and authoritative report concludes:
"Clearly, it was not the intention of Congress
that government should interfere with medical
treatment of addicts."[27] Yet, through a combination of restrictive regulations, attention only
to favorable court decisions, and harassment, the
Narcotics Division of the U. S. Treasury Department (and its successor, the Federal Bureau of
Narcotics) has effectively and severely limited
the freedom of medical practitioners to treat
addict-patients as they see fit--in particular,
to provide addicts with drugs when that is believed medically advisable.

An early test of the Act came in 1919 (Webb
v. U.S.). The facts showed flagrant abuse of

the law by the defendant, Dr. Webb, who had sold
thousands of narcotics prescriptions indiscrim-
inately for fifty cents apiece. The government, however, presented the issue to the U.S.
Supreme Court in the following form:

> If a practicing and registered physician
> issues an order for morphine to an habitual
> user thereof, the order not being issued
> by him in the course of professional treat-
> ment in the attempted cure of the habit,
> but being issued for the purpose of pro-
> viding the user with morphine sufficient
> to keep him comfortable by maintaining his
> customary use, is such order a physician's
> prescription [under the specific exemption
> in the Act]?

Accepting this restrictive definition of "professional treatment," the Court asserted that "to
call such an order for the use of morphine a
physician's prescription would be so plain a
perversion of meaning that no discussion of the
subject is required."[28] Another case three years
later (U.S. v. Behrman) also involved obvious
abuse of the Harrison Act; here the doctor had
given to an addict a huge quantity of narcotics
for use as he (the addict) saw fit. In what one
student of these decisions[29] has termed a "trick
indictment," the government glossed over the
doctor's quite evident bad faith, acted as
though the drugs had been provided in good faith
for the purpose of treating the addict, and obtained a ruling to the effect that any such
wholesale prescriptions (in good faith or not)
violated the law. At the same time, however, the
court indicated that the prescription of a single
dose or even a number of doses--made in good
faith--would not be punishable under the Act.[30]

To this day, the Federal Bureau of Narcotics
quotes with approval the Webb and Behrman decisions, making little or no mention of an important
1925 ruling (Linder v. U.S.) which would seem to
challenge and greatly limit these earlier judgments. In the 1925 case, the government prosecuted a well-established Spokane physician who
had prescribed a small amount of narcotics for
a patient who was actually an agent of the
Bureau. (The defendant claimed that the "patient"
had said she was in great pain from a stomach
ailment and that her regular physician was out
of town; she claimed that she had said she was

an addict.) In a unanimous opinion, the Supreme
Court reversed Dr. Linder's conviction, stating:

> The enactment under consideration...
> says nothing of "addicts" and does not
> undertake to prescribe methods for their
> medical treatment. They are diseased and
> proper subjects for such treatment, and we
> cannot possibly conclude that a physician
> acted improperly or unwisely or for other
> than medical purpose solely because he
> has dispensed to one of them, in the or-
> dinary course, and in good faith, four
> small tablets of morphine or cocaine for
> relief of conditions incident to addiction.

The Court also specifically held that the Webb
and Behrman rulings should not be extended beyond
the facts in those particular cases.[31]

The acceptance of medical discretion embodied
in this decision has in no way been reflected in
federal narcotics regulations:

> An order purporting to be a prescription
> issued to an addict or habitual user of
> narcotics, not in the course of professional
> treatment but for the purpose of providing
> the user with narcotics sufficient to keep
> him comfortable by maintaining his customary
> use, is not a prescription within the mean-
> ing and intent of the act; and the person
> filling such an order, as well as the per-
> son issuing it, may be charged with violation
> of the law.[32]

The Linder decision did not prevent the Bureau of
Narcotics from carrying out what a recent account
has termed a "persecution of the physicians"; at
least during the period 1925-38 there were numerous prosecutions and convictions of physicians
for narcotics violations.[33] There are probably
few such cases today, partly because doctors
have been so effectively cowed by the early
prosecutions and stringent regulations.

The Bureau of Narcotics insists that it does
not attempt to interfere with legitimate medical
practice. Yet the physician's position remains
tenuous. As a joint committee of the American
Bar Association and the American Medical Association has noted, a physician's prescription of
drugs for an addict will probably be upheld if

it is in "good faith" and if he adheres to
"proper medical standards." But these very
questions can only be determined in the course
of an actual court trial of a specific case:

> The physician has no way of knowing <u>before</u>
> he attempts to treat, and/or prescribe
> drugs to an addict, whether his activities
> will be condemned or condoned. He does
> not have any criteria or standards to guide
> him in dealing with drug addicts, since what
> constitutes bona fide medical practice and
> good faith depends upon the facts and cir-
> cumstances of each case....[34]

Over the years the Harrison Act has been
supplemented by many other anti-narcotics statutes
under which the unauthorized possession, sale,
or transfer of drugs is severely punished. Rather
than constituting a rationally planned program
for dealing with the narcotics problem, this
legislation has mainly represented an emotional
response to periodic crises. For example, public
concern about narcotics--aroused by the Kefauver
Committee's 1951 investigation of organized
crime--resulted in a federal law (the Boggs Act)
imposing severe mandatory minimum sentences for
narcotics offenses.[35] Another congressional
investigation four years later, focusing entirely
on the drug traffic, led to the enactment of the
Narcotic Control Act of 1956, which raised the
minimum sentences for offenders and which permits
the death penalty for those who sell narcotics
to persons under eighteen.[36] In addition to the
federal statutes, the various states have enacted
their own anti-narcotics laws.[37]

Many observers, including some prominent
jurists, have condemned the harsh penalties imposed by recent drug laws--objecting particularly
to the fact that such statutes typically draw no
distinction between the non-addict peddler and
the addict. Illustrating these objections was
the 1956 statement of Robert Meyner, former
governor of New Jersey, vetoing a bill which
would have increased mandatory minimum sentences
for narcotics violators and barred suspended sentences and probation even for first offenders.
Stating that he would have unhesitatingly approved if such penalties applied only to non-
addicted suppliers of drugs, Meyner noted:

...although the deterrent quality of
punishment may be conceded in certain
areas, the question remains whether
deterrence may not also be achieved by
severe sentences where the facts so
warrant, without the inherent self-
defeating weakness of laws which are
excessively severe in cases involving
individuals whose offenses do not merit
the punishment commanded by the bills....38

The Failure of Enforcement

What have these legal policies accomplished?
Law enforcement officials often assert that addiction is being kept under control, yet even
government estimates have placed the number of
addicts between 45,000 and 60,000, and almost
all nongovernmental experts feel these figures
greatly understate the problem. In any case,
it is certain that these laws have not come any-
where close to eliminating addiction. They have,
however, greatly influenced the narcotics problem. Cut off from legal supplies of narcotics,
the addict naturally seeks illicit drug sources.
The strong demand of addicts for their drugs
means that there are huge profits to be made in
the black market, and this in turn makes the
risks involved in such an endeavor worthwhile.
According to one account, the retail value of
one thousand dollars worth of heroin may surpass
three million dollars.39 It is understandable,
then, that the endless circle of supply and
demand alluded to in the discussion of abortion
should also be in evidence here. The addict's
position in this exchange is so vulnerable that
not only must he pay exorbitant amounts but
typically he must settle for a highly diluted
product; the repeated adulteration of narcotics
as they go down the line from the original im-
porter to the various distributors and ultimately
to the addict is well known. Many experts contend that no amount of law enforcement effort
could reasonably be expected to stifle the
black market in narcotics. Such observers believe that, given the extreme and continuous
demand of addicts, some way always will be found
to make the drugs available illegally. For, as
Robert Merton has suggested: "In strictly economic terms, there is no relevant difference
between the provision of licit and of illicit
goods and services."40

Most enforcement officials admit that the task of significantly curbing the smuggling of narcotics into the country is a pretty hopeless task. The former U.S. Commissioner of Narcotics himself has been quoted as saying that the combined efforts of the Army, the Navy, the Narcotics Bureau and the FBI could not eliminate drug smuggling. As a customs agent has pointed out, discussing his agency's operations in New York City:

> On normal passenger arrival days it is the policy of the collector of customs at the Port of New York to examine baggage 100 per cent, but when the passenger arrivals are heavy, a spot-check of baggage is performed. Under these circumstances it is not difficult to understand how a passenger using a false-bottom trunk or a suitcase with a false compartment might be able to conceal narcotics and get by the examining inspector; searches of persons are infrequently made and then only as a last resort and only based on substantial reasons.[41]

Again, as in the case of abortion, there occurs the competitive development of enforcement and anti-enforcement techniques.

But, basically, it is the supply-and-demand element and the lack of a complaining victim, rather than the cleverness of the law violators, that render the drug laws so largely unenforceable. Predictably in such a situation law enforcers must resort to special investigative techniques. A major source of evidence in narcotics cases is the addict-informer. Though the addict-informer faces grave danger of underworld reprisal, their eagerness to stay out of jail (and avoid sudden withdrawal from drugs) or simply their need for funds with which to purchase drugs impels many addicts to assume this role. The Bureau of Narcotics is authorized to pay the "operating expenses" of informants whose information leads to the seizure of drugs in illicit traffic; hence, the Bureau at least indirectly supports the addiction (and the "crime") of some addicts in order to uncover others. Despite this fact, and the questionable legal aspects involved in trapping suspects through informers, enforcement spokesmen insist on the propriety and even the necessity of such practices. According to two enforcement experts:

> The police officer who by methodical
> planning, supplemented sometimes by
> happy accident, is able to set up and
> maintain listening posts in the under-
> world, represents one of the finest
> professional developments in the unceas-
> ing war of organized society against
> underworld forces.[42]

Often the informer or even the narcotics agent
himself will directly attempt to obtain a prescription or a supply of drugs from a suspected
doctor or peddler or through an addict. Thus
narcotics investigations frequently tread the
fine line between detection and entrapment. As
in the case of antihomosexuality operations, the
courts will not uphold prosecutions based on acts
or statements directly planned or instigated by
enforcement officers. There is even the danger
that enforcement activities may hinder attempts
by addicts to curb their addiction:

> The case at bar illustrates an evil
> which the defense of entrapment is de-
> signed to overcome. The government
> informer entices someone attempting to
> avoid narcotics not only into carrying
> out an illegal sale but also into return-
> ing to the habit of use. Selecting the
> proper time, the informer then tells the
> government agent. The set-up is accepted
> by the agent without even a question as
> to the manner in which the informer en-
> countered the seller. Thus the government
> plays on the weaknesses of an innocent
> party and beguiles him into committing
> crimes which he otherwise would not have
> attempted. Law enforcement does not re-
> quire methods such as this.[43]

The use of informers and agent-decoys are
not the only unpalatable police techniques used
to combat the drug traffic. Perhaps more than
any other category, narcotics cases have notor-
iously given rise to grave issues of constitutional law--as witnessed by major U.S. Supreme
Court decisions dealing with alleged infringe-
ments of suspects' constitutional safeguards
against improper arrest, illegal search and
seizure, self-incrimination, and the like. One
of the best-known of these decisions was in the
case of <u>Rochin</u> v. <u>California</u> (1952). There the
police, suspecting the defendant of dealing in

narcotics, illegally broke into his room. During the course of a struggle with the intruding officers, the suspect managed to swallow two small objects which the officers had attempted to seize from a table near the suspect's bed. The police then rushed him to a hospital, where--despite his protests--a physician pumped his stomach. As a result, the investigators found morphine which was later used as evidence against him on a narcotics charge. The Supreme Court held unanimously that conviction on the basis of such evidence violated due process of law. Writing for the Court, Justice Frankfurter stated:

> ...the proceedings by which this conviction was obtained do more than offend some fastidious squeamishness or private sentimentalism about combatting crime too energetically. This is conduct that shocks the conscience. Illegally breaking into the privacy of the petitioner, the struggle to open his mouth and remove what was there, the forcible extraction of his stomach's contents--this course of proceeding by agents of government to obtain evidence is bound to offend even hardened sensibilities. They are methods too close to the rack and the screw to permit of constitutional differentiation.[44]

In addition to the questionable nature of enforcement activities, the efforts required to obtain evidence in narcotics cases may lead to an unwarranted expenditure of police energies (and hence, indirectly, of taxpapers' money). In one case five detectives spent a month in Greenwich Village disguised as "beatniks"; one was reported even to have achieved a slight reputation as a poet. According to a news account the entire New York police narcotics squad (then numbering 140 men and women) participated in resulting arrests.[45] If such efforts led to the conviction of leading figures in the drug traffic, they might be worthwhile. Yet it is widely known that current enforcement activities more often serve to ensnare minor violators. The American drug traffic involves at least four classes of sellers: importers (rarely addicts themselves), professional wholesalers (also rarely addicts), peddlers (who may be addicted), and pushers (addicts who sell to get funds for their own drug supplies). As numerous commentators have noted, it is the addicts, pushers, and

perhaps some peddlers who are most affected by
anti-narcotics enforcement. The Bureau of Narcotics and other government agencies protest
that they have in fact managed to convict some
of the major figures in the illegal drug traffic.
But, as Judge John Murtagh has pointed out:

> The Bureau itself admits that there is a
> new dope ring to take the place of every
> one it smashes and that periodic round-ups,
> even if conducted on a national scale,
> while they may serve to weaken the racket
> never effect a killing blow. Perhaps the
> biggest round-up in American history was
> that staged in 1952...which netted a total
> of nearly five hundred suspects. But was
> the syndicate affected by this round-up?
> Hardly at all.[46]

In short, it is evident that the police face
an impossible task in seeking to enforce current
drug laws. The laws are inherently self-defeating.
Even to approximate efficiency in their administration would require the wholesale violation of
legal rights, which the courts will not permit.
Likewise, judges are often unwilling to impose
maximum sentences on addicted drug violators, and
even prosecutors sometimes proceed against them
under the less stringent of several possible
charges. At the same time, enforcement personnel
are under considerable pressure from segments of
the public and from higher officials to produce
results. It is not surprising, under these circumstances, that they exhibit strong hostility
toward the addict, and view themselves as engaged
in a "war" against addiction. With a sharp atti-
tudinal dividing line separating the "good guys"
(law enforcers) from the "bad guys" (those involved in the world of drugs), important dis-
tinctions such as that between the addict and the
non-addicted drug violator, blur or disappear.[47]
These punitive attitudes, in turn, lead to increasingly brutal treatment of the addict, without any
corresponding increase in the effectiveness of
anti-narcotics measures.

144

NOTES

1. Alfred R. Lindesmith, "'Dope Fiend' Myth-ology," _Journal of Criminal Law and Criminology_, 31 (1940), 199-208.

2. D. P. Ausubel, _Drug Addiction: Physiologi-cal and Sociological Aspects_ (New York: Random House, 1958), p. 18.

3. This point has been raised in critical reviews of Jack Gelber's _The Connection_ and other plays and novels about addiction, the critic sometimes maintaining that addicts are not interesting subjects for fictional presentation because "they just sit around and don't really do anything."

4. Isidor Chein, et al., _The Road to H: Nar-cotics, Delinquency, and Social Policy_ (New York: Basic Books, Inc., 1964), p. 356.

5. Helen M. Hughes (ed.), _The Fantastic Lodge: The Autobiography of a Girl Drug Addict_ (Boston: Houghton Mifflin Company, 1961), pp. 113-114.

6. See Alfred R. Lindesmith, _Opiate Addiction_ (Bloomington: Principia Press, 1947).

7. Hughes, _op. cit._, pp. 127-128.

8. Chein, et al., _op.cit._, pp. 246, 347-348.

9. Expert Committee on Addiction-Producing Drugs _Seventh Report_, World Health Or-ganization Technical Report Series No. 116, 1957. As reprinted in President's Advisory Commission on Narcotic and Drug Abuse, _Final Report_ (Washington, D.C.: USGPO, 1963), p. 101.

10. New York Academy of Medicine, Committee on Public Health, "Report on Drug Addiction--II," Bulletin of the _New York Academy of Medicine_, 2nd series, 39 (July 1963), 441-442.

11. See Ausubel, _op. cit._, p. 23.

12. Addict quoted by L. Guy Brown, _Social Path-ology_ (New York: Appleton-Century-Crofts, Inc., 1942), p. 217.

13. Chein, et al., _op. cit._, especially pp. 237-250.

14. For a good summary of the psychiatric approach see Marie Nyswander, _The Drug Addict as a Patient_ (New York: Grune & Stratton, Inc., 1956), Chap. 4; also _Drug Addiction: Crime or Disease?_ Interim and Final Reports of the Joint Committee of the American Bar Association and the American Medical Association on Narcotic Drugs (Bloomington: Indiana University Press, 1961), pp. 50-59.

15. See L. Kolb, "Types and Characteristics of Drug Addicts," _Mental Hygiene_, 9 (1925), 300-313.

16. Alfred R. Lindesmith, "The Drug Addict as Psychopath," _American Sociological Review_, 5 (1940), 920.

17. Lindesmith, _Opiate Addiction_, _op. cit._, p. 69, see also his "A Sociological Theory of Drug Addiction," _American Journal of Sociology_, 43 (1938), 593-613.

18. Chein, et al., _op. cit._, p. 24.

19. Howard S. Becker, _Outsiders: Studies in the Sociology of Deviance_ (New York: The Free Press of Glencoe, Inc., 1963), Chapts. 3 and 4.

20. R.E.L. Faris and H.W. Dunham, _Mental Disorders in Urban Areas_ (Chicago: University of Chicago Press, 1939).

21. John Clausen, "Social Patterns, Personality and Adolescent Drug Use," in A. Leighton, J. Clausen, and R. Wilson (eds.), _Explorations in Social Psychiatry_ (New York: Basic Books, Inc., 1957), p. 238.

22. Chein, et al., _op. cit._, p. 78.

23. _Ibid._, p. 92.

24. _Ibid._, p. 187.

25. _Ibid._, pp. 268, 273.

26. John Clausen, "Social and Psychological Factors in Narcotics Addiction," Law and Contemporary Problems, 22 (Winter 1957), 34.

27. New York Academy of Medicine, op. cit., p. 430.

28. Webb v. U.S., 249 U.S., 96, 100 (1919).

29. Rufus G. King, "The Narcotics Bureau and the Harrison Act: Jailing the Healers and the Sick," Yale Law Journal, 62 (April 1953), 736-749.

30. U.S. v. Behrman, 258 U.S., 280 (1922).

31. Linder v. U.S., 268 U.S., 5 (1925).

32. See U.S. Bureau of Narcotics, "Prescribing and Dispensing of Narcotics Under Harrison Narcotic Law," Pamphlet No. 56 (Washington, D.C.: USGPO, 1956).

33. New York Academy of Medicine, op. cit., p. 432, citing statistics from L. Kolb, Drug Addict-on: A Medical Problem (Springfield, Ill.: Charles C. Thomas, Publisher, 1962).

34. Drug Addiction: Crime or Disease?, op. cit., p. 78.

35. 65 Stat. 767, 21 U.S.C. Sec. 174 (1952).

36. 70 Stat. 567 (1956).

37. For a good survey of state laws see Donald J. Cantor, "The Criminal Law and the Narcotics Problem," Journal of Criminal Law, Criminology and Police Science, 51 (January-February 1961), 516-519.

38. State of New Jersey, Executive Department, Assembly Bill No. 488, veto message of Governor Robert B. Meyner (mimeo, June 28, 1956), p. 5.

39. Vincent Riccio and Bill Slocum, All the Way Down (New York: Ballantine Books, Inc., 1962), p. 145.

147

40. Robert K. Merton, <u>Social Theory and Social Structure</u>, rev. ed. (New York: The Free Press of Glencoe, Inc., 1957), p. 79.

41. Statement of Lawrence Fleishman, U.S. Customs Bureau, in U.S. Senate, Committee on the Judiciary, Subcommittee to Investigate Juvenile Delinquency. <u>Hearings</u>, Part 13. New York City, September 20-21, 1962 (Washington, D.C.: USGPO, 1963), p. 3140.

42. Malachi L. Harney and J. C. Cross, <u>The Informer in Law Enforcement</u> (Springfield, Ill.: Charles C. Thomas, Publisher, 1960), pp. 17-18.

43. <u>Sherman v. U. S.</u>, 356 U. S. 369 (1958), as reprinted in R. C. Donnelly, J. Goldstein and R. D. Schwartz, <u>Criminal Law</u> (New York: The Free Press of Glencoe, Inc., 1962), p. 729.

44. <u>Rochin v. California</u>, 342, U. S. 165, 172 (1952).

45. Robert Alden, "'Beatnik' Police Seize 96 in Narcotic Raid," <u>The New York Times</u>, November 9, 1959, p. 1.

46. John M. Murtagh and Sara Harris, <u>Who Live in Shadow</u> (New York: Ballantine Books, Inc., 1959), p. 99.

47. See Robert M. Lipsyte, "Cops in the World of 'Junk'," <u>New York Times Magazine</u>, October 14, 1962, p. 63 <u>et seq.</u>

WHAT IS DRUG ABUSE? IS THERE A DEFINITIVE ANSWER?
by
Daniel X. Freedman*

This is not an easy topic. There are complex semantic histories behind the term "addict" and international bodies of experts have long attempted to bring some clarity to the terms we use. The simple facts are that there are a variety of settings in which individuals misuse drugs, whether these are prescribed or illicitly procured. Certain drugs are more likely than others to lead to misuse and to a range of consequences from toxicity to dependence and disruption of the conduct of personal or social life.

Behavior which we call misuse may range from unwise self-medication or unwise lay prescription (the wife takes the husband's antibiotic to which she is allergic), to passing, pushing, or consuming pills for kicks, relief, or for avoidance of tension. Certain drug dependencies, called addictions, involve drugs which induce stressful symptoms in their absence and, hence, add a further motive (physiological symptoms and stress) to drug-seeking behavior. There are a variety of toxic, accidental or physical effects (let alone social, religious, legal and economic ones) which may be associated with (or less frequently, a direct consequence of) drug-taking.

The topic does plunge into a variety of what are, in fact, quite different issues. It is clear, however, that the definition of the abuse of drugs is most frequently the definition of an observer. Often we are concerned with whether or not an individual's use of a drug--whether it brings him pleasure or problems, or both, or neither--happens to be offensive to his wife, his family, or his employer, or neighbors. Thus, almost all of us are keenly concerned with the social effects of drug-taking. We judge its desirability (apart from the specific somatic and behavioral effects and the risks entailed) in terms of individual self-regulation, utility, comportment and development, and also in terms of perceptions of others-- which are not always accurate.

If drugs did not simultaneously affect both private and public behavior and provoke value

---

*Dr. Freedman, Professor of Psychiatry, The University of Chicago. Abridged from Drug Abuse in Industry (Philadelphia, Pennsylvania, Halos and Associates, 1970).

judgments about pleasure, and if they did not
influence a gamut of social, legal and economic
interactions, we would neither be as concerned
nor as confused as we are. As a society, we
tolerate a variety of brutal accidents, conditions leading to deprivation and depravity for
segments of the population, and we approach a
range of health issues with far less confusion
and panicked perplexity than we currently show
for drug problems. When "drugs" were equivalent
to narcotics and when both were isolated either
to a few slum areas or to an upper class or in-
tellectual bohemian elite, we could treat the
issues as not really impinging on the fabric of
aspects central to American life. The point is
that drug use, misuse, abuse, dependence, or
physical addiction, all impinge on a variety of
both individual values and social behaviors and
consequences. In defining these issues, we
have fundamentally to grasp precisely what our
specific concerns and questions about drug usage
may be, and expect that individuals will be at
variance if not at odds with groups, and further
that some groups of individuals--cults and cliques-
will oppose general social values whether articulated informally or by law.

It is my thesis that we currently suffer from
an epidemic of drug interest which is far more
distracting than actual patterns of drug use and
misuse. It is further my thesis that we are concerned, if not panicked, by exposure to the unpredictable, exposure of the unwary to all of
this drug interest, and the bewildering variety
of increasingly popular patterns of drug misuse. The topic of drugs has been intruded
(rudely for many of us) upon our normal concerns,
bringing with it uncertainties and alarms and
an expectedly high titer of irritation, as well
as fear. That schools and legislators, and
clinics and law enforcement agents, as well as
industry, should have to confront some of these
bewildering issues is taxing upon our energies.
That young people today have yet another option
for risk-taking about which to formulate attitudes and decisions is a tragic fact of contemporary life and I find it hard to see why anyone
(and some do) would welcome it. Precisely how
our society is going to either "cool it" or
cope with and contain this epidemic of interest
and of use is unclear.

Comprehension and analysis of these issues
are forced upon us. It might help to remember
that it is very difficult to have any kind of a
rational attitude about drugs. It is natural
that we would wish to isolate, avoid, overlook--
or, to counter doubt, overenthusiastically em-
brace--drugs, because we have deep concerns when
we seriously confront them. Every society worries about drugs which are available to it--
whether these are the products of technology or
nature. Every society attempts to rationalize
or socialize their use--either condemning or
demonstrating certain occasions for use.

Recreation is at issue. By the end of the
day, after certain kinds of boredom and work
and labor, one returns home and confronts a
shift in circumstances. He may have a drink or
a talk with his family. Whatever it is, he
seeks a new communion with someone or something
else as a relief from the constraints of the
day. In this attempt to let go and relax, one
shifts attention from one set of concerns to
another. Now almost any drug which changes the
way a part of the body feels can be used to help
the process of shifting attention; some, which
affect the way the brain works or the mind per-
ceives have specific and compelling effects in
this direction. What is dangerous, of course,
is that individual motives can capture the release produced by this holiday from constraints,
and individuals can employ the drug effects for
escape in other than prescribed circumstances.

Further, no society is without deep concern
about man's capacity to overindulge in pleasure.
This is not to say that the addict, incidentally,
is having pleasure; indeed, one of the greatest
oversights of our era has been the failure to
perceive the extent to which the addict is ward-
ing off displeasure. He may have started out
for fun, status, or kicks, or have valued these
drug effects, but his eventual primary use of
the recreational drugs is to avoid displeasure.
A human need to transcend constraints and displeasure is ever present and constructively or
destructively exploited: Utopias are proposed
in each generation; salesmen and prophets have
always threatened establishments with visions,
and lured the lost with proposals and potions
for what they call love and liberation. The
salient point is that every society must have
some means by which to regulate escape (such as

through communion or recreation) and confrontation.
We have, then, been forced to attend to the use
of drugs in our society.

What are the patterns of use which manifest
themselves as drug problems? First of all we see
a pattern of self-medication in which individuals
self-medicate stuffy sinuses and headaches, or
in which the young, in the need to study for
exams or to sleep after overexcitement, are on
occasion attempting to self-medicate with stimulants and sedatives. Secondly, we see experimentation with the available recreational drugs in
which individuals may try in social groups or,
less often, on more private occasions, to "see
what it is like"--and this is the most frequent
kind of contemporary nonmedical drug-taking in
youth. Third, we see the episodic recreational
use of drugs over several years within an individual's biography; this may be an occasional
(weekly or monthly) use of marijuana. People
enter and leave various patterns of using drugs,
so that today's recruits may be tomorrow's vet-
erans and vice versa. Fourth, there is the
dedicated use of drugs in which pharmaceuticals
become central to existence, whether these are
physically-habit-forming drugs or substances
whose effects are habitually sought as a mode
of coping with anxiety or inhibitions (tranquilization), or in the search for escape. This
dedicated pattern of drug-taking may persist or
recur for varying periods in individuals' lives.

Drug dependence may occur with or without
viable harm--or at least disruption. There have
been life-long opiate and alcoholic dependent
persons who were productive and did not "abuse"
their dependence. Many of us have varying
degrees of dependence on coffee or teas, and,
without the intervention of ulcers or coronary
disease, can cite no harm; yet we find it unpleasant to be deprived of our drug. The man who
has his glass of wine and enjoys it may be said
to have a habit--he misses the drug when it is
not available. But, we point out that he has
not lost control over his habit. So individuals
may live and adapt to their dependencies, showing different degrees of control over them. But
the most frequent consequence among dependent
individuals is a variety of evident physical,
psychological and social impairments which few
cultures can value.

Society as a whole, of course, cannot take
into account the gradations with which each
individual may control or regulate or be dominated by his usage of various drugs of choice.
The major socially-sanctioned arrangement has
been a properly regulated medical profession.
Society should additionally be more careful about
the adequacy and relevance of its laws and punitive sanctions (one mode of control), if it is
to avoid creating more problems than it solves.
A mobile and pluralistic society must exert
effort to identify its risks and decide how to
do this. Accordingly, it would be more useful
in our society to make sound assessments of
public health and social dangers which a prevalent pattern of use of one or another compound
may in fact entail than to strictly, moralisti-
cally and abstractly construct definitions of
different abuses or misuses.

What I am suggesting is that there are many
aspects of our attitudes about drugs which are
not only ambivalent and contradictory but which
also lend themselves most readily to unexamined,
tendentious statements and expedient or simple-
minded laws and regulations. For example, if
it is self-medication which generates casualties,
we should perhaps do away with the possibility.
This, again, would mean the strict prohibition
of alcohol. Of course, the facts are that our
society customarily permits consumers, rather
than physicians, to prescribe alcohol, even
though many individuals no doubt use it as a
kind of self-medication. On the other hand,
there is much concern today about the TV pharmacy and over-the-counter drugs which may have
the sedative or stimulant effects that people
seek. Yet we must recognize that people do seek
relief from pain and anxiety; adults have a fundamental task to perform in adjudicating how
their body feels to them and when professional
help is going to be necessary.

This need to diagnose one's own problem, to
learn to tolerate pain on the one hand and to
interpret it and find some relief on the other,
is not an easy topic to resolve through hastily
constructed legislation. We cannot entirely
abolish--nor do I believe we actually should--
the intelligent self-management of everyday ills
and ails. It is possible today to find mother's
medicine cabinet responsible for the contemporary
misuse of drugs--but that well-stocked and

advertised cabinet existed in the 1950's without any apparent epidemic of recreational drug use.

We should be careful about how we displace responsibility for unwanted patterns of drug taking--whether to the Mafia, our own contradictions or youth's. The fact is that our society bears a great burden as to how it will help to educate in attitudes towards reverence for life. If we legislate our network of drug manufacture, advertisement and consumption, we should not overlook some of the basic human needs which are to be dealt with currently.

Thus, we have to separate various quasi-medical uses of drugs, various patterns of drug use and misuse, and the variety of problems entailed where there is drug dependence. We should also be alert to what we mean when we are talking about "an addict" and what we properly should mean. Generally, we equate specific drugs and the addict, even though we know these differ. There are, indeed, many medically useful but socially or psychologically dangerous drugs; among these are those with physical effects producing tissue dependence. By this we mean a tissue reaction in which a second dose of the drug produces some kind of equilibrium (because in the absence of such a dose there is a reaction). The opiates (morphine, heroin, codeine), alcohol and barbiturates, clearly produce patterns of physical dependence in the appropriate dosages. Depending on dosage and dosage schedule (usually excessively high and frequent dosages), certain minor tranquilizers can produce drug-seeking behavior or a drug habit is evident as we use morphine and alcohol on appropriate occasions without producing anything like antisocial drug-seeking behavior. When used medically, addicting opiates are given to "patients."

Further, there are quite different phases (not necessarily sequences) in the use of drugs which produce dependence. This fact is no doubt complicating. Thus some individuals complain that we cannot predict their behavior or eventual demise in addiction simply because they have experimented with heroin, and are indeed not addicted or dependent; this is to a certain extent true. What society does say, of course, is that experimentation greatly enhances risk both to the individual and society; the individual's right to use a potentially dangerous drug

and his right to use a potentially dangerous automobile do not, additionally, include the right to
experimentation with either drugs or automobiles
when this experimentation would increase risks
either to the individual or society. The consequences of dependence or addiction are rarely the
individual's burden alone to bear, and the costs
of liability, even for our highway traffic and
slaughter, is now leading to demands for public
insurance. With regard to drug usage, society
must formulate policies with regard to users and
manufacturers of drugs, distributors, suppliers,
and the abuse of specific drugs.

Many individuals insist that marijuana has
been prevalent for five thousand years, and that
it can be used without risk. This is partly
true; but, of course, no drug can be used entirely
without risk. If an individual employs a drug
such as marijuana in controlled (though legally
risky) circumstances, he is in a controlled phase
of drug usage. The phase at which an individual
begins to self-medicate with marijuana and the
phase at which he begins to rely upon it for
escape and tranquilization may be hard for the
user or observer to differentiate. But the
further phase when frequent daily usage may lead
to cumulative and toxic effects is fairly easy to
define as is the phase at which "more" of an
effect is sought through the use of more potent
forms of cannabis. It is these latter phases
which begin to produce paranoid and hallucinatory
states with some regularity and which represent
more clear-cut stages of danger.

Where controlled pleasure is the purpose of
drug taking and occasional use of low dosage is
the pattern of disease, we do not know the optimal frequency of use over several years' period
of time. This is a matter of dosage schedule and
long-term and cumulative effects. We know some
dangers for single high dosage and continuous
heavy use of low potency marijuana. The dangers
of high potency marijuana in a single or several
dosages--even though we cannot define these
dangers in their entirety--are toxic psychosis
and poor judgment while intoxicated. But we
do not know the dosage interval which is safe or
the problem of cumulative effects with moderately
short intervals over a long period of time. Thus,
while we arrest individuals for mere illicit
possession of proscribed drugs, we are in the
untenable position of finding it difficult to

factually and objectively judge what role drugs
might be actually playing in the possessors'
general behavior. Indeed, we assume a harm that
may or may not be justified on examination of
individual possessors of marijuana. The best way
to protect individuals and society is still to
be determined.

Whatever the rank order of dangerousness,
temptation or lure of a variety of different
classes of drugs, it is clear that our major
public health problem with drugs is alcohol, and
that our knowledge of its misuse can offer us the
general principles by which we could specify what
we will encounter as general problems with other
drugs. Perhaps what is most crucial to any drug-
taking is the way in which individuals tend to
manage the effects of a drug.

Within limits, the effects of any drug depend very much on what purpose one has when taking
the drug and how the occasion of drug-induced
behavior change is to be managed and experienced.
Industry is properly concerned about having any
person high on speed roaming around dangerous
machinery--at the very least it is difficult to
predict his intentions and his judgment. But we
should not forget the governments and armies that
have used pep pills to have pilots fly yet another
mission, nor that our astronauts were trusted to
use amphetamines--indeed instructed to--for
specific purposes. Nor does the presence of an
opiate within the body mean that performance need
be impaired--this depends on tolerance and motivation.

So--within limits--the issue of the intentions of the individual are crucial. His capacity to know, understand and control his intentions (a prediction which intrinsically can
never be too certain) becomes crucial as his
link to habit, judgment and rationality is
loosened by chemical effects on the brain. Thus
we have to assess society's capacity to help
bridge whatever diminution of control a drug in-
duces. Society does this by reinforcing the
definition of specific purposes for which the
drug may be ingested and its effects managed.
The extent to which one can reliably predict that
society's wanted behaviors will be the actual
behaviors of a drugged individual ranges with
individuals, occasions, drugs and groups. Other
calculable variables are the drug (its dosage

and dosage schedules); the drug-taking occasion
and the tasks to be performed in it; the social
constraints or lack thereof in the regulation
of performances; all are complex factors which
would have to go into a prediction.

These various complex links of drugs to behavior and social values means that potentially
the use of drugs affects the whole fabric of
society; for example, legal regulations, workmen's
compensation adjudications, behavior of parents,
teachers, physicians, health workers, scientists
and others, legislation, law enforcement, the
courts and corrections. So, we deal with a broad
public health issue which has involved many different segments of our society. With the present
situation we can no longer lock up the problem
into one or another isolated Federal bureaus
with the hope that the worst of the problems or
the most unwanted of them will stay out of the
sight of the majority of us.

How did we get here? What is it that brought
us to pay attention at last to the issues of drug
misuse? We know that in the early 1900's opium
addicts were often middle-aged, middle-class
women who had been taking tonics which happened
to be laced with a bit of opium. We know that
the Harrison Narcotic Act, passed finally in
1914, was not truly meant to root out these
individual sinners but rather grew out of a
variety of high-level concerns about the problems
of international policy involving our investments
in the Far East and the behavior of oriental
smokers. Few of us clearly comprehend the
history of our drug laws or the ongoing history
of international drug regulations. Yet we can
recall that Commissioner Anslinger and the Bureau of Narcotics had been the sole repository
of judgments on the dangerousness of illicitly
used drugs. He was quoted as being of the opinion that marijuana was not dangerous and again,
in 1937, that it was the chief cause of crime.
The testimony at that time against classifying
marijuana with heroin was opposed primarily by
the birdseed lobby (which used cannabis seeds
for bird food because it made their coats slick,
not because it made them sing). Few medical or
other opponents appeared to testify. The facts
are that a variety of considerations other than
public health or problems of actual crime against
persons and property have dictated our patterns
of drug control.

General ignorance relating to these matters
has had consequences; drug problems were largely
left to a handful of "experts" in law enforcement and other agencies. It was when the
children of the culture-bearing elite began to
use drugs--and more crucially when commentators
in the media reacted--that the current drug
problem surfaced and engaged knowledgeable
psychopharmacologists and educators. The
media--such as _Time_ and _Life_ or _Playboy_ and the
daily press--advertised the chief drug of interest. Between 1960 and 1966, this was LSD.
What was a fairly small and localized epidemic
of drug interest and use among select populations was rapidly disseminated. This subsequently
had the effect of stimulating a style or a fad as
these various journals continued to mythologize
(hence prescribe) what was the prototypical youth
and their culture. This was also linked with all
the trappings and trippings of psychedelic go-
go, with its emphasis on immediacy, "now," vivid-
ness and self-centeredness, and salient spoofing
of smugness.

LSD is essentially no different in its
effects than mescaline. It was vividly described
by Havelock Ellis in 1898, and was tested in this
country in the 1930's without any epidemic of
drug trials, experimentation, misuse or excessive interest. It is difficult to account
for the fact that this did not happen; an editorial in Lancet on Ellis' report indicated
that if the public ever did get ahold of this,
it would be a problem for the streets. Why is
it that we have a problem at this time? No one
is clear on the answer to this. But given the
rapidity with which styles and information can
be conveyed--or reacted to--it can become significant, imitated and consequential in terms
of public style and habits.

Serious early experimenters were either
curious or attempting to seek some special
inner-comprehension, new perception, or mystical state. But we should not be so gullible
as to believe that this is any longer the key
motive for current drug experimentation. The
message has been replaced by fad.

The epidemic quality of drug excitement
which precedes drug use and misuse is important
to comprehend. With excitement will come a
variety of invested social roles--drug experts

(whether they be writers, scientists, physicians,
ex-addicts, do-gooders or users). The consequences are a wealth of activities, ranging from
conferences and half-way houses and various
groups to press reports. None are unlikely to
make it possible to accurately define the nature
of problems which are talked about with such intensity.

It was clear that by 1966 LSD use was peaking
out (not, of course,disappearing), and that the
rate of increase of use was at least being contained. Most experts today agree that any small
subgroup of LSD users will have about a two-
year history of concentrated usage; the drug
itself becomes less interesting to the users;
some grow into other interests or responsibilities
or both; some perceive various risks for themselves in the drug life, and all have perceived
casualties.

Between 1966 and 1968, penalties escalated
for LSD possession and use; there was intense
publicity about possible chromosomal damage.
Attention shifted to discussions about marijuana
and the practice of trying marijuana became
topical. There was an unanticipated consequence
both to the intense propaganda that marijuana was
not as dangerous as our laws indicated (true) and
to the increasing experimentation with it on the
part of college youth. An attitude of careless-
ness and a disbelief in "authority" escalated;
the patina of safety and accusation of establishment hypocrisy around marijuana spread to all
drugs. There followed the increased use of
amphetamines ("speed"), intravenous experiments
generally, and "pot and pills" (multiple drug-
taking emerged as critical). In general, there
was an increased interest in a life style which
incorporated experimenting with drugs. Between
1968 and the present, multiple drug experimenta-
tions on the one hand, and marijuana experimentation especially, have spread to a variety of
ages and subgroups and locales in this country.

It is crucial to understand this epidem-
iology. We find experimentation on both Coasts
with a number of new compounds, and through the
press and youthful travelers, they spread from
the Coasts to the heartland's urban centers and
from there to the various campuses and counties;
from older drug experimenters, the pattern and
interest in playing with drugs drifts down to

younger age groups. The epidemic in part is sustained by the panic reactions of observers; the press and legislators, and the excitement of a new thing which blends so well with all the highly publicized mythology about youth subcultures (from the psychedelic to the hippie, from the radical to the protester).

What should be focused upon is the role of the individual carrier and propagandizer. Many populations and subcommunities stay immune from any particular drug problem--not because supplies could not be tapped--but because there are no individuals who are demonstrating and carrying the drugs. The astonishing mobility of individuals in our society can rapidly carry a drug subculture with all its follies and ferment into schools, factories, clubs or wherever subgroups of people are related.

To have drug abuse, drugs must be available, interest must be generated, and a market created. Where this occurs, the unwary are exposed simply because of another group's demands for drugs. As the population at risk enlarges so, too, will the casualties and unwanted patterns of drug-taking. So, while an individual's biography with respect to drugs should not in itself alarm industry or any other group, it does seem pragmatic explicitly to define unwanted behaviors. These need not be labelled criminal, sinful, or medically dangerous. Rather, they simply should be labelled as undesirable.

Given all the unpredictabilities and risks entailed even in socially sanctioned drug-taking, the industrial plant or school is not the place for proselytizing for or consuming recreational chemicals. There is no reason for an organization dedicated to work or learning to have to adapt to new drug problems. Even in their highest and most developed forms, recreational drug-taking belongs in some other time and segment of society than the work arena. Thus, while defining undesirable behaviors such as "drug abuse," it should be possible to deal realistically with issues in one's household or community with regard to proscribed behaviors without at the same time unduly restricting individual rights. Upset to the community, as well as certain limits on the degree of acceptable individual inefficiency or danger, provides a warrant for proscribing the occasion of nonmedical drug use. The proscription does not also proscribe rehabilitative efforts, preventive efforts, and humane counseling.

We have today an unhealthy and exaggerated, if not lurid, interest in drug issues. We shall have to foster an environment where there is less interest in self-experimentation with drugs, more interest in self-respect and more awareness about our careless use of alcohol, nicotine and psychotropic agents. We shall have to convert drug panic into concern, and both into patterns of more selective and sufficient methods of encouraging healthy drug-taking and of dealing with the victims of unwise drug use.

While we can define unwanted drug use and differentiate it from unwise or unhealthy drug use, the issue is always that of human behavior. While any group can readily define appropriate and inappropriate behavior according to its own needs, it seems imperative that all groups in our society go to the trouble and confusion of sorting out the issues of drugs, persons, occasions, desired and undesired outcomes, and appropriate social responses, if society is to deal effectively with the drug problem. It is to be hoped that we can do this with some attention to reason, with some comprehension of human folly and human potential, and of our individual roles in it.

DRUG ABUSE AND LAW ENFORCEMENT
by
Charles Delaney*

The word "protection" in the minds of many
citizens has come to mean the same thing as
"law enforcement." Citizens believe that their
property and lives will automatically be protected if the laws are enforced by the police.
But by "enforcement" what the average citizen
means is that he wants police officers to arrest
someone else before they break a law. During
the course of a day, police officers do not
look around neighborhoods and other public places
in order to arrest people who might break the
law; however, in the minds of many citizens that
is exactly what they expect police officers to
do.

A woman who calls the police station, when
she is in the middle of an argument with her
husband, often does so in order to get the
police to "protect" her from what her husband
might do, not what he has done. If young people
are out late at night, law-abiding citizens
expect the police to "pick them up," not because
they have done anything to harm the lives or
property of others, but on the general pre-
cautionary principle that if they are not
"picked up" they _might_ get into trouble. Citizens want police officers to arrest or jail an
alcoholic, not because he has hurt himself or
anyone else, but just to "be on the safe side"
in the event that he _might_ do so.

A badge, a uniform, a night stick, a gun,
and modern means of investigation and communication do not transform an ordinary human being
into an omniscient one. The police officer
cannot tell from looking at people whether or
not they _might_ break a law. However, the
assumption on the part of citizens that they have
a right to expect police officers to "protect"
them from _probable_ harm or loss of property has
placed police departments in the position of
having to _predict crimes_ or illegal acts before
they occur. Since it is impossible for police
officers or anyone else to know the motives of
people simply by looking at them, talking with
them or questioning them for short periods of

time, and since it is very unlikely that someone
about to commit a crime will come up to a police
officer to tell him his intentions, the police
have been forced, in order to meet citizen
demands, to become "prediction" officers. Police
departments have generally responded to "prediction" demands by forming "special units" within
the department to <u>uncover crimes before they
happen</u>. Because citizens want to be "protected"
from what <u>might</u> happen to them, police have moved
into the paradoxical position of now having the
capability of knowing through "special units"
when there is a higher degree of probability some
crimes <u>may</u> happen but being unable to legally
enforce the law (make arrests, etc.) until the
crime has <u>actually</u> been committed. "Special"
police units may give psychological reassurance
to the citizenry when they believe that these
units will be able to act as a crime deterrent
and keep some crimes from being committed, but
the crime statistics remain virtually the same--
even with a high degree of probability that a
crime may be committed, the police are still in
the position of having to make arrests <u>after
criminal behavior has actually been exhibited</u>.
The result is that the same number of crimes
are probably committed with "special units" in
police departments as are committed without them.
This is particularly true if the "undercover"
agents within special units remain anonymous
(or undetected) among potential law breakers.

Even when mass arrests can be made from
"undercover" or "special unit" activities, it
is not at all clear that this has a significant
impact on such massive problems as drug abuse
in our society. If everyone who uses drugs or
is a part of the drug problem were to turn
himself in to the police tomorrow, we would
still have drug problems as long as there are
people in our society who want to take drugs.
Drug injection, regardless of the type or
amount, except in rare instances, is a voluntary
decision. As long as people want to take drugs
all the laws and "special" police units in the
world won't make any difference. If glue sniffing is made illegal, they'll try marijuana; if
marijuana is made illegal, they'll try amphetamines; if amphetamines are made illegal, they'll
try some other substitute. There are any of a
variety of ways people can drug themselves if
they are determined to do so. Therefore, when
the police make arrests, even massive arrests,

citizens are not protected from the possibility
that their own children <u>might</u> ultimately decide
to use drugs. This fact is becoming somewhat
more accepted now that middle-class, well-edu-
cated young men and women are becoming drug
abusers. The drug-user in today's society cannot
be identified by the way he dresses, the way he
talks, the kinds of professions he may be in,
etc. The use of drugs is not limited to any socioeconomic group within our society.

Some citizens still think of the drug problem as being related to a few junkies, pushers,
drug addicts, drug freaks, etc. They believe
that if the police arrested all of the "weirdos"
the drug problem would be a thing of the past.
But, as it turns out, many drug addicts and drug
users in today's society are not "weirdos." The
housewife who takes several aspirin a day, drinks
10 cups of coffee, and takes a sleeping pill at
night is just as much in the drug scene as a
young high school student who occasionally smokes
marijuana. In order to enter the drug scene,
all that most children have to do is open the
door to the home medicine cabinet or take a
pocket full of change down to the local pharmacy
or grocery store.

The job of decreasing drug abuse problems will
not automatically come about with the passage of
additional drug laws or formation of "special"
police units. Laws will not prevent a young
person from experimenting with drugs he finds
in the home medicine cabinet; laws will not prevent people who want to take drugs from taking
them.

Responsibility for solving the drug problem
has been placed at the feet of local law enforcement officers and agencies when, in most instances, that responsibility should lie elsewhere. Perhaps one of the most difficult aspects
of police work is the readiness with which people
shift responsibility to the police officer for
solving their problems. As soon as the police
officer arrives upon a scene, the responsibility
for making decisions usually shifts from those
directly concerned to the police. When someone
has a car accident, responsibility shifts to
the police officer to decide what happened in
the accident and to make the proper report;
when a child runs away from home, the police
officer is given the responsibility for finding

the child and returning him. Now that our
society is worried about drug abuse, the responsibility for doing something about that
problem has been shifted to a large extent to
the local police, who are expected to "protect"
people from further drug problems. But the experienced police officer knows that if the drug
problem is to be alleviated citizens themselves
must assume the major responsibility for their
own behavior.

NARCOTIC ANTAGONISTS: NEW METHODS TO
TREAT HEROIN ADDICTION
by
Allen M. Hammond*

The rising incidence of heroin addiction and
the generally discouraging record of attempts to
rehabilitate addicts has fostered the hope that
modern chemical wizardry will provide some means
of inoculating addicts or potential addicts
against the effects of heroin, thereby preventing
drug addiction. But if a drug to block heroin
addiction could be developed, to what extent
would it help solve the drug problem, and would
it be beneficial, to the addict and to society,
to administer it?

The questions are not hypothetical because
such drugs, known as narcotic antagonists, do
exist; but neither are the answers obvious.
Skeptics who doubt the clinical effectiveness
of narcotic antagonists point out that drug addiction is a behavioral response to deep-seated
emotional problems, and that administering yet
another drug to "cure" those problems is a naive
and simplistic approach. Others think that
blocking heroin use with the antagonists will only
cause addicts to switch to different drugs and
will leave untouched the deeper problem of drug-
seeking behavior. Those who have used narcotic
antagonists in treatment do not promote them as
a cure for addiction, but they do believe that
these drugs can be a useful adjunct to psycho-
therapy and a significant means of preventing
heroin addiction, especially among adolescents.
The whole issue is likely to receive much more
attention; President Nixon's newly appointed
coordinator for drug abuse prevention, Jerome
Jaffe, has included antagonists on his list of
potentially important treatment options. Fund-
ing for research on these drugs will apparently
increase.

Narcotic antagonists are effective against
heroin and other narcotics because they prevent
those drugs from reaching the nervous system;
antagonists differ, for example, from methadone,

*Allen M. Hammond, "Narcotic Antagonists: New
Methods to Treat Heroin Addiction," Science,
Vol. 173, pp. 503-506, 6 August 1971.

a synthetic narcotic, in that they themselves do
not have narcotic effects and are not addictive.

The two narcotic antagonists now being used
in experimental treatment programs are cyclazocine (a benzomorphine compound) and naloxone
(N-allylnoroxymorphone). A daily dose of about
4 milligrams, given orally, of cyclazocine, which
is the more widely used, will block both the
habituating effects and the euphoria, or "high,"
from heroin for 24 hours. Patients are built up
to this blocking dose gradually over a period of
several weeks and in the early stages often experience dizziness, headaches, and other side
effects--sometimes including hallucinations. Once
established on the blocking dose, patients who
miss their daily dose report experiencing headaches and sensations akin to "electric shocks."
At two and three times the doses normally used in
treatment, cyclazocine apparently can have an
effect similar to LSD, only more unpleasant. Cyclazocine is slightly habituating, in the sense
that mild withdrawal symptoms (the electric shocks)
occur when its usage is discontinued; but neither
it nor naloxone is addictive. The narcotic antagonists, unlike methadone, do not satisfy an
addict's craving for drugs, and, despite side
effects, treatment with these drugs is for the
addict very much like being drug-free. In fact,
many former addicts reportedly test the antagonist
from time to time by injecting heroin, because
they "don't feel anything" with the antagonist.

Naloxone has far fewer side effects than cyclazocine and apparently does not require a period
of gradual accommodation. Pharmacologically, it
is in many ways an almost perfect antagonist. It
can be used to treat heroin overdose and has been
licensed for this purpose by the Food and Drug
Administration; *recovery from the effects of
heroin overdose usually begins within a few minutes after naloxone is injected. For the treatment and prevention of addiction, however, the
drug is not ideal because its antagonist effects
do not last as long as those of cyclazocine;
more than one dose per day, or clinical supervision during part of the day, is necessary.
Naloxone is not very effective in oral form, thus

---

*Neither cyclazocine nor naloxone has been approved
for the treatment of addiction, and both are available for this purpose as investigative drugs only.

doses of 1,000 milligrams or higher must be used. According to those who have used it, the drug has a noxious taste that is impossible to hide.

Cyclazocine and naloxone are believed to work by attaching themselves to sites in the central nervous system known as morphine receptors. Because the antagonists have a greater affinity for these receptors than the narcotic drugs do, the latter are prevented from reaching the nervous system, and their effects are blocked. This blockade can be surmounted, but only by injecting extremely massive doses of narcotics. Several drugs other than cyclazocine and naloxone are known to have antagonistic properties, but many of them have unacceptable side effects as well. In contrast, the so-called pure antagonists, such as naloxone, have apparently no pharmacological properties in their own right except to block narcotics.

Clinical experience with narcotic antagonists at the present is limited--a consultant to the newly constituted Drug Abuse Prevention Office of the White House estimates that only about 200 persons have been treated with these drugs. Nor are the antagonists ideal, in the forms available today, because they have a relatively short active lifetime within the body. Other possibilities for blocking drugs may exist, and it may be possible to chemically modify cyclazocine and naloxone to obtain forms that will act longer. Even in their present form, the drugs can probably be packaged in a plastic time-release capsule or in some other preparation that would allow sustained action--from a few days to a month. But very little research has been done on these possibilities to date, in large part because of a lack of funds. The drug companies that developed the antagonists (Stirling-Winthrop for cyclazocine, and Endo Laboratories, a subsidiary of DuPont, for naloxone) are reluctantly making the drugs available for experimental use, and are doing some research as a "public service" and public relations gesture; but they have no great interest in narcotic antagonists because the potential market for these drugs is not large.

The federal government supports most current research on antagonists, although some state governments, notably New York, also finance research. In the fiscal year just ended, the

National Institute of Mental Health (NIMH) funded some 32 research projects totaling $524,000, with the largest chunk of money devoted to clinical studies. More federal money is likely to become available, however, since the White House Drug Abuse Prevention Office, headed by Jerome Jaffe, is apparently going to recommend a major research and development effort aimed at finding a 30-day blocking drug for heroin, as well as expanded clinical trials.

But NIMH may lose some of its initiative and control over the research effort. By earmarking funds for specific purposes at the White House level, Jaffe and his staff will have a lot to say about how the research is done. One plan that is currently under discussion, for example, is to bring together several research groups, including some from the drug industry, and contract with them to develop the long acting forms of the antagonist. Contract research, although common in other areas of research, would be a novelty in the pharmaceutical field. Several major drug firms have indicated an interest in the project, even though nothing definite has been agreed upon yet.

Supply Problems

The new drug office in the White House will also have to contend with a variety of problems in supplying the narcotic antagonists. For example, one constraint on any operational program using naloxone is its expense and lack of availability. Naloxone is derived from thebine, a chemical present in small amounts in opium; it is correspondingly expensive, and, according to most investigators, hard to come by. It took one New York research group some 18 months to obtain sufficient quantities from DuPont for a clinical trial. Federal officials insist that adequate supplies are available for experimental use, and officials at the Bureau of Narcotics and Dangerous Drugs, which establishes production quotas for investigative use, maintain that closing the Turkish poppy fields will not make it possible for individual companies to get enough raw materials in the future. But difficulties in obtaining a supply of opium may well provide companies with another disincentive to produce naloxone and similar compounds and a convenient excuse for not doing so.

Some research into new narcotic antagonists
is already under way, with promising early results. One compound being studied is closely
related to naloxone and is also derived from
thebine, but it appears to have some advantages
over both naloxone and cyclazocine. The new drug,
known as EN-16-39 (N-cyclopropylmethylnoroxy-
morphone), is undergoing preliminary tests at the
Addiction Research Center (ARC) of NIMH in Lexington, Kentucky, where the use of antagonists
for the treatment of narcotic addiction was first
suggested and tried. The compound has already
been tested in animals at Endo Laboratories on
Long Island and is being tested in human subjects
during the current ARC trials. According to
William R. Martin of ARC, the drug is about twice
as long-acting as naloxone, and, although it does
have some side effects, they appear to be far
fewer and less severe than those associated with
cyclazocine. Because it is also more effective
orally than naloxone, the required dose (and the
cost of the drug) appears to be about one-twentieth
that of naloxone.

Most of the treatment programs using narcotic
antagonists (see below: "Addict Treatment Programs") are restricted to patients who appear to
be highly motivated to stop using drugs. But
even with these patients a wide variety of problems are often encountered, including high dropout rates during the early stages of treatment
and the use of other drugs. One of the chief
causes appears to be that patients are compelled
to face their problems and to deal with the real-
ities of their social situations, however impossible. This may well be beyond the capability
of large numbers of addicts, many of whom presumably use narcotics to avoid just those situations.

For how many addicts, then, are the antagonists likely to be useful? Methadone, because of
its narcotic effect, is more appealing to many
addicts, and the relaxed, jovial atmosphere of
a methadone ward contrasts sharply with the
tension, frustration, and anxiety that charac-
terize a cyclazocine ward, according to one
psychiatrist who has worked in both. Since there
are more patients needing treatment than there
are facilities available, antagonist therapy
and methadone maintenance are not competitive
methods of treatment at present. Yet it is still
uncertain how many addicts can be induced, in the
long run, to seek the more demanding type of
treatment.

170

Three major roles have been proposed for
narcotic antagonists in the treatment of heroin
addiction. They might be useful in a preventive
role in the treatment of the casual user of
heroin who has a high likelihood of becoming
addicted. They might be useful in the rehabilitation of addicted individuals who do not wish
to be maintained on methadone--both those who
want to end a period of methadone maintenance
and those just entering treatment for whom neither
methadone nor a therapeutic community is acceptable.
In this regard, antagonists might be a significant
option in combination with a therapeutic community, perhaps making possible a shift to nonresi-
dential programs. Third, the narcotic antagonists might be used prophylactically, more or less
as a vaccine, in high drug risk areas during a
crisis. An example of such a use would be to
vaccinate large numbers of teenagers at a high
school that was experiencing an epidemic of
heroin use. Large-scale prophylactic use of
antagonists in the armed forces has also been
proposed--as a kind of social experiment.

A number of objections have been raised to
the use of narcotic antagonists, either in treatment or in the prevention of heroin addiction.
Multi-drug use appears to be an increasingly
common practice, even among heroin addicts, and
the effect of widespread administration of antagonists might be to switch heroin users to
amphetamines, cocaine, alcohol, or other drugs.
Barbiturates, in particular, seem to be the drug
of choice for many who would otherwise "mainline" heroin, because the calming, sedative
effect is somewhat similar. But barbiturates
are more addictive than heroin, and withdrawal
much more dangerous--apparently the mortality
rate for unassisted withdrawal is as high as
15 per cent.

Conflicting Views

There appear, in fact, to be two basic
points of view among those who work with the
drug problem. Critics of both the antagonists
and methadone believe that the attempt to treat
drug addiction medicinally, rather than by
educational preventive measures and other "soft
social programming," is characterized more by
a concern for the welfare of society than for
the welfare of the patient. Psychologists and

ex-addicts involved with therapeutic communities
have charged that the therapy provided in the
antagonist programs amounts only to hand-holding,
and that the addict's basic problems are rarely
tapped and dealt with. (The situation is complicated by the tendency of many partisans of a
particular rehabilitative approach to be so
committed to their own method that they cannot
see the value of any other approach.) Some observers fear that antagonists, especially in
their long-acting forms, will have a high potential for being used in socially irresponsible
ways, whether or not those who developed them
intended it.

Supporters of the narcotic antagonists
believe that the urgency of the drug problem
does not admit of waiting for ideal solutions
and that the antagonists can provide help--if
not a cure--for many who desperately need it.
The psychiatric director of at least one antagonist program, while admitting that the cyclazocine
and supportive therapy that she administers is
little more than a crutch for the patient, points
out the practical advantages--the addict is not
down in the gutter, not narcotized past the
point of coping with daily problems, and not
compelled to steal. Others point out that,
while antagonists as presently administered will
not stop those who want to use heroin, they can
help prevent the impulse "fix," which may be of
particular help to the adolescent in resisting
peer-group pressure to use drugs.

Antagonists are not the solution to the
drug problem. But since the problem seems unlikely to go away, the antagonists, as is true
of other methods, can play a potentially important role in treatment. They can be, as one
addict put it, "like having a friend in your
pocket."

Addict Treatment Programs

Clinical trials of narcotic antagonists in
the treatment of heroin addicts are taking place
in a number of small programs that usually involve no more than 15 patients at a time. At
Kings County Hospital in New York City, for
example, cyclazocine is administered on an out-
patient basis, although patients must come in
daily to take their dose. Before being admitted

to the program, patients are required to attend group therapy sessions as part of an orientation and screening process to select likely candidates. Once admitted, they must spend 6 weeks in the hospital, being withdrawn from heroin with decreasing doses of methadone and then being gradually built up to the proper dosages of cyclazocine. Most dropouts from the program occur during this period, when patients try to face life without narcotics. Thereafter, they enter the out-patient program, which includes daily urine samples to check for drug use, counseling, and biweekly group therapy sessions in addition to the cyclazocine.

Perhaps the largest and oldest cyclazocine program in the country is that at the Metropolitan Hospital in New York City. After a hospital stay for detoxification, medical treatment, evaluation, and accommodation to the cyclazocine, the patients are treated on an outpatient basis. Patients come in only two or three times a week, rather than daily, and urine samples are spot-checked on the average of once every couple of weeks. The length of time required to build up to the prescribed dose is shortened to 4 days, by treating the initial side effects of cyclazocine with naloxone. But because it is still an experimental rather than a treatment program, patients commonly are kept in the hospital a total of 3 to 9 weeks.

One of the narcotic antagonist programs using naloxone is that at the Connecticut Mental Center in New Haven. The program gets around the problem of naloxone's limited period of action by operating as a day-patient facility. The patients, adolescents in this case, take part in therapy and vocational and recreational activities; at the end of the day, they receive their naloxone and leave for the night. But the antagonist is not the only method of treatment. The program relies heavily on what its director calls psychosocial intervention--the attempt to replace the drug culture for the addict by making available to him alternative life styles, goals, and opportunities.

Although essentially all of the existing antagonist programs are still experimental in character and design, many of them report encouraging results. In some cases, patients who

are still being treated with cyclazocine are
working and living an apparently drug-free
existence some two years after entering the program. The patients themselves appear to be
satisfied that treatment with an antagonist is
a good thing--those contacted by <u>Science</u> expressed
fears about being on the street again and said
that they were glad to have that extra bit of
security.

MIND-ALTERING DRUGS AND THE FUTURE
by
Wayne O. Evans*

A study of man shows that throughout recorded
history, and in almost every culture, people have
taken chemical substances to change their mood,
perception and/or thought processes. The earliest
recording about such drugs seems to be the hymns
of praise sung to "Soma," the magic mushroom of
the Aryan invaders of India, found in the Vedas.
These indicate its use came from northeastern
Europe and had existed since 2000 B.C. Later,
about 1500 B.C., the Eber Papyrus documents the
use of wine by the Egyptians. The opium poppy,
Papaver Somniferum, appears in records as early
as 1000 B.C., and documents from Mesopotamia
indicate the use of cannabis (Indian hemp) as a
psychotropic drug at least 500 B.C. The ancient
Indian civilizations of Mexico and South America
used mind-altering chemicals, e.g., cocaines,
tropines, harmines and indoles of various types.
Farther west, the natives of the Pacific islands
used betel and kava kava, while in Asia, natural
products which yield ephedrine and reserpine were
common in medical practices. Closer to home, we
can consider our own history of opiate usage,
laughing gas or ether sniffing parties, cocaine
epidemics and a tradition of excessive use of
alcohol. Obviously, man always has sought chemical methods to alter his mind and this tendency
has not abated and may even have grown in modern
times.

Psychotropic Drugs Pour into Market

Today, medicinal and biochemistry, animal
and clinical psychopharmacology, neurophysiology
and neuroanatomy are advancing at the same rapid
rate as the other biological sciences. Thousands
of chemicals are tested each year for potential
psychotropic properties. Expeditions have been
launched to such dissimilar environments· as the
upper Congo and the continental shelf in search

*Wayne O. Evans, Ph.D., "Mind-Altering Drugs and
the Future," The Futurist, Vol. V., No. 3, June
1971, pp. 101-104. Published by the World Future
Society, P.O. Box 19285, Twentieth Street Station, Washington, D.C.

of new plants or animals which might yield chemicals to alter the mind. New psychotropic drugs have the highest rate of entry onto the market of all types of drugs. Further, our techniques of testing new chemicals for psychotropic properties, in both animals and man, have been refined to the point that one would be hard pressed to name a mood, mode of perception, or mental function which now is not testable and roughly quantifiable.

Due to this heightened skill in science and technology, we are achieving a potency and specificity of action in drugs which previously would have been impossible. As an example, K. W. Bentley has synthesized an opiate-like substance which is ten thousand times as potent as morphine. This means that the average effective dose for a human being is 1.5 micrograms to achieve an analgetic equivalence with the usual dose of morphine given for postoperative pain relief. Another example of the capability to produce more potent and specific drugs is the development of certain diazepoxides (Librium Ⓡ) which can induce sleep at a dose as low as 0.5 mg. We finally may have produced a compound which will live up to the fabled "knock-out" drops of spy fiction.

This greater potency and specificity of drugs comes from a knowledge of the interaction of chemical molecules with receptors on cell membranes, understanding of the affinity and activity of drugs for specific receptor sites, by using molecules with optimal, rigid shapes and appropriate positioning of ionic and polar groups, and by blocking metabolism or facilitating procursor formation. Drug molecules now are better behaved than they were in the past.

A convincing demonstration of this increased specificity of psychotropic drugs is seen in some of the anti-depressant agents, e.g., tricyclic amines. At the proper dose and rate of administration, they do not produce euphoria, but do ameliorate depressive states by reducing the uptake and inhibiting the binding of brain norepinephrine in storage granules of neurons.

Developments in neurophysiology also have contributed to our capacity to design novel and potent psychotropic substances. The chemical and electrical mapping of brain systems for the basic drives, e.g., hunger, thirst, pleasure, fear, sex, excitement, sleep, etc. are well

advanced. The faith held by psychopharmacologists that a person's mood and his neurochemical
state were equivalent terms from different viewpoints seems to be on the road to justification.

Public Acceptance of Drugs is Growing

Science alone is not responsible for the
development of new drugs used in a culture. In
order for a drug to be developed, people must
want it and a social condition favorable to its
use must exist. From the evidence of an ever-
increasing consumption of psychotropic substances
by people today this condition appears to be ful-
filled. To gain a perspective in regard to our
present social situation, we should remember the
resistance to the introduction of anesthetics
for childbirth, with its implicit assumptions
that pain is "good" and that the "natural" inherently is "virtuous." Anti-psychotic tranquilizers
were introduced into our mental hospitals as recently as 1955; in 16 years the previously ever-
growing number of hospitalized mental patients
has dwindled, to the point where in 1968 occupied
mental hospital beds were at the same level as
in 1947 in the United States. A more general
public acceptance of psychotropic drug use is
shown by the number of over-the-counter pharmaceuticals that are purchased. At a local super-
market one can buy drugs reputed to relieve
tension, produce sleep, make one become more
alert, relieve all sorts of pain, reduce motion
sickness, fight fatigue, etc. Most people do
not realize that aspirin is the second largest
cause of acute drug death in the United States,
that caffeine poisonings do occur from the
tablets bought in drugstores or supermarkets,
that anti-histamines in cold tablets can slow
reflexes, or that the "safe, non-barbiturate,
non-habit forming" sedatives they purchase can
induce severe hallucinations at high doses.
Finally, we must not forget the most prevalent,
socially destructive and personally harmful
psychotropic drug of them all, alcohol. To call
a drug a beverage does not change its chemistry.

Public attention constantly is directed toward psychotropic drug use by mass media advertising, drug education programs, peer group
pressures and advice from physicians. Consider
how many ads you see on television, newspapers
and magazines during a single day for chemicals

to make you feel better, become more beautiful,
or be the life of the party. Think of the recent flood of opinions you have heard about
drugs from both the establishment and from the
youth. In almost every town in the United States,
drug abuse education programs have sprung up.
Energetic, well meaning, but unfortunately, often
relatively uninformed people have decided to tell
"the truth" about drugs to young people who think
they already know everything there is to know
about them (4,300 scientific articles were published on psychotropic drugs in 1968 alone).
Evidence of this information gap can be seen by
considering references to "drugs" without mention
of purity, dose, route of administration, schedule
of use, situation-person-behavior-drug interactions, etc. The fact is that drugs qua drugs are
not inherently "evil" nor do they convey "universal truth." Indeed, we have no data to show
whether any of the social programs and educational
schemes now underway will help to reduce the
harmful use of drugs. This lack of evidence has
not deterred these activities. Indeed, the programs could be increasing drug use by adding to
drug advertisement.

Adults Who Warn Youth Against Drugs Are Using Drugs Themselves

Peer group pressures for drug use are not
confined to the young. Recent studies have shown
that almost half of middle class adults in the
suburbs who occasionally have taken psychotropic
substances did not receive them from a physician
but from a neighbor or friend who told them that
this was "just the pill to make them feel good."
Ninety per cent of all psychotropic drugs in
the United States were not prescribed by a
trained psychiatrist, but rather by some other
type of physician who may be less aware of drug-
behavior interactions. Further, many physicians
are not current in their information about these
new drugs. The deaths resulting from a use of
certain anti-depressants witness this fact.
Also, few physicians have been trained in the
pharmacology of marijuana, heroin, LSD, STP,
etc. Non-medicinal drugs aren't taught in medical schools. Indeed, parents and physicians
who are telling children not to use drugs are
themselves using mind-altering chemicals on a
massive basis and, frequently, the drugs are
not even received legitimately by prescription.

When we give up alcohol and tranquilizers, we will reduce the hypocrisy of which the youth accuse us. Perhaps, then, a dialogue can begin.

Even physicians are not totally free from some responsibility for the present extensive use and misuse of psychotropic drugs. Studies have shown that young people who often were ill as children and were taken regularly to a physician and there received pills form the group most likely to enter the drug subculture during late adolescence. Yet some physicians prescribe psychotropic substances merely to satisfy the desire of their patients for some form of chemotherapy, without considering the full psychiatric implications of the complaints or the potential efficacy of the compounds.

In the United States in 1969, 90 million new prescriptions were issued for minor tranquilizers, 17 million new prescriptions for antidepressive drugs, 12 million people had used marijuana at least once, and one calculates the consumption of diet pills, stimulants, aspirin, sleeping compounds with scopolamine and other psychotropic drugs by the boxcar load. We have lived up to the famous comment, "Man is the pill-taking animal."

Potent, Safe Euphorics and Aphrodisiacs Are Foreseen

In the near future--say 20 years hence--we could have available highly potent, minimally hazardous antipsychotics, tranquilizers, analgesics, antidepressives, euphorics, psychedelics, stimulants, sedatives, intoxicants, aphrodisiacs, as well as combinations of these drugs to expediently produce most mood states. There now are over 900 drugs listed as psychotropic by the National Institute of Mental Health and the list is rapidly increasing.

The production of non-sedated states of tranquility has advanced since the discovery of meprobamate (Miltown ®) to its present form in the diazepoxide series (Librium ®). It seems almost inevitable that this trend will continue. The introduction of pentazocine (Talwin ®), a potent analgesic which produces a relatively minimal degree of physical dependence, heralds the probable development of a new class of

potent, analgesic drugs which do not have physical dependence as a side effect. This development is continuing so that physical dependence
should not be a major medical problem in the
near future. Also, research has demonstrated
that by combining an opiate with an amphetamine,
one produces a greater potency of analgesia without an accompanying depression of vital bodily
functions, sedation, or mental incapacitation.
These two developments portend that shortly we
shall have potent analgesic substances which
will interfere minimally with one's daily life.
Oral forms of these new analgesics with little
dependence or sedation are under development.

The introduction of lithium into manic-
depressive therapy is an exciting recent development. Although some types of manic-depression
are refractory to any treatment and some depressive states respond best to a short series of
electroconvulsive shocks, it appears that a combined therapy of tricyclic amines with a long-
term administration of lithium will reduce the
impact of this disorder. Further, lithium use
has advanced our knowledge of "affect" disorders at a cellular level.

Need for Drugs Less Harmful Than Alcohol

Compounds to produce euphoria or psychedelic
states seldom are discussed in "proper" pharmacological or medical circles. Yet, a member of
the National Institute of Mental Health has
stated that an urgent need exists to search for
compounds which can relieve the tensions of
daily life by giving a person the occasional
opportunity to become intoxicated without the
severe problems associated with the excessive
use of alcohol. As population expands and
recreational possibilities shrink; as the im-
personality of a specialist-run, counter-intui-
tive society increases and meaningfulness of
community life lessens; the tensions easily
might cause an episodic desire by some to become
intoxicated for a short while to feel wise,
strong and loved. If we accept this unpleasant
truth, the least we can do is develop compounds
less hazardous for use than alcohol (potentially
an addicting, physically harmful drug). Additionally, we must provide places and circumstances where these bouts of intoxication could
take place, while minimizing the harm a person

might do himself or his fellow man. Can we continue to tolerate the fatalities on the highways,
overweight, liver damage, psychosis, broken homes,
sex crimes, and crowding of public hospitals and
jails caused by the unwise use of alcohol? The
explorations of the cannabinols, and the extraction of tetrahydracannabinol as the active principle of Indian hemp, may be a possible first
step in a search for new, less hazardous "anti-
alienation" drugs and the creation of socially
approved, peer-monitored "drag strips" for rac-
ing may be our best models for effective social
control of intoxicant use.

Recent research on sleep, coupled with data
from studies on depressed patients who have received a combination of an amphetamine and a
monoamine oxidase inhibiting, antidepressive
drug, has demonstrated that man can live quite
well on four hours of sleep a night--a fact well
known to the Mogul Emperors. This, considered
with the development of relatively safe sedatives of the diazepoxide type, should let us
arbitrarily decide whether and when to be awake
or asleep--as long as we stay within the apparent
physiological constraint of at least four hours
of sleep per day. Consciousness may become op-
tional and a matter of convenience, personally
or for a society run in shifts to prevent over-
crowding of limited facilities.

Hedonists' Dream May Be Fulfilled Through Sex Drugs

Aphrodisiacs have a fascinating history. Perhaps for no other chemical has man sought so long
and avidly. In examining a recent dictionary of
purported aphrodisiacs, it was interesting to
note that chemicals to aid the flagging potency
of the male outnumbered those to aid the female
by about 20-1. Mass media publicity of L-DOPA
and PACA have alerted the public to the fact
that the brain centers responsible for the trig-
gering and maintaining of the sexual act already
have been discovered. It is possible in animals,
by either chemical or electrical means, to ini-
tiate the sexual act and have it continue without
satiation for prolonged periods. Whether these
sexual acts are pleasurable or not to the animal
is difficult to know. However, if we combined
a euphorogenic agent (to make the sexual act
pleasurable), with a cholinergic stimulant (to

provide the male an increased capacity for potency without ejaculation), and finally, stimulated the brain centers responsible for the initiation and continuation of the sexual act, we may be approaching the hedonistic philosopher's dream. In some sense, we already have aphrodisiacs (see Aphrodix ®, Bennet Pharmaceutical). The only questions remaining are the particular combination of drugs, their ratios and the production of oral forms. If these drugs are developed and widely used, I cannot help but wonder what types of human interactions may result. Where is the warmth, affection and subtlety in a chemically driven liaison?

Peer Group Control Might Limit Drug-Induced Harm

The social consequences of chemically alterable behavior depends on the nature and source of the imposed sanctions. Thus far, through history, we have seen admonitions for individual self-control, prohibitive legal sanctions, peer group control, and, on occasion, imposed use of mind-altering drugs. Individual control is, I believe, a lost battle. The present evidence of the quantity of drugs consumed is proof enough. Prohibitive laws have been attempted since the Empress of China proclaimed the death sentence for opium users and, in Turkey, the use of tobacco was punishable by death in "a means acceptable to God." Our own more recent experience with prohibition of alcohol is additional evidence of the lack of efficacy of this type of sanction. Finally, 12 million people in the United States have used marijuana—though many of the states have harsh laws against its possession. This seems to demonstrate that the threat of harsh punishment does not work well to deter use of psychotropic drugs. Few physiological effects of drugs could be as severe as their legal effects. Peer group control has been used as a sanction for chemical users—sometimes to limit use to special situations and acceptable doses. Presently, in small groups, some young people learn to "guide" each other in drug use and can exercise a rather superb degree of control so that group members seldom become too "high" on marijuana. Similarly, in Italy, a tremendous amount of alcoholic beverages are consumed, yet, there are relatively few cases of alcohol dependence or the various other ill effects that sometimes result from continued use of this drug. It appears that introduction of children to the consumption of alcohol in a family situation, during mealtimes, "immunizes" them against later excessive use. In Italy, the family encourages drinking but does not tolerate drunkenness. Perhaps, we should take note of this method in order to reduce drug-induced harm.

Drugs Could be Used to Slow Social Progress

A frightening possibility exists that psychotropic chemicals could be imposed upon people without their consent or by social pressure. One must wonder if some of child psychopharmacology, as sometimes practiced, is not a form of chemical warfare against our children, and the spread of LSD from one spouse to another demonstrates that pressures for drug use are both close and powerful. Again, the development of incapacitating warfare agents of a psychotropic nature, by the United States and other countries, shows what can be done with these chemicals. At least most of the young have accepted the creed "Thou shalt not alter the consciousness of another without his consent." Are we as honorable? It is not difficult to envision a possible future in which tranquilizers, hallucinogens or euphorogenics, effective in the micro or nanogram range, could be distributed in an aerosol to quiet a "pre-riot" area. What would be the possibility of any social progress in a society in which the authorities might reduce people's level of agitation or disgust by chemical means? We must ask ourselves if agitation, conflict and violence are necessary precursors of social progress, or are these behaviors no longer tolerable in an inter-dependent, urbanized society?

Drugs Might Produce Dreams or Induce Forgetfulness

The distant future holds many promises—or threats—of memory drugs, amnesia chemicals, dream-producing agents, pills to increase suggestibility, and all manner of other chemicals to make one's phenomenological state a matter of convenience. Although much discussion has revolved around the possible development of drugs to improve memory, people seem to have overlooked the advantages of drugs which will destroy it. Heinz Lehmann has pointed out that the most pathetic aspect of old age is the sense of already having experienced everything. At a recent meeting, he quoted a patient as saying "a pickle doesn't really taste like a pickle anymore." Old age is a state of constant déjà vu and déjà entendu. To overcome this apathy of experience, we might use drugs to heighten the sensations of the elderly and re-establish their sense of novelty to experiences by producing a temporary condition of amnesia. Why not allow an elderly person to rest and conserve his resources for most of the week, but on weekends or special occasions, allow him the excitement produced by a stimulant and/or psychedelic compound with an amnesic drug as a bonus? Certainly, with this group, we are not concerned about dependence, or the other, usual fears associated with drug use by young people. Why should their lives be a constant, grey boredom waiting for death?

We can, if we wish, produce an individualistic "choose your mood" society or a chemically controlled tyranny or an age of ultimate hedonism by chemical manipulation——or any other variant desired. Perhaps the real questions should be: "Can we choose? If so, who should choose? and Who will choose?" Technology is doing mankind a great service: It has forced him to define his morals, goals, and future. It has exposed him to his ultimate choice: "What shall I become?"

SOME CONSIDERATIONS FOR THE TREATMENT OF
NON-NARCOTIC DRUG ABUSERS
by
Carl D. Chambers and Leon Brill*

Introduction

There has been no determination of the prev-
alency of non-narcotic drug abusers in the United
States, nor have we had the means of ascertaining
how much of these legally manufactured and distributed drugs have found their way into the
illicit market. Independent figures and estimates do indicate this abuse is widespread, and
that there is a constant supply of non-narcotic
drugs in the illicit market:

1. Each year in the United States, 100,000
    pounds of amphetamines and amphetamine-
    like products are manufactured. This
    is enough for fifty 5 mg doses for every
    person in the entire nation irrespective
    of age. During the same period of time,
    over 1,000,000 pounds of barbiturate
    derivatives are manufactured--the equiv-
    alent of approximately 24 one and one-
    half grain doses for each person in the
    nation--enough to kill them twice.

2. Half of the annual production of amphe-
    tamine base finds its way into the
    illicit market.

3. It has been estimated that in 1957 seven
    per cent of our adult population was
    regularly using one or more of the
    psychotropic family of drugs, e.g.,
    tranquilizers, sedatives and stimulants;
    but by 1967, 27 per cent were doing so.

4. There are as many, and probably more
    high-dose intravenous amphetamine
    users in our large cities than there
    are heroin addicts.

*Carl D. Chambers, Ph.D. and Leon Brill, M.S.W.
Dr. Chambers and Mr. Brill are currently with
the Department of Psychiatry, Division of
Addiction Sciences, University of Miami, School
of Medicine. Their remarks here are reprinted
from Industrial Medicine, Vol. 40, No. 1,
pp. 29-36, 1971.

Two general facts about current abuse of
the non-narcotic drugs--amphetamines, barbiturate-
sedatives and tranquilizers--emerge from the
available patchwork of figures and estimates.
First, amphetamines appear to be more widely
abused than the barbiturate-sedatives and the
barbiturate-sedatives more widely than tranquilizers. Second, of the three classes of drugs, the
barbiturate-sedatives appear to inflict the most
damage on the abusers' health and conventional
functioning.

Barbiturate Abusers

The first barbiturate, Veronal, was introduced into clinical medicine in 1903 and the
short-acting barbiturates, which abusers in the
United States tend to prefer--pentobarbital,
secobarbital and amobarbital--became popular during the late 1930's and early 1940's.

It has been our experience that barbiturate
abusers can be grouped into three fairly distinct
types:

1. There are persons who, in order to deal
   with states of emotional distress, will
   abuse the barbiturates solely for their
   sedative-hypnotic effects, and in so
   doing remain constantly in a highly
   sedated state.

2. There are persons who, during the
   course of therapeutic usage, have discovered the paradoxical reaction which
   occurs when sufficient tolerance has
   been developed with the barbiturates.
   At these dose levels, barbiturates
   stimulate rather than depress, and the
   person begins now to take the drug for
   exhilaration effects.

3. There are persons who, during the course
   of abusing another class of drugs, in-
   gest large amounts of barbiturates to
   alter the effects of the other drugs,
   e.g., to counteract the abuse effects
   of amphetamines. This frequently sets
   up a consecutive cycle of abuse to
   enhance the effects of intravenous use
   of opiates, to substitute for an opiate
   during the times when opiates are unob-
   tainable, etc.

While the barbiturates were believed to be capable of producing a psychic dependence (habituation), it took nearly half a century to convince the practitioners of clinical medicine that the barbiturates were indeed drugs of addiction if abused. Even with indisputable evidence of the addiction liability of the drugs, they did not come under effective control until the mid-1960's.

Treatment Considerations

The Detoxification Phase

As with the narcotic addict and the alcoholic, the barbiturate abuser, regardless of type, does not ordinarily seek treatment until such time as his abuse has precipitated some crisis, e.g., the loss of a drug supply, etc. Once the abuser does seek treatment or it is imposed, the detoxification phase of treatment, since it can be life-threatening, should occur on an inpatient basis.

...Withdrawal of persons with strong physical dependence may be life-threatening, and can only be accomplished satisfactorily, and with reasonable safety, in a drug-free environment where hospital and nursing facilities are available. (A.M.A.[1])

The gravity of the barbiturate abstinence syndrome is indicated by the occurrence of death following the withdrawal of secobarbital from a patient who had been using 50 gm of the drug daily (Fraser, et al.[2]).

The contraindication of abrupt withdrawal of barbiturates and the specific symptoms to expect from physically dependent persons are widely documented in the literature. Even a rapid reduction of the dose to which the person has become tolerant is considered dangerous. The general procedure for the medically controlled withdrawal process dates to the pioneering work done by Isbell et al.[3]

...The amount taken also varies over a wide range, but most chronic habitués probably take between 0.5 to 2.0 gm of the drug daily (Isbell[4]).

This initial process is, of course, to establish with some degree of certainty the amount of drugs the person has been ingesting. After the

"test dose" procedure of gradually increasing
doses of barbiturates has ascertained the "stab-
ilization dose," a gradual reduction in daily
intake from that dose is indicated.

If the barbiturate abuser has concurrently
abused other drugs which require a separate withdrawal regimen, the evidence is that multiple
withdrawals can be conducted simultaneously without increasing the danger of abstinence from
either.

Treatment During Initial Abstinence

The literature would indicate that once primary withdrawal has been completed--in two to
three weeks--the rehabilitative and psychother-
apeutic treatment of the barbiturate abusers is
identical with that for the narcotic addict.
While there is, of course, some pragmatic expediency in this approach, the authors' experiences
would indicate some variation may be warranted.

Post-detoxification treatment should be
guided by the type of barbiturate abuser the
patient has been. For example, it would probably
be appropriate to treat the concurrent barbitur-
ate-opiate abusers as you would an opiate addict.
It would, however, be clinically inappropriate
to treat the individual who has kept himself in
a constant hypnotic stupor the same way as the
individual whose sole abuse was for the exhilaration effects of the drugs. While both types
of individuals perceive themselves to be inadequate, how they used the drug to counteract this
inadequacy, e.g., what the drug was doing for
them, provides the cues for the focus of the
therapeutic process. In the one case, the individual abuses the barbiturates not only to avoid
interacting and competing, but also to block out
anxiety or worry about this non-interaction and
non-competitiveness. In the other case, the
stimulation derived from the drugs and the increased activity which follows are interpreted
as increasing one's efficiency and effectiveness
in interactions and competition.

During 1969, the authors had an opportunity
to collaborate in the collection of detailed life
histories of seven barbiturate abusers who had
voluntarily sought treatment for this drug-taking
behavior in an experimental unit at the National
Institute of Mental Health Clinical Research

Center at Lexington, Kentucky. This experience
has provided us with some insight into the nature
of the problems which must be therapeutically
resolved during treatment.

Most of these barbiturate abusers had become
addicted while being legitimately treated for
an undefined anxiety, stress or depression. This
psycho-social symptom typically appeared after
an inadequately resolved crisis in their life
left them unable to cope with their problems.
These abusers were able to maintain this "medicine" orientation throughout their drug careers,
and were thus able to purchase their drugs legally
and relatively inexpensively. In contrast to
narcotic addicts, they were able to escape involvement in both the criminal and illicit drug
subcultures even though they had been abusing the
drugs for an average of 5.6 years.

Extensive experimentation with other drugs
was prevalent among these barbiturate abusers.
All had experimented with drugs other than the
addicting drug. This extra-experimentation was,
however, focused upon other sedatives, tranquilizers and anti-depressants. Once addicted, this
experimentation subsided.

Although all of these barbiturate abusers
were being treated for the consequences of their
drug-taking behavior, the abuse of drugs was
only one visible indication of an inadequacy in
coping with, or resolving, various psycho-social
problems.

Specific Psycho-Social Problems
Requiring Therapeutic Attention

Suicidal Gesturing

All seven of these patients reported a crisis in their lives that led them to consider
seriously suicide as an alternative to coping
with their difficulties. Two of the seven
addict-patients reported actual suicide attempts.
Commonly, there were several suicidal gesturings
prior to the onset of drug abuse as well as
following drug abuse. As would be expected,
the gesturing following onset usually consisted
of taking excessive doses of a sedative. An
analysis of each life history indicated the
gesturing seemed crisis--rather than process--
precipitated.

Alcohol

Several of these addict-patients reported excessive drinking as having been a factor in their lives. These alcohol abusers reported their disruptive drinking behavior had terminated after they began using drugs. These addict-patients first abused alcohol in an attempt to cope with their problems and when this was unsuccessful, they began to "cope with" their problems by abusing non-narcotic drugs.

Prior Psychiatric Hospitalization

All of these non-narcotic addicts reported a history of at least one psychiatric hospitalization. The data indicate that this type of addict-patient should be viewed as a psychiatric patient--as indeed they view themselves. These non-narcotic addicts rigidly retained a self-concept of a "sick person," and even after becoming aware of their drug dependency, viewed this addiction as a medical problem to be treated with medicines.

Interpersonal Relations

All but one of these addict-patients had been married and they all reported they had experienced serious marital difficulties. The marital problems resulted in various child-rearing difficulties that left some of the children with obvious problems of their own. Further inquiry established that none of the patients had ever achieved a satisfactory interpersonal relationship with a member of the opposite sex. It can be stated that, although the patient may have been surrounded by "families" and "friends," they related only on a superficial level with minimal involvement. They appeared to be emotionally starved individuals continually pushing others from them when they became involved in an interpersonal affair. For the most part, these addict-patients presented an appearance lacking in warmth and acceptance. However, their self-imposed isolation bothered them. This was an area where a large number of psycho-social problems seemed to emanate.

It has been our experience that high-frequency, individual supportive counselling is a valuable procedure during the initial abstinence phase of treatment. The main therapeutic emphasis should be on the acquisition or sharpening

of coping skills. While these abusers are more
likely to have more competitive skills, e.g.,
education, jobs, status, intact families, etc.,
than the narcotic abusers, they seem to be
deficient in their ability to adapt and adjust
to new or stressful situations. While it is
possible to impart and acquire these coping skills
in group settings, individual sessions are probably more appropriate for initiating the process.
Once some minimal insight and success are accomplished, the group setting where testing can occur
and be analyzed is usually indicated.

Treatment During Extended Abstinence

Barbiturate abuse is best viewed as a chronic
relapsing disease. As a relapsing disease, contact with the ex-abuser should be maintained for
an extended period of time. While our experience
is somewhat limited, the management of patients
during this extended "after care" phase can be
effectively accomplished in regular, but infrequent group sessions. Groups with enduring
histories appear most appropriate for the rapid
discovery of anxieties or depression, which too
frequently signal relapse in these patients.
Multiple-diagnoses groups, as well as groups
comprised only of barbiturate abusers, have produced favorable results. Neither, however, has
been rigorously studied for measures of outcome.

Special Considerations for the
Treatment of Barbiturate Abuse

1. There is sufficient evidence to warrant
the implementation of special suicide prevention
procedures during the initial detoxification and
abstinence phases of treatment. The incidence
of suicide during these phases of treatment is
apparently much greater than that found among
narcotic addicts.
2. If chemotherapy appears indicated after
detoxification, there is evidence that these
"former drug abusers" will be less inclined to
abuse the phenothiazines, reserpine, or the
tricyclic anti-depressants than the minor tranquilizers.
3. Except for the persons who abuse barbiturates concurrently with other drugs, e.g.,
opiates or stimulants, most barbiturate abusers
should not be treated in close proximity with
the narcotic addicts. These barbiturate abusers
normally will not have had any involvement in

either the criminal or illicit drug subcultures.
One can, therefore, treat these abusers with the
narcotic addicts without the concerns of seduction
and contamination.

4. Individuals addicted to non-narcotic
drugs may be beginning to seek out public and
private mental health facilities for treatment.
Not only will the addicted individual need extensive treatment, other family members may also need
concurrent treatment. It was noted in one study
(Moffett and Chambers[5]) that the incidence of a
family member's concurrently abusing drugs was
high (30.0%), with most of the abusers being
spouses. The mental health agency must be therapeutically prepared to accept these patients _and_
their families into treatment.

5. While we, like others, have tended to
treat the barbiturate-narcotic abusers as narcotic abusers, and the barbiturate-amphetamine
abusers as amphetamine abusers, we have done so
on the basis of expediency. Well-designed clinical research needs to be accomplished to validate these procedures.

The Non-Barbiturate
Sedative-Hypnotic Abusers

Several of the newer non-barbiturate sedative-
hypnotic drugs when abused have been shown to produce intoxication, dependence, coma and/or death,
resembling those due to barbiturate abuse.

Drugs		Intoxica-	Depend-	Coma/
Generic	Brand	tion	ence	Death
Meprobamate	Miltown, Equanil, etc.	Yes	Yes	Yes
Glutethimide	Doriden	Yes	Yes	Yes
Ethinamate	Valmid	Yes	Yes	Yes
Ethchlorvynol	Placidyl	Yes	Yes	Yes
Methyprylon	Noludar	Yes	Yes	Yes
Chlordiazepoxide	Librium	Yes	Yes	--
Diazepam	Valium	Yes	Yes	--
Oxazepam	Serax	Yes	--	--

While these drugs are indeed addicting when
misused, the available evidence would suggest
this addiction will occur only at dose levels
considerably in excess of those therapeutically
prescribed. Essig,[6-8]through his own work and
through reviews of other researchers' works, has

2

documented the abstinence effects of certain dose
levels.

While our experience with treating the non-
barbiturate sedative-hypnotic abusers is too
limited to permit general action, we would anticipate the treatment process to parallel the three
treatment phases which have been effective with
the barbiturate abusers: initial detoxification,
initial abstinence and extended abstinence.

Drug	Daily Dose	Duration	Significant Withdrawal Effect
1.Meprobamate (Miltown, etc.)	4 gm	3 mos.	Convulsions
	10 gm	--	Death
	3.2-6.4 gm	40 days	Convulsions, psychotic behavior
2.Glutethimide (Doriden)	2.5 gm	3 mos.	Convulsions, delirium
3.Ethinamate (Valnid)	2-13 gm	24 mos.	Convulsions, psychotic behavior
4.Ethchlorvynol (Placidyl)	1,500 mg	months	Convulsions
	4-5 gm	1 1/2- 2 yrs.	Convulsions, violent behavior
	2-3 gm	6-7 mos.	Convulsions
	2-2.5 gm	10 mos.	Convulsions, psychosis
5.Methyprylon (Noludar)	7.5 to 12 gm	18 mos.	Death
6.Chlordiazepoxide (Librium)	300-600 mg	5-6 mos.	Convulsions
7.Diazepam (Valium)	100-150 mg	--	Convulsions
	120 mg	--	Convulsions

Essig,[6-8] one of the major contributors in
the assessment of abuse potential and addiction
liability for these drugs, has provided the clinician who is confronted with the necessity for
detoxifying this type of abuser with an appropriate regimen for doing so.

Post-detoxification treatment, at least with
glutethimide (Doriden) abusers, has been effective
when conducted in the same manner as indicated
earlier for the barbiturate abusers--high frequency individual supportive counselling sessions
during the initial abstinence phase and less

frequent group therapy sessions during the extended aftercare phase.

Specific research needs to be accomplished to validate which therapeutic techniques are most appropriate for which type of abuser. While we are acutely aware that therapeutic success, regardless of the technique, is intimately related to the skills of the therapist, it should be possible at some future date to predict with a greater degree of success which patients will relapse and why.

The Amphetamine Abusers

While there are indeed large numbers of persons who will use small doses of amphetamines without a physician's supervision for a temporary expansion of energy, e.g., students, athletes and truck drivers, this use most frequently does not occur with sufficient regularity for a dependency upon the drug to develop.

Amphetamine abusers appear to fall into two somewhat distinct contrasting types. While the authors are, of course, aware that a dichotomous characterization of amphetamine abusers would not be totally distinct and that there will be many gradations and exceptions, it does provide an appropriate frame within which to provide treatment services. We have chosen to label these two types of abusers as adaptive and escapist.

The adaptive abusers can be generally characterized as using the amphetamines to bolster their functioning within conventional interpersonal and social activities. This type of abuser tends to deny the abuse upon initial confrontation and when the denial is no longer possible will contend the drugs prevent or eliminate "problems" rather than cause them. This type of abuser usually has enjoyed some success in his interactions and social competitiveness, but mistakenly believes the drug permits him to recapture or increase this success. In contrast, the escapist abusers can be generically characterized as using the drugs so they will not have to function within conventional interpersonal and social activities. This type of abuser does not tend to deny the abuse when confronted, but has multiple ready rationalizations why it occurs. He readily admits that drugs are a problem to him. He had not normally enjoyed any success in his interactions and social competitiveness, and escapes these

activities, at least at the conventional level,
through his abuse of drugs.

The Three Phases of Treatment

The authors have found the treatment of amphetamine abusers, regardless of type, should
include three distinct phases: the initial physiological detoxification phase, the initial abstinent phase and the long-term after care phase.
The advocation of these three distinct phases and
the therapeutic content of each is based more
upon the authors' clinical deductions than extensive clinical experience. It is presented with
a full awareness of patient variation and exception, but with the aim of providing an appropriate
frame within which experience can be accumulated.

The initial detoxification phase of treatment
is basically a medical process and should be accomplished on an inpatient basis. While there
is apparently no harm in the abrupt withdrawal
of amphetamines, the psychiatric reactions to
amphetamine abuse, which reportedly range from
acute anxiety to full-blown psychosis, may require
medication, e.g., sedatives or phenothiazines.
Concurrent medical problems primarily associated
with the intravenous high-dose abusers may also
require attention during this phase of treatment.

Excluding those cases which require extensive attention for concurrent medical problems,
the initial detoxification phase should be completed within one week. This initial phase will
be characterized by sleepiness. Social withdrawal,
severe depression with suicidal ideas and neur-
asthenia have also been reported.[9-12] These characterizations appear to be appropriate for both
the adaptive abusers as well as the escapist
abusers and at least during this phase of treatment, the treatment procedures are basically the
same for both types of abusers.

Even though there is evidence that portions
of the primary withdrawal distress may continue
for several weeks, it is recommended that the
second phase of treatment--initial abstinence--
be conducted on an ambulatory basis. The recently
detoxified amphetamine abuser of both types can
be expected to display chronic fatigue, which
continues for several weeks, has been interpreted
variously as a lack of initiative, apathy and
lethargy. In our experience and others,[10] an

Dichotomous Typology of Amphetamine Abusers
(Selected Characteristics)

Adaptive Abusers	Escapist Abusers
1. Onset was accidental medicine abuse and the medicine rationale continues	1. Onset was deliberate experimentation for a predefined euphoric effect and the euphoric rationale continues
2. Onset occurs after adulthood and after the acquisition of most major individual and social roles	2. Onset occurs prior to adulthood and before the acquisition of most major individual and social roles
3. Extensive experimentation with other drugs	3. Extensive experimentation with other drugs
4. Nonaggressive reaction to amphetamines	4. Aggressive reaction to amphetamines
5. Amphetamine of choice is not methamphetamine	5. Amphetamine of choice is methamphetamine
6. Oral use of drugs from a legal source	6. Intravenous use of drugs from an illicit source
7. Solitary abuse (hidden)	7. Group abuse (highly visible)
8. Regular--noncyclical abuse with any mood elevation a byproduct	8. Spree--cyclical abuse specifically for euphoric-stimulating effect

exaggerated sense of guilt occurs in most patients during the initial abstinence phase. The authors have had success with individual high-frequency supportive counselling during this phase of treatment. The main therapeutic emphasis during the frequent contacts, e.g., three one-hour sessions per week, has been on counselling only on present and future behavior. While both types of abusers profit from intensive supportive counselling in the areas of drug usage, general attitudes, domestic relations, peer relations and employment difficulties, the primary focus is somewhat different.

Supportive counselling for the adaptive abusers should be focused upon the alleviation

of neurotic-like reactions to normal interpersonal relations and social activities. It has
been our experience that this type of abuser
frequently is unable or unwilling to recognize
his drug use as being causal to any of his
problems. His rationale, of course, is that the
drug eliminates his interaction difficulties,
etc. Coping with the awakening feelings, which
were dormant throughout the period of heavy drug
use, becomes a primary therapeutic task.

In contrast, the escapist abusers have more
frequently presented psychotic-like reactions to
their interactions and activities. As opposed to
the "uncovering" techniques utilized with the
adaptive abusers, a "covering" frame of reference
has proven to be effective with the escapist
abusers. Other contrasts which should be considered are: (1) the escapist abuser tends to
blame all of his problems on the drug with an
assertion that if the therapist can assist in
the maintaining of abstinence, he will have no
problems and (2) being younger, as a rule, the
escapist abuser has not acquired educational or
occupational skills nor the values our system
attaches to them.

Our experience has been that this disability
usually continues beyond detoxification resulting, in part, from disabilities in functioning
which pre-date drug use. Competitive skills,
both at the individual and social levels, must
be acquired. Habilitation, rather than rehabilitation, too frequently is the case.

In summation, during this abstinent phase
of treatment, the patient should receive frequent supportive sessions as he explores his
intrapersonal and interpersonal capacities without the use of drugs. The ambulatory situation
with frequent therapeutic contact seems best
suited for these explorations, which will probably occupy several months.

As in any type of drug abuse which produces
a dependence, amphetamine dependence is most
appropriately conceptualized as a chronic relapsing disorder. Once the individual patient
has demonstrated some degree of continuity in
conventional functioning, therapy should continue, but within a different context and
within a different frame of reference.

The long-term after care phase of treatment
appears to be managed most appropriately in regular but somewhat less frequent group sessions.
Indices of anxiety or depression, inappropriate
changes in mood or affect, inabilities to cope
with stresses, etc., any of which may signal a
relapse episode, seem to be more readily detected.
In addition to early detection, concentrated support and guidance are more available in group
therapy settings. Our experience has been that
the reality therapy techniques are appropriate
during this "continuous care" phase until such
time as a crisis is presented or detected. At
that time, the more buffering techniques or supportive therapy have produced favorable responses.

In summary, after the initial detoxification
is completed, very frequent individual supportive
counselling provides the therapeutic mode for re-
integration. When the patient demonstrates adequate functioning, the mode can be switched to
less frequent, but reenforcing group therapy
sessions.

It has been our experience that the amphetamine abusers of the adaptive type should not
be treated in proximity with the escapist type
of amphetamine abusers or most narcotic addicts.
It would appear appropriate to treat them in
proximity with other "medicine abusers," e.g.,
abusers of tranquilizers, antidepressants, and
some analgesic addicts who had medical or accidental onsets.

There seems to be little reason to segregate
the escapist type of amphetamine abusers from
narcotic addicts. Both have shared common drug
experimentation patterns, illicit subcultural
involvements, etc., and seduction from one group
to another is unlikely. While both have their
preference drugs, heroin users will also "shoot"
amphetamines to enhance the effects of the opiate
and amphetamine abusers will "shoot" heroin to
"taper a run and prevent crashing."

Special Considerations in the Treatment
of Amphetamine Abusers

1. Amphetamine abusers of the escapist type
characteristically abuse their drugs in a cycle.
The cycle has two basic phases--an up, or active
phase, and a down, or reactive phase. The two

phases are approximately equal in duration. Typically, an experienced abuser will inject the
drug, usually methamphetamine, at two- to four-
hour intervals for four or five days (the action
phase), during which time he will remain awake
continuously, and then collapse from exhaustion
and remain in a semicomatose state sleeping in-
termittently for the next four or five days (the
reaction phase).

At the onset of a "run," doses are relatively
small, e.g., 50 to 100 mg, but as the run progresses, the doses increase. Kramer, et al[11]
reported the highest maximum dose known to us--
a dose in excess of 1 gm taken every two hours,
probably close to 15,000 mg in one day. At the
peak of a "run," no quantity of drug produces
the desired effects. Throughout the "run," the
abuser will continue to desire to function in all
of the conventional roles, but his ability to do
so will deteriorate in direct proportion to the
time he has been in the action phase of the
cycle.

The adaptive abusers do not abuse their drugs
in such a cycle. This type of abuser ingests
drugs in a very steady, regular, and at a fairly
stabilized dose level for extended periods of
time. As indicated earlier, in contrast to the
escapist abuser, his subjective desires to
function in conventional activities and his
objective ability to do so also remain fairly
stable. This, of course, is not meant to suggest
that this type of abuser doesn't "think" he is
functioning better than he is.

2. There is considerable disagreement concerning the incidence and degree of permanent
organic damage to the brain with amphetamine
abuse. Representing one extreme, Lemere[9] reported that clinical, pathological and experimental studies had demonstrated permanent organic
brain damage; and, for this reason, the associated psychiatric condition would be even more
difficult to treat than spontaneous disorders.
Kramer, et al[11] while not testing specifically
for brain damage, did discover that about a third
of their respondents indicated memory and concentration impairment after their experience
with high doses of amphetamines. Most recently,
Connell[12] summarized the question in the following manner: . . ."The present position would
seem to be that there is no conclusive evidence

of permanent brain damage, but there may well be
a basis for such an eventuality in terms of the
clinical, animal, physiological, neurochemical,
and neurophysiological findings."

If indeed permanent brain damage does occur,
the clinician should consider this when establishing treatment expectations and goals with the
patients. In the few cases where standardized
psychological tests were available, the authors
have not encountered any organic brain damage
which could be attributed to drug use. Large-
scale dose- and time-related research studies are
needed to determine the incidence and degree of
permanent organic brain damage among amphetamine
abusers.

3. Numerous writers have addressed themselves to the aggressiveness of what we have
labelled the escapist type of amphetamine abusers.[9,11-16] This behavior, variously labelled as
aggressive, assaultive, violent, compulsive, suspicious, paranoid and impulsive, may in some
patients present a major management problem.
While the physical danger to other patients or
treatment personnel is probably no greater than
that encountered in the treatment of psychotic
patients whose problems were not drug induced,
it does warrant the clinician's awareness.
Smith[15] has suggested that these high-dose mainliners of amphetamines are the most--and probably
the only--dangerous drug abusers to treat. Our
own experience would support this contention. Unfortunately, it has not been possible to predict
when a violent eruption will occur with this
type of abuser. While paranoid reactions and
impulsive violence most frequently occur during
the initial detoxification phase of treatment,
episodes have been encountered throughout the
treatment process. Violence during the initial
detoxification phase seems best countered with
a general nonthreatening calmness. Our limited
treating experience would indicate that the
episodic eruptions which occur after detoxification are best countered with more direct
methods, e.g., by the direct use of authority
and the labelling of the behavior as inappropriate
and not to be tolerated. This authoritative setting of limits does not appear to "feed" the
paranoid delusions or suspiciousness, and this
is undoubtedly related to the insights gained
during treatment. Other writers[11,16] have also
noticed the "pseudodelusional" character of these

abusers' paranoid ideas. The degree of conviction
with which the abuser holds these "pseudode-
lusions" and the impulsivity with which he reacts
to them is probably related to the amount of
elapsed time abstinent. The greater the amount
of time abstinent, the less the conviction with
which the delusion is held, and the less likely
an impulsive aggressive reaction to the delusion.

4. The question as to the incidence and
whether amphetamine psychosis is dose-related
deserves close clinical and research attention.
At the present time, the literature reflects both
polar positions. Ellinwood's[17] work would indicate that this psychosis is dose-related, e.g.,
the greater the dose the greater the probability
of producing the psychosis. Lemere's[9] work, on
the other hand, suggests this relationship is not
so predictable. He presents the case history
of a 47-year-old who had ingested a daily dose
of only 30 mg of destroamphetamine, ostensibly
for weight reduction, over a period of four
years. A paranoid psychosis reportedly ensued
with some organic deterioration that had per-
sisted even after discontinuation of the drug.

If indeed a paranoid psychosis does occur
with any regularity at such low doses, a special
problem is presented to the social system. For
example, at these low doses the person taking
the drugs will still be capable of conventional
functioning throughout his drug-taking career
until the paranoid psychosis erupts. If this
eruption should include the all-too-common components of aggressiveness and violence, a significantly dangerous situation could ensue
involving those around the abuser, e.g., his
fellow workers, his family, fellow commuters, etc.

Large-scale, carefully controlled dose-and
time-related research is of the highest priority, to determine the incidence and degree of
amphetamine psychosis. Well-designed, time-
related follow-up studies are also indicated,
which would determine the recovery potential during abstinence. These research efforts also need
to include studies to isolate those psychoses
which were essentially toxic reactions to the
abuse, and the others which were precipitated or
triggered in the borderline individual.

5. Clinicians must be constantly alert to
the possibility of a multi-dependent patient.

These abusers will use a wide variety of drugs, together or sequentially, according to the vaporous notions of the person and the availability of the drugs. Heroin addicts have long combined their drugs to produce prolonged or intensified reactions, e.g., cocaine, amphetamines and barbiturates, but the multidependent abuser appears to be much more prevalent than in the past. Opiate addicts who "boost" their injections with sedatives and high-dose intravenous amphetamine abusers who "taper runs" with various analgesics, frequently are unaware of their multiple dependencies. Carefully detailed drug histories, including all drugs and the extent of their use, are necessary components of the intake examination. While an opiate withdrawal can normally be conducted safely on an ambulatory basis, the superimposition of a sedative, tranquilizer or stimulant dependency would indicate an inpatient detoxification.

Probably as many as 5% of all heroin addicts are also high-dose amphetamine abusers, and as many as 35% of all heroin addicts are concurrently addicted to a sedative.

The Hallucinogenic Abusers

The Drugs

Hallucinogenic drugs include LSD, a semi-synthetic derivative of ergonovine, whose effects were first accidentally discovered by Albert Hofmann in 1943; mescaline, a phenethylamine present in the buttons of a small cactus (mescal, peyote); psilocybin, an indole found in a mushroom (teonanacatl); DMT (dimethyltriptamine), a synthetic indole found in the seeds of a South American plant; DOM or dimethoxyamphetamine, otherwise known in Haight-Ashbury as STP, an abbreviation for "serenity, tranquility, and peace"; and the seeds of some morning glory varieties (Oloiuqui), the active principle of which is closely related to LSD. Marijuana, which has hitherto been mistakenly classified as a narcotic and with hard drugs, is increasingly being viewed as a mild hallucinogen. Most of our knowledge concerning these drugs has been accumulated with LSD. This section is, therefore, directed primarily to the LSD abusers.

LSD, in crude form, is relatively simple to synthesize given a supply of lysergic acid or

one of the ergor alkaloids. Lysergic acid can,
in turn, be produced by deep fermentation processes fairly readily, if there is suitable
equipment and knowledge. The synthesis of
lysergic acid is very difficult, however. DMT
is a newer synthetic, with a shorter and harsher
action than LSD, a "trip" usually lasting about
two hours.

LSD was first described as a "psychotomimetic" drug, producing a "model psychosis" because it was assumed to have many similarities
to psychosis; i.e., it "mimicked" psychosis.
A similarly inaccurate description used has been
"hallucinogenic" though it is agreed LSD does
not produce true hallucinations since the subject
may be aware of what is happening, i.e., there
is a "spectator ego" witnessing all the excite-
ment--a sort of split of self, with one part
observing, the other participating. The most
recent term of "psychedelic," meaning "mind-
manifesting," is deemed more acceptable today
though it too raises a question as to whether
LSD is indeed generally consciousness-expanding
in the sense implied by some advocates.

The Effects of Abuse

LSD is not physically addicting in the sense
of barbiturates and opiates. The dependence is
psychological, not physical. Tolerance develops
rapidly after a few days of repeated use, but is
usually lost in two or three days. Some users
have built up their LSD doses to 1000 and 2000 mcg
over a period of days. The first or threshold
dose is about 25 mcg and an average dose is 200
to 400 mcg. Cross-tolerance exists among LSD,
psilocibin and mescaline, though tolerance to
mescaline develops more slowly than to the other
two. Paradoxically, some users report a state
of increased sensitivity to LSD once they have
lost their tolerance. Unexpected return of the
drugged state without ingestion of LSD for months
or even a year later has been reported. Some
people in the drugged state may pay attention to
auditory frequencies they normally ignore and
thereafter continue to be sensitive to these
frequencies.

To date, neither the mode nor site of action
of LSD is known, but it has central, peripheral
and neurohumoral effects. Physiologically, the
effects of psychedelic drugs resemble those

produced by sympathomimetic drugs such as: increased pulse rate and blood pressure, dilated
pupils, tremor and cold, sweaty palms, and at
times, flushing, shivering, chills, pallor,
salivation, dysrhythmic breathing, nausea,
anorexia and urgency.

Drug-induced activity lasts 8-12 hours, with
the most intense changes in sensation, mood and
perception occurring during the first half of
the experience, the latter part being marked by
introspection and hypersuggestibility. A change
in mood is the first obvious behavioral change
observed. Along with this, is a tremendous increase in sensory input, a kind of flooding, with
perceptual distortions and hallucinations. "Syn-
esthesia" often occurs, i.e., a crossover of the
different senses: subjects can "hear" colors,
visualize music as colors, or "taste" sounds.
There is also "tunnel vision," the focusing in
on minute details not observed before.

The literature reports three different kinds
of experiences under LSD: (1) the good trip--
a predominantly pleasing experience; (2) the bad
trip--a dysphoric experience characterized by
anxiety, panic, feelings of persecution, fears
of loss of ego boundaries, loss of control and
time perception, and impaired performance; and
(3) an ambivalent state where the subject may
simultaneously experience contrasting feelings as
of happiness and lightness, relaxedness and
tenseness (Mayer[18]).

The bad trip has been well documented in the
literature. It has been described as psychological and attributable to the panic emergency
upon experiencing a host of overwhelming sensations. Learning was entailed and described in
relation to marijuana use. Frosch[19] reported
that, in a 2 1/2 year period, some 250 persons
were admitted to Bellevue with mental disorders
either directly attributable to LSD or where the
drug played a major role in bringing about the
disorder. Patients admitted remained from a few
days to several months, and a few were transfer-
red to State hospitals.

Another study[20] was made of 70 post-LSD
psychiatric admissions during a 6-month period
in a Los Angeles medical center, these patients
representing 12% of all admissions. One-third
of the LSD patients were psychotic on admission

and two-thirds required more than one month of
hospitalization.

The negative experiences which a clinician
may encounter during the management of these
patients have been summarized[18] as follows:

Acute Reactions

The acute reactions--the bad trips--are of
two types:

1. Psychotoxic reactions which are characterized by confusion and/or acute paranoia,
   feelings of omnipotence and invulner-
   ability, which may cause the user to
   expose himself to dangers resulting, at
   times, in injury or death.

2. Panic reactions which occur as a secondary response to the drug-induced symptoms.

One may anticipate fairly rapid recovery
from these two acute states. Remission usually
occurs within two or three days with the recommended treatment of sedation and verbal support.

Recurrent Reactions

These reactions are the spontaneous return
of perceptual disorders or feelings of depersonalization, occurring up to a year after the
last use of the drug. Frosch[19] believes these
recurrent symptoms are associated with stress or
anxiety in the patient. Others[21] feel they may
be symptomatic of brain lesions. Blacker[22] found
no EEG evidence of classically defined organic
brain damage in chronic LSD users.

Prolonged Reactions

These reactions are the chronic anxiety
states and chronic psychoses resulting from LSD
administration, persisting beyond the period of
acute intoxication.

Significant variables determining the cause
of any LSD trip are: the personality and expectations of the subject, the presence of a depend-
able guide, the nature of the setting in which
the drug is taken, and the age of the subject.
Younger subjects were noted to have experienced

acute reactions more frequently.

Smith[23] has described a cultogenic "psychedelic syndrome" among hippies in the Haight-
Ashbury area. Members do not feel themselves
to be mentally ill, and are not considered ill
by fellow members of their community. As long
as the individual remains in the hippie subculture, he can survive and handle his internal
conflicts, and treatment of any kind becomes impossible. Some observers believe that chronic
use brings about sharp personality changes, a
greater receptivity to excitement and stimuli,
magical thinking and poor organization which
cannot be explained psychologically alone.

<u>Treatment</u>

For the acutely intoxicated state, the
American Medical Association[24] recommends the
LSD abuser have an immediate trial with pheno-
thiazine medication, preferably administered
intramuscularly since the phenothiazines block
the action of LSD. He further suggests barbiturates can be used in lieu of, or in addition to
the phenothiazines. Because the hallucinogens
do not cause physical dependence, there are no
physical complications of withdrawal. Care
should be exercised, however, to learn whether
other addicting drugs were taken concurrently
with the LSD, which may require a separate detoxification regimen. Once the acute reaction
or panic has subsided, sedatives or tranquilizers
have been recommended.

Some clinicians place more emphasis upon
pleasant surroundings and psychological supports
during the initial treatment phase than upon
medication.

The duration of the initial treatment of
the acutely intoxicated abuser is relatively
short--12 to 72 hours. Once this period of intoxication is over, and if symptoms of mental
illness are apparent, any medication prescribed
should be on the same basis as for a similar
type of mentally ill person who has not been
involved with hallucinogens.

Post-detoxification treatment during initial
abstinence is probably best managed if it is
focused upon coming to grips with any psychological dependency produced by the abuse. As with

any drug which produces a psychological dependency, the dependency produced by LSD abuse continues long after the physiological effects have
dissipated. Sympathetic supportive counselling
seems to be most effective during post-detoxification treatment.

Extended therapeutic contact with the ex-
abuser of LSD is imperative for two reasons. First,
after psychedelic intoxication there is always
the possibility of spontaneous recurrence, and
second, this contact is the only way in which the
clinician can ascertain if the acute reactions are
indicative of a chronic abuse pattern.

Special Considerations for the Treatment
of LSD Abusers

1. While our information about the biologic
hazards of LSD and other hallucinogenic drugs
must be considered incomplete and requiring additional research, the evidence is such that women
in the childbearing age should be cautioned concerning this possibility.

2. Clinicians must be continuously alert
for symptoms other than those anticipated from
the drug history taken from the patient. It is
becoming apparent that large numbers of patients
cannot be certain which drugs they have been
taking. Recent studies[25] have shown many of the
hallucinogens sold on the illicit market are
"mislabelled" and vary widely in potency. What
was thought to be mescaline or psilocybin may
indeed be LSD which will greatly panic the users.
If DOM (STP) has been ingested rather than LSD,
phenothiazines, especially in high doses would
be contraindicated since they seem to prolong
the acute reactions. In addition, spontaneous
recurrence of the acute reactions is more frequent with DOM (STP) than with LSD.

207

References

1   A.M.A. Committee on Alcoholism and Addiction:
    Dependence on barbiturates and other sedative
    drugs, J.A.M.A., 193:673-677, 1965.

2   Fraser, Havelock F., et al: Death due to with-
    drawal of barbiturates, Ann. Intern. Med.
    38:1319-1325, 1953.

3   Isbell, Harris, et al: Chronic barbiturate in-
    toxication: an experimental study, Archives
    of Neurology and Psychiatry, 64:1-28, 1950a.

4   Isbell, Harris: Manifestations and treatment
    of addiction to narcotic drugs and barbitur-
    ates, The Medical Clinics of North America,
    34(2):425-438, 1950b.

5   Moffett, Arthur D., and Chambers, Carl D.:
    The hidden addiction, Social Work, 1970.

6   Essig, Carl F.: Addiction to nonbarbiturate
    sedative and tranquilizing drugs, Clin.
    Pharmacol. Ther. 5:334-343, 1964.

7   Essig, Carl F.: Newer sedative drugs that
    can cause states of intoxication and de-
    pendence of barbiturate type, J.A.M.A.,
    196:714-717, 1966.

8   Essig, Carl F.: Addiction to barbiturate and
    nonbarbiturate sedative drugs. In Asso-
    ciation for Research in Nervous and Mental
    Disease: The Addictive States, Baltimore:
    Williams and Wilkins, 1968.

9   Lemere, Frederick: The danger of amphetamine
    dependency, Amer. J. Psychiat., 123(5):
    569-572, 1966.

10 Griffith, John: Psychiatric implication of
    amphetamine drug use. Paper presented at
    the Non-narcotic Drug Institute, Southern
    Illinois University, Edwardsville, Illinois,
    June, 1967.

11 Kramer, John C., Fischman, Vitezslav S.,
    and Littlefield, Don C.: Amphetamine abuse:
    patterns and effects of high doses taken
    intravenously, J.A.M.A., 201(5):305-309, 1967.

12 Connell, P. H.: Some observations concerning
    amphetamine misuse: its diagnosis, management,
    and treatment with special reference to re-
    search needs. In Wittenborn, J. R., et al
    (Eds.): Drugs and Youth, Springfield, Charles
    C. Thomas, 1970.

13 Tatetsu, S.: Methamphetamine psychosis,
    Folia Psychiatry Neurology Japan, Supple.
    7:377-380, 1963 as quoted in Kramer, et al:
    Amphetamine abuse, J.A.M.A., 201:305-309,
    1967.

14 Carey, James T., and Mandel, Jerry: A San
    Francisco Bay area "speed" scene, J. Health
    Social Behavior, 9:164-174, 1968.

15 Smith, David: The trip, Emergency Medicine,
    pp. 27-42, December, 1969.

16 Cohen, Sidney: The psychopharmacology of
    amphetamine and barbiturate dependence. In
    Wittenborn, J. R., et al (Eds.): Drugs and
    Youth, Springfield, Charles C. Thomas, 1970.

17 Ellinwood, E. H.: Amphetamine psychosis:
    I. description of the individuals and pro-
    cess, J. Nerv. Ment. Dis., 144:273-283, 1967.

18 Mayer, Roger E.: LSD--the conditions and con-
    sequences of use and the treatment of users.
    In Wittenborn, J. R., et al (Eds.): Drugs
    and Youth, Springfield, Charles C. Thomas,
    1970.

19 Frosch, W. A., et al: Untoward reactions to
    lysergic acid diethlamide (LSD) resulting in
    hospitalization, New Eng. J. Med., 273:
    1235-1239, 1965.

20 Ungerleider, J. T., et al: The "bad trip"--
    the etiology of the adverse LSD reaction,
    Amer. J. of Psychiat., 124:1483-1490, 1968.

21 Lettvin, J.: You can't even step in the same
    river twice, Natural History, 76:4-12, 1967.

22 Blacker, K. H., et al: Chronic users of
    LSD: the acidheads. Speech presented at
    the 1968 National Meeting of the American
    Psychiatric Association. Publication in
    process.

23 Smith, David: The psychedelic syndrome,
    <u>Clin. Toxic.</u>, 2:69-73, 1969a.

24 A.M.A. Committee on Alcoholism and Drug
    Dependence: Dependence on LSD and other
    hallucinogenic drugs, <u>J.A.M.A.</u>, 202:47-50,
    1967.

25 Creek, Frances E.: Illicit drugs found to be
    "mislabelled" as well as to vary widely in
    potency, <u>Medical Tribune</u>, 11:1 and 20,
    April 13, 1970.

21021

DRUGS AND THE LAW
by
Thomas J. Maroney*

I. The Drug Problem: Youth, Authority and Harm-
    ful Substances

    No consideration of drug use and abuse would
be complete without an examination of one of the
most crucial and vexing aspects of the problem--
the relationship between drugs and the law. That
relationship will be examined after a brief pre-
fatory discussion of the societal setting in which
drug use and the law interact.

    A. An Historical Perspective on the Drug
        Problem

    The contemporary drug problem revolves to a
great extent around the relationships between
youth and authority and youth and harmful substances. It may help us keep the present problem
in perspective to view today's drug use as a reflection of relationships that are age-old.

    The relationship between youth and authority
has never been an easy one. A 4,000 year old
Egyptian hieroglyphic, recently discovered said:
"Children no longer respect their parents." And
in ancient Greece, Socrates lamented that the
youth had lost its respect for the law, for man
and for the Gods. For more modern examples,
music fans may recall the catalog of youthful
irresponsibilities and evidences of lack of respect for authority found in the song "You Got
Trouble" from the play and motion picture "The
Music Man." And the reader, whatever his age,
can search his memory for his own (or his children's) youthful transgressions against authority.

    Similarly, there is a long and illustrative
history in the relationship between man--includ-
ing youth--and harmful substances. A recent study
by an Australian psychiatrist, Dr. D. S. Bell,
reveals that opium, marijuana and cocaine were
almost certainly known to Stone Age peoples and
that ways of cultivating and preparing opium,
as described by the Sumerians on stone tablets
in 7,000 B.C., were substantially the same as

----
*Thomas J. Maroney, B.A., LL.B., is an Associate
Professor of Law at Syracuse University College
of Law.

those used today. Furthermore, Dr. Bell reported
that epidemics of drug addiction such as the
world is now experiencing have repeated themselves
down through history. One specific example of
what Dr. Bell describes can be drawn from ancient
China. As Norman Taylor points out in "Narcotics:
Nature's Dangerous Gifts," the ancient Chinese
were startlingly modern about drugs and medicines.
In about 2737 B.C. the Emperor Shen Nung wrote a
pharmacy book which contained a quite sophisticated explanation of Indian hemp. For more
modern examples, the reader may again call to
mind "You Got Trouble" from "The Music Man."
Also instructive is a survey taken of the Yale
University Class of 1873. Of 114 men in the
class (in those pre-women's-liberation times),
62 drank alcoholic beverages, over half the class
smoked and 16 even chewed tobacco. Parents and
school authorities especially, may be amused to
know that 76 of the class said they had worn some
form of beard or moustache, 92 were poker players
and various members of the class spent their time
"sleeping, loafing, drinking beer, fighting with
girls, and camping out with girls." Finally the
reader can examine his own (or his children's)
attraction toward substances of varying degrees
of harmfulness.

    B.   Drug Education and the Generation Gap.

    None of the above is meant to condone drug
use in any form at any time by anyone. Indeed
the harm to individuals and society from drug
abuse is self-evident. The historical background
is simply an attempt to establish a common perspective for some very diverse readers. One of
the difficulties in attacking the drug problem
is an education gap. And one of the difficulties
in closing this education gap is the existence
and breadth (especially concerning drugs) of
"The Generation Gap."

    The Generation Gap is hardly a new phenom-
enon. As John Kaplan writes in "Marijuana--the
New Prohibition," conflict between the young
and old is an attribute of all but the most
stagnant societies. The cleavage is epitomized
by countervailing cliches. The oldster longs
for "the good old days" as the youngster retorts
that "you just don't understand." Each may be
partially correct. In any event the relationship
today, as revealed especially by attitudes toward
drugs, is different, more strained. Kaplan says:

It is hard to escape the feeling that
today's conflict between the young and
the old over methods and expressions and
values is deeper, more pervasive and more
emotional than in any previous era in our
memory.

As an example, one can contrast the attitudes of
the Amherst College class of 1959 and the late
Janis Joplin toward drugs.

A portion of the Amherst class of 1959, as
Kaplan reports, was polled at its tenth reunion
in 1969. Those polled took, by a substantial
margin, "progressive" or "liberal" attitudes
toward a number of social issues. There was one
exception, however, and that concerned the use
of marijuana. Those present stood 76 to 50
against relaxing marijuana laws. Contrast their
stance with that of the late Janis Joplin. Some-
time before her death, the cause of which was rul-
ed to be an accidental overdose of heroin, Joplin
was asked what she wanted out of life. Her reply
was straightforward:

To be stoned, staying happy and having
a good time. I'm doing just what I
want with my life, enjoying it.
When I get scared and worried, I tell
myself, 'Janis, just have a good time.'
So I juice up real good and that's what
I have.

From this comparison it should be obvious
that very different values are held, even by
people only a few years apart in age. As Kaplan
states, by reference to the music revolution,
"The distance between the Kingston Trio and the
Beatles, though just a few years in time, is
great indeed." How much greater the distance
between the Beatles and Lawrence Welk. And how
great the need for all generations to be flexible and to work together toward a common goal
of adequate drug education.

II. The Law--Defined and Explained

Explaining "The Law" to non-lawyers is often
not an easy task; in this instance it is further
complicated by the readers' diversity. Some may
have known and long since forgotten certain
fundamentals about what law is, the sources from
which it is derived and how it is actually applied.

Others may not yet have been exposed to such con-
cepts. Thus a primer on "the law" should aid
all in understanding the discussion in Part III
of drug laws and laws on drug-related problems
likely to be encountered in the schools.

A. "The Law" Defined and Characterized.

For our purposes "law" can probably be defined simply as the body of rules governing the
affairs of man within a community. It comes in
a number of varieties: (1) "common law," that
is, law made by judges; (2) "statutory law," that
is, law made by legislators; and (3) "constitutional law," which is probably most accurately
viewed as a limitation upon the two other types
of law. Thus in some instances judges are competent to make law by themselves. An example of
this judge-made "common law" is the legal principle in contract law that (with certain important
exceptions) a legal contract does not have to be
in writing. In other instances the legislature
is competent to make law. An example of this
legislatively made "statutory law" is a law
passed by the New York State legislature which
makes it a crime to possess even one marijuana
cigarette. Whether a law is "common law" or
"statutory law" it may be that there is some "constitutional law," or more accurately, constitutional limitation, which makes it invalid. Examples of these constitutional limitations are
the ban on unreasonable searches or seizures and
on the taking of someone's property without due
process of law. As the discussion below will
show, drug laws are "statutory laws" and there
probably are not many constitutional limitations
upon them.

In addition to the above definitions, it may
be useful to give some characterizations of the
law. Law is a very human system which works
better on some occasions than on others. Not
surprisingly, people's estimates of the law and
its performance have varied widely. Sir Edward
Coke, a prominent English lawyer and judge once
said, "Reason is the life of the law...Law...
is the perfection of reason." Coke's fellow
Englishman Charles Dickens did not think so
highly of the law as some of his novels reveal.
In "The Pickwick Papers" the character Mr.
Bumble refers to the law as "a(n) ass, a(n)
idiot." These contrasting points of view are
helpful in reminding us that although we have

"a government of laws," the laws are created and applied by men and women.

    B.   The Creation and Application of "the Law."

       1.   The Source of the Law.

It can be said that in a constitutional democracy such as the United States, the people are the source of the law. The documents upon which our system of government was founded make this clear. The Declaration of Independence says that, "To secure these rights, governments are instituted among men, deriving their just powers from the consent of the governed." And the Preamble to the United States Constitution says that "We the people...do ordain and establish this Constitution for the United States of America."

Since the people are the source of law and the legislators are their representatives, it should be clear that the legal process is not a science and that the legal system is not a computer which can be programmed to spew forth mathematically exact solutions to society's thorny problem. Mr. Justice Oliver Wendell Holmes, Jr. was ahead of his time in recognizing this reality. In 1881 Holmes said:

> The life of the law has not been logic: it has been experience. The felt necessities of the time, the prevalent moral and political theories, intuitions of public policy, avowed or unconscious, even the prejudices which judges share with their fellow-men, have a good deal more to do than the syllogism in determining the rules by which men should be governed.

The law, Holmes continued, "Embodies the story of a nation's development through many centuries" and thus "it cannot be dealt with as if it contained only the axioms and corollaries of a "book of mathematics."

       2.   The Process of Creation.

Since the law in Holmes' words, "is not a brooding omnipresence in the sky" it falls to human beings to attempt to fashion legal solutions to society's problems. The primary focus of this activity is in the legislatures, at the federal

and state levels. The legislator in performing
his task is moved--consciously or unconsciously--
by a number of influences. Two of the most crucial are mores and politics. Before discussing
these two influences, it should be noted that
the legislator's being so moved is an inevitable
and--assuming the legislator's integrity--per-
fectly proper aspect of the legislative process.

a. The Passage of New Laws.

The first stage at which mores and politics
may come to bear is in the passage of new laws.
At this stage social mores--the community's
moral attitudes--may lead the members of the
legislature to outlaw certain conduct. The community's moral judgement that certain conduct is
undesirable thereby becomes the government's
judgement that such conduct ought to be forbidden.
Examples which come immediately to mind are the
use of alcohol and the use of other kinds of
drugs. In the words of William Eldridge, author
of "Narcotics and the Law," "It must be recognized that ultimate philosophical and religious
tenets play a large part in the social judgement
concerning narcotics."

Politics may also influence the legislator
in his task of passing new laws. Election campaigns reveal the impact of politics especially
upon criminal laws. It never hurts a candidate
to be against crime and in favor of "law and
order" as the 1968 campaign illustrated. In the
wake of the campaign came new restrictive federal
and state criminal laws.

Eventually the conscious and unconscious
melding of mores, politics and other factors
results in legislation, which if approved by the
chief executive officer, becomes a law. After
the law takes effect a question may arise whether
it violates any constitutional limitation. For
example, someone arrested under a certain law
may claim as part of his defense that the law is
unconstitutional. As noted previously, even a
statutory law which the Legislature has the
unquestioned power to pass may be invalid if it
violates a constitutional limitation. If a
question of constitutionality is raised it is to
be resolved by the courts (up to and including
the United States Supreme Court) and the process
is referred to as judicial review.

In reviewing legislation for constitutionality, the courts begin with a presumption which
may or may not hold up. Courts presume that a
law passed by the legislature represents that
body's rational judgement as to a proper solution
to a particular problem, in light of the information available to the legislature when the law
was passed. Not the only solution; not necessarily the best solution; merely a proper and
"rational" solution. A shorthand formulation is
to say that the courts will presume that "whatever legislative choice is rational is constitutional."

The determination of which choice is rational
and which is not, is hardly a predictable process.
Consider, for example, the classification of
marijuana. Suppose that a state legislature
passes a statute which classifies marijuana as a
narcotic. Since narcotics are generally agreed
to be highly dangerous substances, narcotics offenses, including marijuana offenses, would be
treated as quite serious crimes and offenders
punished accordingly. Someone arrested for a
marijuana offense in this situation would probably argue that the law is invalid; that it violates a constitutional limitation; that it is not
based upon rational judgement since, pharmacologically speaking, marijuana is not a narcotic.

The illustration is not a hypothetical one;
at least two recent cases have involved this very
issue of marijuana classification. The decisions
of the courts are flatly inconsistent. The first
case, known as Rener v. Beto, 447 Fed 20 (5th
Cir. 1971) involved a Texas law against the possession of a narcotic drug. The definition of
"narcotic drug" included marijuana. Rener was
convicted of violating this law because he had in
his possession a single marijuana cigarette.
(He had tried unsuccessfully to swallow it when
approached by two policemen.) Since it was his
second marijuana offense, Rener was sentenced to
thirty years in prison.

As his defense, Rener argued that the classification of marijuana as a narcotic drug was
not a rational legislative choice and that the
law violated two constitutional limitations, the
Due Process and Equal Protection clauses in the
United States Constitution. The court rejected
his argument. The court said that it was not its
job to decide whether the classifications in the

law were wise or desirable. It said that, "Legislatures have been given wide powers of discretion when it comes to classifications in the
adoption of police laws and it is limited only
when such classification is without any reasonable basis." The court then reviewed the arguments of Rener and the State of Texas as to
whether marijuana was in fact a narcotic in a
pharmacological sense. The court did not specifically rule on that point. It simply upheld the
law, stating, "We are unable to say that the Texas
legislature acted arbitrarily and without a reasonable basis when it classified marijuana,
together with addictive drugs, as a narcotic."
Incidentally, the court also upheld Rener's sentence.

The second case, known as <u>People</u> v. <u>McCabe</u>,
10 CrL 2074 (Ill. Sup. Ct. 1971) involved an
Illinois law which classified marijuana as a
narcotic drug. The significance of the classification lay in the punishment provisions. The
penalty for a first offense of selling a narcotic
drug (including marijuana) was a mandatory minimum ten year sentence. In contrast the penalty
for a first offense of selling a stimulant or
depressant drug was a maximum, non-mandatory,
one year sentence.

As his defense McCabe argued that the classification of marijuana as a narcotic drug, especially in light of the disparity in sentences
for narcotics offenses on the one hand, and
stimulant and depressant offenses on the other,
was not a rational legislative choice and violated
two constitutional limitations, namely the Equal
Protection clauses of the Illinois Constitution
and the United States Constitution. The court
agreed.

Excerpts from the majority opinion and two
dissenting opinions show the contrasting judicial approaches to determining "rationality."
The majority said:

> If any state of facts may reasonably be
> conceived which would justify the class-
> ification, it must be upheld...We are
> aware that any compilation and examination
> of materials cannot comprehend all studies
> that have been made. We know, too, that
> knowledge in this whole area is not nearly
> complete. We proceed not to determine

scientific questions, but to judge whether
the data presently available provides a reasonable basis for the described classification of marijuana....The consideration
of this data, of course, will not extend
to the wisdom or unwisdom of the legislative
classification. We confine our examination
to the question whether the challenged
classification can be supported on any
rational basis....The consensus is that
although marijuana has been commonly associated with the opiates, such as morphine
and heroin, there are important differences
between the so-called abuse characteristics
of the two. Heroin and morphine are true
narcotic analgesics in the sense that their
use produces a marked indifference to pain.

Cocaine, which is placed with marijuana
and the opiates in the Narcotic-Drug Act,
is a powerful stimulant, whereas the
morphine-type drugs have a depressing action.
Too, cocaine is further unlike the opiates
in that it does not have effects of tolerance
or physical dependence and abstention does
not cause acute withdrawal symptoms. However, because of its potent nature, it in-
duces intense physical and mental excita-
tion and a marked reduction in normal
inhibitions which often results in aggressive and even violent behavior. Intense
hallucinations and paranoid delusions are
common and, because of this, cocaine users
frequently attempt to dilute the experience
with a depressant such as heroin or morphine.

The properties and consequences of the use
of marijuana differ from those attending
the use of opiates or cocaine.

Almost all authorities agree that marijuana
is not a narcotic or addictive in the sense
that the terms are precisely used. Unlike
the opiate drugs, it does not produce a
physical dependence, and upon abstention
there are no withdrawal symptoms. A tolerance to the drug does not develop.

The depressant and stimulant drugs within
the Drug Abuse Control Act includes the
barbiturates (depressants), the amphetamines (stimulants), and the hallucinogens.
The drugs psilocybin, peyote, mescaline

and what is commonly called LSD are examples
of the hallucinogens. Frequent use of the
barbiturates at high dosage levels leads
invariably to the development of physical
dependence, tolerance and severe withdrawal
symptoms, similar to those associated with
heroin use. The effects of barbiturate
intoxication resemble those of alcoholic
intoxication....Accidental death from an
overdose also can occur.

The consensus of the amphetamines (stimulants) is that, unlike the barbiturates,
their abuse does not lead to a physical
dependence, but the development of a high
tolerance and a strong psychological dependence are common.

Special mention should be made of one particular amphetamine, methamphetamine, commonly called "speed." Its effects are
generally the same as other amphetamines,
only markedly intensified. There is evidence that large doses result in permanent
brain damage. The drug's lethal qualities
are well documented. The potential for
violence, paranoia and physical depletion
are substantially more severe.

As with marijuana usage, a true physical
addiction does not occur with LSD, in that
withdrawal effects do not follow abstinence.
Frequent use of LSD will lead rapidly, however, to the development of a high tolerance. Psychological dependence develops as
it does with exposure to almost any substance which alters the state of consciousness. During LSD-intoxication severe panic
and paranoid reactions are encountered.

Against this background of comparison one
would conclude that neither the chemical
properties of the drugs nor their effects
on the behavior of the users provides any
justifiable or reasonable basis for the
sharply disparate penalities which are
imposed for a first sale of marijuana and
for a first sale of a drug under the Drug
Abuse Control Act. Too, the consequences
of abusive use of marijuana certainly
appear not to be comparable to the demonstrated and profound ill-effects of opiate
or cocaine addiction. Marijuana, in terms

of abuse characteristics, shares much more
in common with the barbiturates, amphetamines,
and, particularly, the hallucinogens than it
does with the "hard drugs" classified in
the Narcotic Drug Act. Marijuana does differ
from the barbiturates and amphetamines in
that it has no established medical use, but
neither do LSD, peyote, or mescaline. Thus,
one cannot reasonably distinguish marijuana
from the substances under the Drug Abuse
Control Act on this basis.

Nor is there any reasonable basis for placing marijuana under the Narcotic Drug Act
and not under the Drug Abuse Control Act
because of any compulsion to abuse. The
compulsion associated with marijuana has
been described as moderate or mild. The
same is true of the amphetamines. The
opiates and cocaine, on the other hand,
have a maximal compulsive quality in this
regard. Barbiturates, too, have this quality. Thus, in this respect, marijuana is
dissimilar from the other drugs in the
Narcotic Drug Act. Indeed, from this limited standard of comparison it is the barbiturates under the Drug Abuse Control Act,
and not marijuana, which approximate the
characteristics of the true narcotics.

Another factor which has been frequently
advanced to provide a justifiable basis for
classifying marijuana under the Narcotic
Drug Act rather than under the Drug Abuse
Control Act is that the use of marijuana
progresses to heroin use and addiction.
This thesis, once broadly entertained, has
recently encountered serious challenge.
Today it is reported that the vast majority
of marijuana users do not graduate to the
use of heroin....Whatever can be said of
marijuana use leading to the use of other
and so-called harder drugs can be applied,
and to a probably greater extent, to barbiturates, methamphetamine and LSD.

The thesis that marijuana use, as does the
use of the opiates and cocaine, leads to
criminal activity cannot provide a basis
for distinguishing marijuana from the
depressant and stimulant drugs or the
hallucinogens.

Observations to be drawn on marijuana are
that it is not a narcotic and it is not
truly addictive. Its use does not involve
tolerance, physical dependence or the withdrawal syndrome. Physical ill effects from
its use are, so far as is known, relatively
moderate. Its abuse does not have the profound and ill consequences observed in the
use of some of the other drugs considered.
Its use does not singularly or extraor-
dinarily lead to opiate addiction or to
aggressive behavior or criminal activity.

Against the entire background of the drugs
considered we judge that the classification
of marijuana under the Narcotics Drug Act
rather than under the Drug Abuse Control
Act has been arbitrary....We do not find a
rational basis for the classification, a
consequence of which is that one first
convicted of the sale of marijuana must
without qualification receive a sentence ten
times greater than one permitted to be imposed on one convicted for the first time
of a sale of drugs under the Drug Abuse
Act....The present classification of marijuana offends the equal-protection clause
of the United States constitution and our
new constitution of Illinois and was in
violation of section 22 of article IV of
the former constitution of the State.

In concluding its opinion, the majority noted
that it was aware of decisions such as <u>Rener</u> v.
<u>Beto</u> and disagreed with them.

Two judges dissented and each wrote an opinion of his own. The first dissenting judge said:

Since the majority concludes that the inclusion of marijuana in the Narcotics Drug
Act is an unconstitutional classification,
it is necessary to state my...disagreement
with that conclusion. Defendant concedes
that when the first Illinois drug act was
passed in 1931, the combining of marijuana
with "hard drugs" seemed to be legitimate,
and that if only "hard drugs" were prohibited in Illinois, it still might not
be irrational to put marijuana in that
category. Defendant contends, however, that
after the legislature created a second and
lesser category of prohibited drugs by

enacting the Drug Abuse Control Act in
1967, it was no longer rational to continue
"to assign marijuana to the category with
which it has much less in common."

Medical and scientific opinion is even now
by no means unanimous in condemnation of
classifications of marijuana with "hard
drugs" and, as the majority notes, "knowledge in this whole area is not nearly complete." In the absence of more nearly
conclusive evidence that the legislative
judgement was devoid of any rational basis,
a finding of unconstitutionality is unwarranted, for few rules of law are more
soundly bottomed than that which proscribes
judicial interference with legislative discretion.

The second dissenting judge said:

The majority opinion does not focus on what
I consider to be the critical aspect of the
question of classification. The majority
is concerned with characteristics of the
various drugs discussed and their effects
on the human body and behavior pointing out
similarities and differences. I do not consider these comparisons important. Instead
we must be concerned with the purpose of
the classification and the problems the
legislature was attempting to alleviate
thereby....The legislature was not attempting to classify drugs of similar characteristics and effects but was attempting to
classify these drugs for the purpose of
combating the social evil found in the
illegal sale, possession and use of the
same.

The conclusion of the majority ignores the
fact that traffic in marijuana had been a
social problem of sufficient magnitude to
warrant legislative action for many years.
Material submitted with the briefs indicates that although a relatively small
percentage of marijuana users become addicted
to the so-called "hard drugs" a high percentage of "hard drug" addicts first became
acquainted with the use of drugs through
the use of marijuana.

The defendant's brief has also focused on
the characteristics and effects of the
various drugs and has ignored the problem-
to-be solved approach. The burden is on
the defendant to present evidence which
shows that the apparently reasonable basis
for this classification does not exist....
The defendant has failed to produce any
evidence concerning the nature of the
traffic in the various drugs or the need to
control the same. The presumption of the
validity of the classification must therefore prevail.

   b.   The Modification or Repeal of Existing
        Laws.

A final note about the impact of formative
influences on the legislator. They also come to
bear at the stage when modification or repeal of
existing statutory law is being considered. Drug
laws are a good example. Increasingly, proposals
are being made to ameliorate drug laws, especially concerning first offenses involving marijuana. Such proposals are subjected to the
influences of mores and politics and often suf-
focated in the process. As Kaplan noted in
"Marijuana: the New Prohibition," "It is clear
that moral opposition to a life-style inhibits
any change in the marijuana laws."

   3.   The Application of the Law.

Once a law has been properly enacted and has
passed constitutional muster, if such a challenge is made, it must be enforced. The law
enforcement process operates in essentially two
stages: non-judicial and judicial. Though
sequential and different in form, both stages share
a common characteristic. At neither stage is the
process inexorable: on the contrary, it is
flexible and discretionary. This flexibility is
essential for the operation of any legal system.
But it presents possible dangers, especially
with regard to non-judicial law enforcement, which
is in the hands of the police.

   a.   Non-Judicial Law Enforcement.

Although we desire equal application of the
law, in candor it must be admitted that the
actual application of the law may sometimes vary
with the views that society and the police

officer hold toward an offense or an offender.
The variation takes the forms of non-enforcement,
selective enforcement or zealous enforcement.
Non-enforcement means that a valid statutory law
is seldom if ever enforced. Adultery is a particularly clear example. It is common knowledge
that, although adultery is and has long been a
crime in New York State, the adultery law is almost never enforced. The writer has never, in
his personal experience or in conversations with
other attorneys, heard of an arrest (or prosecution) for adultery in this state.

Selective enforcement means that a valid
statutory law is enforced solely or at least primarily against a certain segment of society. The
enforcement of the flag desecration law is an
example. In recent years in many areas of the
country flag desecration laws have been enforced
against young adults at the same time as business
firms using flags in advertising were not being
proceeded against. In a number of instances
with which this writer is personally familiar the
young adult should never have been charged and
the business firm just as certainly should have
been.

Zealous enforcement is often carried out in
conjunction with selective enforcement and means
that valid statutory laws are enforced in a
hyper-intensive fashion. Any conceivable ground
for arrest is used in every arguably proper instance. Flag desecration could again be used
as an example. Every symbol, design or repre-
sentation which might conceivably be taken to
be a desecration is used as the basis for an
arrest, even though the law was obviously not
intended to be applied in such a fashion.

The vagaries of non-judicial enforcement are
illustrated not to denigrate law enforcement
officials but simply to stress that the unjust
exercise of police discretion can breed dis-
respect for the law and thus further complicate
the task of solving difficult social problems.

        b. Judicial Law Enforcement.

The second stage of the law enforcement
process can be termed judicial and begins after
an arrested person is first brought in to court.
This stage of the process is also, to some extent, flexible and discretionary. It is first

in the control of the prosecutor (district attorney) and eventually in the control of a judge and jury. The prosecutor must first decide exactly what crime a person is to be charged with and in some instances must submit his case to a grand jury for an indictment. Some time thereafter he must either obtain a guilty plea or submit the case to a court and jury in an attempt to obtain a conviction. To obtain a plea he may quite legitimately agree with the accused person's attorney to allow the accused to plead guilty to a less serious offense than that originally charged.

If no such arrangement can be arrived at, the case goes to a judge and jury. The jury is to decide guilt or innocence by first determining the facts of the case and then applying the controlling law to them. Its task is not nearly so simple as this description makes it sound. Nor is it so detached and mechanical. The jury is not only trier of fact; it is also to some extent "the conscience of the community" and its decision will usually reflect its hybrid nature. One notorious example was the performance of large city juries during Prohibition. In some instances they simply would not return guilty verdicts in liquor violation cases. Their sympathies too obviously lay with the accused.

If the jury does find the accused person guilty it is usually the judge's function to impose a sentence. With some important exceptions, the judge normally has a great deal of latitude in sentencing. Needless to say fair and sound sentencing decisions are required if there is to be any prospect for rehabilitation of those convicted of crime.

III. The Law of Drugs.

The foregoing societal background and legal primer form the underpinnings for the discussion herein of drug laws. The origin, evolution and current state of American drug laws will be summarized, followed by an analysis of New York State drug control laws and laws governing drug-related problems which may arise in the schools.

A. American Drug Laws.

1. Origin.

American drug laws are a twentieth century
phenomenon, although drug abuse problems were
evident in the latter half of the nineteenth
century. Examples include narcotic addiction
stemming from the administering of pain-killing
drugs to military personnel wounded in combat;
opium smoking among Orientals in San Francisco;
and drug problems caused by the consumption of
patent medicines. The impetus for drug control
laws came from a 1912 treaty whereby the United
States obligated itself to control the domestic
sale, use, and transfer of opium and cocoa products. Two years later federal drug laws were
passed and eventually the states also passed such
laws.

2.   Evolution and Current State.

Despite the obvious risks, two generalizations
can fairly safely be made about the drug laws
passed up until the past few years. One is that
they were sometimes based upon misinformation or
incomplete information on some critical points.
The other is that the laws were of a decidedly
punitive, almost vindictive cast. More than one
drug law was based upon shaky premises about drug
taxonomy; the effect of various substances upon
mind and body; the actual extent of drug use; or,
the effectiveness of harsh legal sanctions. To
illustrate: William Eldridge in "Narcotics and
the Law" shows that although Michigan (as of
1962) believed strongly in severe mandatory sentences in drug cases (e.g., a twenty year mandatory minimum sentence for a first offense of
narcotics sale), the state maintained no central
repository of data on drug sentences. As Eldridge
points out, concrete information was not available to those making unqualified pronouncements
about the success or failure of the preventive
methods theretofore employed in the United States.

Drug laws were also of a strongly punitive,
almost vindictive cast. Many provided for
severe sentences and, as in Michigan, removed the
judge's discretion in sentencing an offender,
requiring instead the imposition of a mandatory
minimum sentence. In addition the laws reflected
a peripheral punitiveness. For example, a New
Jersey law required that anyone who had ever
been convicted of a narcotics offense must register with the police in any place where he intended
to remain more than twenty-four hours.

There are a number of signs today that the
punitive precedents just described are being
superseded and that drug control laws are being
"humanized" and "rationalized." In a number of
jurisdictions (federal government and the states)
new drug laws have been passed recently or are
being considered presently. One especially sym-
bolic focus is the marijuana laws. As Kaplan
states, the movement to increase penalties for
marijuana violations seems to have spent most of
its force. Although there are still some quite
substantial penalties in effect, at least for
more serious marijuana offenses (see tables in
9 Crim. Law Reporter 2438-44, August 25, 1971),
the clear trend in the legislatures is toward a
reduction of penalties for marijuana offenses.
For example, on August 8, 1971, "The New York
Times" reported that in the three years past,
twenty-six states had revised their marijuana
laws--in twenty-four the penalties for possession
of marijuana were reduced, usually to make the
first offense a misdemeanor, with a one-year
maximum sentence that can be suspended by the
sentencing judge.

In addition to such changes, there are also
recommendations for further reforms by various
well-respected public and private groups. Three
such groups have recently recommended further
amelioration or eventual elimination of criminal
penalties for some marijuana offenses. A study
of the National Institute of Mental Health concluded that the penalties for use and possession
of marijuana are much too severe and much out of
keeping with knowledge about its harmfulness.
Dr. Bertram S. Brown, Institute Director, said
he did not think scientific opinion yet justified
legalization; he recommended instead, "decrimin-
alization." The American Bar Association's Committee on Alcoholism and Drug Reform has recommended that all criminal penalties for marijuana
possession be eliminated. Finally, and of greatest significance, The National Commission on
Marijuana and Drug Abuse has unanimously decided
to recommend that all criminal penalties for the
private use and possession of marijuana be eliminated. The political significance of its position lies in the fact that nine of its thirteen
members were appointed by President Richard M.
Nixon and in the further fact that President
Nixon said on May 2, 1971, "Even if the commission
does recommend that it (marijuana) be legalized,
I will not follow that recommendation." it

will be interesting indeed to see the legislative
reaction, shaped by mores and politics, to these
latest proposals.

Other evidence of the "humanizing" trend can
be found in the flexibility being built in to
sentencing provisions (disposition other than
jail or prison for certain types of offenders);
in commitment rather than imprisonment for certified narcotics addicts, and in the mergence of
Methadone maintenance programs.

Along with "humanizing" has come a "rationalizing" of the structure of drug laws. The
term is used here in a non-technical, non-legal
sense to mean simply that the drug laws are
being revised to accord with common sense, medical knowledge and community sentiment. The above-
mentioned developments relating to marijuana are
evidence of this "rationalizing." So too is the
trend to increase penalties for offenses involving amphetamines, barbiturates and hallucinogens,
in recognition of their dangerous potential and
the social and law enforcement problems resulting from their usage.

The above legislative developments point up
what may be emerging cross-currents in drug control. At a time when legislators and governors
are displaying a genuine interest in obtaining
adequate information upon which to base humane
and rational laws, some members of the judiciary
are acting upon an emotional premise that harsh
sentences are what the drug problem demands. A
number of federal and state commissions (and
private groups as well) are engaged in extensive
investigation of the medical, societal and legal
aspects of drug use with an intensity and sin-
cerity that evidences their realization that
drug use will neither be wished away nor solved
by harsh criminal sanctions. Some judges, on the
other hand, are meting out twenty or thirty year
sentences for marijuana offenses or a thirty year
sentence for the sale by an admitted narcotics
addict of a fraction of an ounce of heroin. The
writer believes that such a response can only
exacerbate an already difficult situation.

B. The Laws of the State of New York.

The laws of probable interest to the reader
can be divided into (1) the drug control laws
and (2) laws governing drug-related problems

likely to be encountered in the schools. The
former category includes drug offenses and their
punishment and the latter, school-based problems
such as search of a student or his locker and the
confidentiality of disclosures by a student to
school personnel.

1. Present Drug Control Laws and their
   Application.

An examination of present drug offenses and
penalties reveals the hand of the formative influences discussed in Part II (B) in the specific
setting of this state. The magnitude of the
drug problem in New York State, especially the
hard drug problem in large metropolitan areas,
has had a unique impact. Legislators have been
deprived of the "luxury" of passing overly-mor-
alistic laws and on the whole the legislative
response has been pragmatic. The tone is illustrated by a Declaration of Purpose included in
a 1966 law establishing a civil commitment procedure for certified narcotics addicts. It
reads in part:

The legislature finds and determines as
follows:
1. The human suffering and social and
economic loss caused by the disease of drug
addiction are matters of grave concern to
the people of the state. The magnitude of
the cost to the people of the state for
police, judicial, penal and medical care
purposes, directly and indirectly caused
by the disease of drug addiction, makes it
imperative that a comprehensive program to
combat the effects of the disease of drug
addiction be developed and implemented
through the combined and correlated efforts
of federal, state, local communities and
private individuals and organizations.
2. A comprehensive program of compul-
sory treatment of narcotic addicts is
essential to the protection and promotion
of the health and welfare of the inhabitants
of the state as well as to discourage the
violation of laws relating to the sale,
possession and use of narcotics and other
dangerous drugs. Narcotic addicts are estimated to be responsible for one-half the
crimes committed in the city of New York
alone and the problem of narcotic addiction
is rapidly spreading into the suburbs and

other parts of the state. This threat to
the peace and safety of the inhabitants of
the state must be met. Not only crime, but
unemployment, poverty, loss of human dig-
nity and of the ability to fill a meaningful and productive role in the community,
as well as damage to the physical and mental
health of the addict himself are all by-
products of this spreading disease. The
narcotic addict needs help before he is
compelled to resort to crime to support his
habit. The narcotic addict who commits a
crime needs help to break his addiction.
A comprehensive program of treatment, rehabilitation and aftercare for narcotic addicts
can fill these needs.

The legislative scheme is not perfect, however,
as will be seen below.

> a. The Primary Drug Offenses and
> Punishment.

The present laws, texts of which are appended
to this article, went into effect in 1967 and
have been revised somewhat since then. A thor-
oughgoing revision is being considered by the
State Legislature at its 1972 session. The present offense structure contains a detailed and
sophisticated breakdown based upon who has what
drug in what quantity for what purpose. The
laws are well-drafted and well-conceived, with
one glaring exception--the comparative treatment
of marijuana on the one hand and amphetamines,
barbiturates and hallucinogens on the other.

Under the law any illegal drug is called a
"Dangerous Drug" and that term is subdivided
in three: "Narcotic Drug," "Depressant or
Stimulant Drug" and "Hallucinogenic Drug." The
prohibitions of the law are against possession
and sale of Dangerous Drugs; it is no crime
simply to use one. The term "sell" is broadly
defined and covers any transfer of a drug or
offer or agreement to do so, whether or not
money is received in return.

The first major category of offense is
possession offenses. Possession of Dangerous
Drugs is forbidden whether it is the high school
student's single marijuana cigarette or the
pusher's bulk supply. Potential sentences range

from a maximum of one year to a maximum of life imprisonment.

The least serious offense (Possession Sixth Degree, N.Y. Penal Law § 220.05) is simple possession of any Dangerous Drug. It is a Misdemeanor punishable by a maximum of one year imprisonment. Thus possession of any quantity of any Narcotic, Depressant or Stimulant, or Hallucinogenic Drug can be prosecuted. One marijuana cigarette, one pep pill, one L.S.D. cube; possession of each is forbidden.

The remaining five possession offenses are felonies and of increasing severity. Possession Fifth Degree (Penal L. § 220.10) is possession of any Dangerous Drug with intent to sell and is punishable by one to four years imprisonment. Thus possession of any quantity of any Narcotic, Depressant or Stimulant, or Hallucinogenic Drug with intent to sell can be prosecuted. Possession with intent to sell of one marijuana cigarette, one pep pill or one L.S.D. cube is forbidden.

Possession Fourth Degree (Penal L. § 220.15) is possession of any Narcotic Drug with intent to sell or simple possession of a specified quantity of certain Narcotic Drugs and is punishable by two and one-third to seven years imprisonment. At this point the Penal Law's definition of "Narcotic Drug" becomes significant. "Narcotic Drug" is defined in the N.Y. Public Health Law § 3301 (38) and that definition incorporated into the Penal Law as a sub-category of Dangerous Drug. "Narcotic Drug" is defined to include not only truly narcotic substances (heroin, opium, etc.) but also marijuana, or more precisely:

marihuana (cannabis, sativa and all other substances, whether synthetic or in plant form, which contain the active ingredients of cannabis, sativa or delta-1-tetrahydro cannabinol, monoterpene numbering system as used by Mechoulan or delta-3-tetrahydro cannabinol or delta-6-tetrahydro cannabinol or delta-8-tetrahydro cannabinol or delta-9-tetrahydro cannabinol as numbered by Korte and Isbell or cannabidiol or cannabinol).

Thus under the first part of this possession

offense, possession with intent to sell of even
one marijuana cigarette can be prosecuted, although a prosecutor has discretion to treat
such conduct as a less serious Possession Fifth
Degree offense. The second part of this offense
consists of simple possession of specified
quantities of Narcotic Drugs: twenty-five or
more cannabis cigarettes; one-eighth ounce or
more heroin, morphine or cocaine; one-fourth ounce
or more of cannibis; and one-half ounce or more
of raw or prepared opium. The significance of
this provision lies in what it does and does not
cover. It includes marijuana but not Depressant
or Stimulant or Hallucinogenic Drugs. Their
possession, in however great a quantity, can be
no more than a Possession Fifth Degree offense.
And if intent to sell cannot be established, it
can be no more than a Possession Sixth Degree
offense.

Possession Third Degree (Penal L. § 220.20)
is simple possession of a specified quantity of
certain Narcotic Drugs and is punishable by
five to fifteen years imprisonment. The previous covers the same group of Narcotic Drugs
(including marijuana) as does the prior offense
and is different in that it prosecutes possession
of greater quantities; for example one hundred
cannabis cigarettes as contrasted with twenty-
five such cigarettes.

Possession Second Degree (Penal L. § 220.22)
is simple possession of a specified quantity of
certain "hard" Narcotic Drugs and is punishable
by eight and one-half to twenty-five years imprisonment. Thus possession of eight or more
ounces of heroin, morphine, cocaine or opium can
be prosecuted.

Possession First Degree (Penal Law § 220.23),
the most serious possession offense, is simple
possession of a specified quantity of the "hard"
Narcotic Drugs referred to in Possession Second
Degree. It is punishable by fifteen years to
life imprisonment. Under this provision possession of sixteen or more ounces of heroin, morphine, cocaine or opium can be prosecuted.

The other major category of offense is sale
offenses. "Selling" is forbidden whether it is
the high school student's gift of a marijuana
cigarette to a classmate or the pusher's profit-
motivated transfer of drugs in return for cash.

Possible sentences range from a minimum of two and one-half to seven years imprisonment to a maximum of life imprisonment. In considering the sale offenses the reader should again be reminded that "sell" as defined by law includes any transfer or offer or agreement to transfer a Dangerous Drug, whether or not money is received in return.

Selling Fourth Degree (Penal L. § 20.30), the least serious sale offense, is the sale of any Dangerous Drug and is punishable by two and one-third to seven years imprisonment. Thus the sale or gift (or offer or agreement therefore) of any quantity of any Narcotic, Depressant or Stimulant, or Hallucinogenic Drug can be prosecuted. Even the gift of one marijuana cigarette is forbidden.

Selling Third Degree (Penal L. § 220.35), is the sale of any Narcotic Drug and is punishable by five to fifteen years. Thus the sale or gift (or offer or agreement therefore) of any quantity of any Narcotic Drug can be prosecuted. As indicated in the discussion of possession offenses, "Narcotic Drug" includes marijuana. Thus the gift of even one marijuana cigarette can be prosecuted here, although a prosecutor has discretion to treat such conduct as a less serious Selling Fourth Degree offense.

Selling Second Degree (Penal L. § 220.40) is the sale of a Narcotic Drug to anyone less than twenty-one years of age or the sale of a specified quantity of certain "hard" Narcotic Drugs and is punishable by eight and one-third to twenty-five years imprisonment. Under the first part of this provision, the sale or gift (or offer or agreement therefore) of one marijuana cigarette to a person less than twenty-one years of age can be prosecuted here, although a prosecutor has discretion to treat such conduct as a less serious Selling Third or Fourth Degree offense. Under the second part of this provision the sale or gift (or offer or agreement therefore) of eight or more ounces of heroin, morphine, cocaine or opium can be prosecuted.

Selling First Degree (Penal L. § 220.44) the most serious sale offense, is the sale of a specified quantity of certain "hard" Narcotic Drugs and is punishable by fifteen years to life imprisonment. Thus the sale or gift (or offer or

agreement therefore) of sixteen or more ounces of
heroin, morphine, cocaine or opium can be prosecuted.

In addition to the possession and sale of-
fenses there are other miscellaneous drug offen-
ses: Criminally Injecting a Narcotic Drug
(Penal L. § 220.46); Criminally Possessing a Hy-
podermic Instrument (Penal L. § 220.45); Crimin-
ally Using Drug Paraphernalia in the Second
Degree (Penal L. § 220.50) or First Degree (Penal
L. §220.55); Loitering for the Use of Drugs
(Penal L. § 240.36); and Growing Marijuana (Pub.
Health L. § 3315).

b. Application of the Laws.

As with any other laws, enforcement of drug
control laws is first non-judicial, in the hands
of law-enforcement officials and subsequently
judicial, in the hands of the prosecutor and the
courts. At the non-judicial stage there can be
the temptation above mentioned for police officers
to engage in selective and/or zealous enforcement.
The temptation has not always been resisted in
drug cases. In a number of instances with which
the writer is personally familiar vehicles have
been stopped with or without justification and
thoroughly searched without justification, in
the hope of uncovering drugs. Long hair and an
oddly-painted conveyance seem to some enforcement officials to be reasonable ground to suspect
the driver of something. If drugs are then found
a court must decide if they have been seized
legally. If not, they may not be used in a
criminal prosecution. If no drugs are found
the damage to respect for law is done.

At the judicial stage drug law enforcement
retains the element of flexibility. The prosecutor must decide where police and prosecution
resources should be concentrated. The answer,
normally, is upon the hard drug traffic, with
less strenuous effort being made against less
serious offenses. Such a decision is appropriate
and perfectly proper in light of the magnitude
of the problem and the financial and human resources available to combat it.

If a drug case goes to the judge for sentencing there is considerable discretion available
to make the punishment fit the crime. In this
state there is no punitive mandatory minimum

sentence for drug offenses. By and large the
applicable punishments are the same as for other
offenses of the same degree of seriousness. And
within that penalty structure the judge has latitude to act with mercy toward an undeserving one.
In one instance there is a special provision for
drug offenses. A law passed in 1971 (N.Y.Crim.
Procedure L. § 3170.56) provides that if the
offense charged is simple possession of marijuana
or loitering for the use of marijuana and the
accused has no previous conviction, the judge may
adjourn the case for up to one year, in contem-
plation of its eventual dismissal. During the
adjournment the accused must comply with conditions set by the court, the purpose of which is
to give him an opportunity to mend his ways.

> 2. Proposals for Reform of the Present
>   Drug Control Laws.

Although the present drug control laws were
passed in 1965 and became effective in 1967 they
were in danger of becoming outmoded even then.
The surge in drug abuse in the late 1960's had
as perhaps its only beneficial side-effect an
increase in knowledge of drugs, their taxonomy
and effects upon mind and body. This newly crys-
talized knowledge made clear the substantial
dangers in abuse of amphetamines, barbiturates
and especially hallucinogens and the comparatively
less substantial dangers in the abuse of marijuana.
In this light the present laws on Possession or
Sale of these substances have stood reality on
its head. Possession of an unlimited supply of
L.S.D. is a less serious offense than possession
with intent to sell of one marijuana cigarette
or simple possession of twenty-five marijuana
cigarettes. Similarly the sale or gift of any
quantity of L.S.D. to a person of any age is a
less serious offense than the sale or gift of
one marijuana cigarette, especially to someone
under twenty-one.

These and other anomolies of the present law
may be responsible for galvanizing a reform effort. In 1970 the State Legislature and Governor
Nelson A. Rockefeller agreed to the creation of
a Temporary State Commission to Evaluate the
Drug Laws. The Commission's mandate was broadly
phrased in recognition of the many facets to
the drug problem and in reflection of the Legislature's desire to accumulate information upon

which to base rational, effective legislation.
The Commission was ordered to:

> ...make a comprehensive study of present
> state laws dealing with the use, possession
> and sale of narcotics, and such other drugs
> as amphetamines, barbiturates, hallucino-
> gens, marijuana and related substances de-
> rived from the cannabis plant and other chem-
> ical substances, in order to determine what
> meaningful sanctions will be effective, cap-
> able of enforcement and yet realistically
> related to the offense involved. The com-
> mission shall also examine the nature of
> drug effects upon the individual, and the
> roles of drug taking and experimentation
> as part of the fabric of a total life pat-
> tern.
> More specifically, the commission shall
> (1) concern itself with the development of
> systems of laws and regulations, that op-
> timize the freedoms of the individual and
> minimize harm to the individual and to
> society from himself and those around him,
> (2) to provide a consistent application
> of all knowledge to rational judgments
> regarding the real hazards and positive
> potentialities inherent in narcotic and
> non-narcotic drugs and other chemical sub-
> stances, (3) to make an objective analysis
> of the effects of the penal law as it re-
> lates to narcotic and non-narcotic drug
> use, possession and sale, (4) to provide
> the executive department and the legis-
> lature with comprehensive information on
> the social, fiscal, and health problems
> associated with narcotics addiction, and
> drug abuse, (5) to study the emerging
> patterns of mixed drug abuse which com-
> plicate present legal approaches, (6) to
> develop a meaningful public information
> program utilizing all forms of modern com-
> munication, (7) to prepare for submission
> to the legislature such changes in exist-
> ing laws and such other measures necessary
> to deter the use of narcotic and non-nar-
> cotic drugs and other chemical substances.

The first fruits of the Commission's efforts
may ripen into new laws in the 1972 session of
the Legislature. The Commission has proposed a
realignment of the possession and sale offenses
reflective of the newly-emergent knowledge of

the comparative harmfulness of drugs. Some general observations can be made without going into specifics. First and very important is a scientifically accurate definition of the various dangerous drugs. Of great interest is the Commission's proposed ameliorations of the penalties for marijuana possession or sale (in some instances) and its proposed stiffening of the penalties for possession or sale of amphetamines, barbiturates and hallucinogens. The fate of these proposals will be interesting to observe.

3. Drug-Related Problems in the Schools.

Of even more interest to school personnel than drug prohibition and penalties may be the laws governing drug-related problems that may be encountered in the schools. Perhaps the two most likely problems will be investigation of drug use and confidential relationships.

School authorities will quite rightly desire to investigate suspected drug use. Indeed it is probably their obligation to do so. The highest court in the state has said that, "It is the affirmative obligation of the school authorities to investigate any charge that a student is using or possessing narcotics and to take appropriate steps if the charge is substantiated." People v. Overton, 20 N.Y. 2d 360 (1967); 393 U. S. 85 (1968); 24 N.Y. 2d 522 (1969).

In the course of investigation the school authorities may desire to search a student or his locker, by themselves or in conjunction with the police. Their right to search a locker has been established by the Overton case just mentioned. In its opinion the course said:

> A school does not supply its students with lockers for illicit use in harboring pilfered property or harmful substances. We deem it a proper function of school authorities to inspect the lockers under their control and to prevent their use in illicit ways or for illegal purposes. We believe the right of inspection is inherent in the authority vested in school administration and that the same must be retained and exercised in the management of our schools if their educational functions are to be maintained and the welfare of the student bodies preserved.

The search of a student's person presents a
more complex and sensitive issue. A police officer cannot stop and search someone at will; a
high degree of suspicion will not suffice. Without a search warrant he may ordinarily search
someone only incident to a valid arrest. (In
addition he has a limited right to frisk a suspect, limited to an exterior search to discover
a weapon.)

The question which arises in the schools is
whether personnel who are not police officers are
bound by the same strictures if they undertake
to search a student. The answer is in some
doubt. In 1970 the State Education Department
of the University of the State of New York published a booklet entitled "Education's Role in
the Prevention of Drug Abuse: Guidelines for
School Programs." As to search of a student's
person the Guidelines state:

> While the inspection of a locker, with or
> without a warrant, is permissible, the
> rule is otherwise with respect to the
> search of the individual. To search an
> individual unless the search is the inci-
> dent of a lawful arrest and not the mere
> occasion which gives rise to the arrest,
> a search warrant should be obtained. School
> authorities should refrain from searching
> individual students, or requiring the empty-
> ing of pockets or removal of clothing. The
> same would apply to a student's automobile
> parked in a student parking lot. (United
> States v. DiRe, 332 U.S. 581; State v.
> Bradbury, 243A 2d 302; People v. Cohen,
> 57 Misc. 2d 366.)

The writer concurs in this advice but calls
the reader's attention to two court decisions to
the contrary. Although not decisions of the
highest court of the state they are nonetheless
significant. The first case is People v. Jackson, 65 Misc. 2d 909 (App. T. 1st Dept. 1971).
The case resulted from an incident in a New York
City high school. As the court summarized the
facts:

> ...On October 27, 1969 the Coordinator of
> Discipline at a city high school received
> information which caused him to proceed
> to a certain classroom. He sought out
> the defendant, a student, in the room and

requested that he accompany him to his
office. This the defendant did willingly.
En route, the Coordinator observed a bulge
in the defendant's left pants pocket and
further observed him continually putting
his hand in and taking it out of the pocket.
As they neared his office, the defendant
bolted for the door at the outside of the
school. As he did this, the Coordinator
noticed a policeman standing in front of the
office and called out to him, "He's got
junk and he's escaping." With that he pur-
sued the defendant and caught up with him
three blocks from the school. The Coordinator grabbed the defendant, who still had
his left hand in his left side pants pocket.
Grabbing defendant's wrist, the latter's
hand came out revealing the nipple of an
eyedropper with other material clenched in
his fist. The Coordinator held defendant's
wrist and said, "Give that to me"; there-
upon the Coordinator opened his hand and
found a set of "works," syringe, eyedropper,
etc. This material, the subject matter of
the motion to suppress, was then turned
over to the police officer who also had pur-
sued the boy and came upon the scene at that
moment.

The trial court suppressed the seized drug evidence, on the ground that the Coordinator of
Discipline, a governmental official, had searched
the student without the prerequisite of probable
cause, in violation of his constitutional rights.
A majority of the appellate court disagreed,
although one judge agreed with the trial court
judge. The opinions are worth quotation.

The judge writing the majority opinion said:

Here, the Coordinator of Discipline of
a city high school, acting with a high
degree of suspicion, but short of probable
cause, searched this student and found him
in possession of a set of narcotics "works."
While a student has the right to be free
of unreasonable search and seizure, school
authorities, in view of the "distinct
relationship" between them and their students and the right of parents to expect
that certain safeguards will be taken,
have "the affirmative obligation to investigate any charge that a student is using

or possessing narcoties," which "becomes a
duty when suspicion arises" (People v. Overton, 20 N.Y. 2d 360, 362-363; see, also
Moore v. Student Affairs Committee, 284 F.
Supp. 725, 729-730). A school official
standing in loco parentis to the children
entrusted to his care, has, inter alia, the
long-honored obligation to protect them
while in his charge, so far as possible,
from harmful and dangerous influences, which
certainly encompasses the bringing to school
by one of them of narcotics and "works,"
whether for sale to other students or for
administering such to himself or other students. I have read the citation of authorities given in the dissenting opinion relating to the "philosophy of loco parentis."
Those cases are not affected by the doctrine
and are inapposite.

What the Constitution (Fourth Amendment)
forbids is not all searches and seizures, but
unreasonable searches and seizures (Elkins
v. United States, 364 U.S. 206, 222). Each
search must be determined in its own setting.
The amendment, as it relates to seized property, after search, does not apply to private
persons. Classifying the Coordinator as a
governmental official, in his capacity and
sphere of responsibility embracing the purpose and duties he is called upon to perform
with respect to his charges, it would not be
unreasonable or unwarranted that he be permitted to search the person of a student
where the school official has reasonable
suspicion that narcotics may be found on the
person of his juvenile charge. Such action,
of an investigatory nature, would and should
be expected of him. Being justified, he
would still be performing this important
function, though three blocks from school,
necessitated by the flight of this errant
boy. As I view the incident, the Coordinator's function and responsibility went with
him during the chase that took the boy
away from the school. In loco parentis
purpose did not end abruptly at the school
door. The need to fulfill that purpose--
including the making of a search--extended
uninterruptedly beyond the school limits
since the defendant chose to run away.
This is a far cry from a situation not stemming from the school, without the nexus
existing here. Absent that nexus, the

search and seizure by the Coordinator would
be unreasonable and unlawful for the obvious
reason that his duties and responsibilities
originate within the school.

To circumscribe the official's action,
in these circumstances, within school limits
would be akin to the incident where the
cinematic county sheriff stops in hot pursuit of the wrongdoer at the county line,
ruefully watching him cross over, powerless
to do anything more.

The dissenting opinion emphasizes that
the search and seizure happened away from
the school and that the action of the policeman and the school official conjoined in
making the search and seizure. This is mis-
placed emphasis, because proper place is not
given to the official's right and duty to
act as he did in the circumstances, originally and independently, in fulfillment of
a quasi-parental obligation. Moreover,
this right and duty did not make him a law
enforcement officer as the dissent suggested.
Rather as the doctrine suggests, and simply
stated, he was acting in a limited manner,
in place of the defendant's parents. In
the landmark case, relating to the duty of
teachers in the supervision of school children, the Court of Appeals in <u>Hoose</u> v.
<u>Drumm</u> (281 N.Y. 54, 57-58) stated: "At
recess periods, not less than in the class
room, a teacher owes it to his charges to
exercise such care of them as a parent of
ordinary prudence would observe in comparable circumstances."

Stated differently, a school teacher, to
a limited extent at least, stands in loco
parentis to pupils under his charge, and
may exercise such powers of control, restraint
and correction over them as may be reasonably
necessary to enable him properly to perform
his duties as a teacher and accomplish the
purposes of education (79 C.J.S., School
and School Districts, #493).

This doctrine is imbedded in the common
law and has received implicit recognition by
our State Legislature through the enactment
of section 35.10 of the Penal Law, which
restates the former Penal Law, section 246
(subds. 4, 6). The section declares: "The
use of physical force upon another person
which would otherwise constitute an offense
is justifiable and not criminal under any

of the following circumstances:

"1. A parent, guardian or other person
entrusted with the care and supervision of
a minor or an incompetent person, and a
teacher or other person entrusted with the
care and supervision of a minor for a
special purpose, may use physical force, but
not deadly physical force, upon such minor
or incompetent person when and to the extent
that he reasonably believes it necessary to
maintain discipline or to promote the welfare of such minor or incompetent person."

Without proper recognition of the doctrine, the reasonableness of the official's
conduct toward the defendant cannot be
properly viewed and concluded. With full
recognition, however, the action of the
official toward the student, taken in school
and away from school, partaking of their
"distinct relationship," may be better understood and accepted as necessary and reasonable in light of loco parentis and in jux-
taposition with the Fourth Amendment (see,
generally, _Terry_ v. _Ohio_, 392 U.S. 1).

As was expressed in _People_ v. _Overton_
(24 N.Y. 2d 522, 526) the school official,
therefore, was performing the "fulfillment
of the trust and responsibility given him by
the city residents" in relation to a high
school student. On remand from the Supreme
Court (292 U.S. 85), the Court of Appeals
held, in effect, that the inspection of the
locker, under attack was not the result of
"legal coercion" but was permissible conduct
in conformity with the in loco parentis
doctrine, conditioned only by reasonable
suspicion. As I view the present incident,
the school official was fulfilling a comparable "trust and responsibility" and similar approval of his conduct should be
accorded without imposition of probable
cause.

Also, appropriate analogy may be made
from section 180-a of the Code of Criminal
Procedure, known as the "Stop and Frisk"
law which permits a police officer to stop
any person in a public place for temporary
questioning when he reasonably suspects
such person is committing or is about to
commit a felony, and to frisk the suspect
for weapons if he reasonably suspects that
his life is in danger. This law is not
cited for comparison of any factual pattern

suggested by that law. The section points
up, however, that one of the absolutes
under the Fourth Amendment, namely, probable
cause, is   displaced by reasonable suspicion
for the reason that a frisk, sometimes liken-
ed to a lesser invasion of a search, is necessary as an incident to inquiry upon grounds
of elemental safety and precaution which
might not initially sustain a search (see
People v. Taggart, 20 N.Y. 2d 335; see, also,
People v. Peters, 18 N.Y. 2d 238; People v.
Sibron, 18 N.Y. 2d 603).

As stated in People v. Peters (supra,
p. 247) "The Fourth Amendment protects not
against all searches and seizures, but
'against unreasonable searches and seizures.'
The doctrine of 'stop and frisk upon reasonable suspicion' does not produce unreasonable
searches and seizures."

The in loco parentis doctrine is so compelling in light of public necessity and as
a social concept antedating the Fourth
Amendment, that any action, including a
search, taken thereunder upon reasonable
suspicion should be accepted as necessary
and reasonable. Seemingly, like rationale
founded on extreme public purpose was used
in Sibron, Peters and Taggart, supra, dispensing with probable cause as a requirement
in the circumstances of those cases.

In Camara v. Municipal Court (387 U.S.
523, 528) the Supreme Court, discussing the
Fourth Amendment declared: "The basic
purpose of this Amendment...is to safeguard
the privacy and security of individuals
against arbitrary invasions by government
officials."

As noted, the rigid standard, probable
cause, may not be imposed upon a school
official if he is expected to act effectively
in loco parentis. While we are far advanced
from the days of the little red schoolhouse,
such advancement has also brought great ills.
Rampant crime and drug abuse threaten our
schools and the youngsters exposed to such
ills. Much could be written about the
ponderous problems that beset parents and
school authorities in their efforts to prevent and stave off the conditions all about
us. We are well aware of the gravity of
these conditions. There is no need for
enlargement. In consequence, greater responsibility has fallen upon those charged

with the well-being and discipline of these
children. What they may do in that regard
should be weighed, on balance, with full
appreciation of their duties and the nature
of that greater responsibility. Only then
can reasonableness be concluded in the context of the prevailing circumstances relating to the Fourth Amendment. Of course,
absolute control should not be handed over
in the everyday dealings with these children.
Reasonable restraint is imposed, less what
the school officials do shall take the
form of authoritarian behavior, trammelling
the rights of the students entrusted to them.
Toward that end, a basis founded at least
upon reasonable grounds for suspecting that
something unlawful is being committed, or
about to be committed, shall prevail before
justifying a search of a student when the
school official is acting in loco parentis.

I, therefore, conclude that within the
framework of this happening, no arbitrary
invasion of the defendant's privacy resulted.
On the contrary, the search and seizure,
based at least upon reasonable grounds for
suspecting that something unlawful was being
committed, or about to be committed, must
be deemed a reasonable search and seizure
within the intendment of the Fourth Amendment as applied to the "distinct relationship" of the high school official to his
student.

The order should be reversed on the law
and the facts. Motion to suppress hypodermic needle and "works" denied and the
case remitted to the court below for further
appropriate proceedings.

The dissenting judge said:

I view this occurrence in a different light.
As my brethren and the District Attorney
concede, the Coordinator of Discipline
acted "with a high degree of suspicion short
of probable cause" when he pulled defendant's
hand from his pocket and seized the hypodermic needle from defendant's clenched
fist. This was not done in the school or
on its grounds; it occurred three blocks
from the school. As the Coordinator and
the defendant had approached the door of
the former's office, defendant had bolted
toward the building's exit and the

Coordinator had taken off in pursuit. The
patrolman regularly assigned to the school
joined the chase when told by the Coordinator that defendant had "junk" and was
escaping. With both of them in pursuit,
the Coordinator, as noted, caught defendant
three blocks away, grabbed defendant's
wrist, pulled defendant's hand from his
pocket and seized the hypodermic syringe,
eyedropper, etc. As the District Attorney
also states, "Had these acts been performed
by a police officer, the evidence obtained
would have been admissible in a criminal
proceedings" (see Mapp v. Ohio, 367 U.S. 643).

When defendant was seized, the Coordinator
was not enforcing a school regulation but,
as a law enforcement agent, was chasing
defendant to make an arrest--and he had no
basis to make the arrest.

I cannot agree that in this context, the
Coordinator was acting as a private citizen
or merely as a teacher, at the place of arrest.

Furthermore, had the policeman searched
defendant, fruits of the search would have
been suppressed. There is no logical reason
to grant the teacher greater rights outside
the school than the patrolman had (see
Dixson v. State of New York, 54 Misc 2d 100;
People v. Williams, 53 Misc 2d 1086). He
was not then acting alone, he was acting in
co-ordination with the patrolman. As such,
his search partook of the infirmity applicable had the arrest been by the patrolman
directly (cf. People v. Horman, 22 N.Y. 2d
378).

The Coordinator of Discipline saw no
crime committed in his presence. Concededly,
he acted on suspicion alone, short of probable cause. Part of his duties as Dean of
Boys, was to maintain security and order at
the school, a facility belonging to the City
of New York. While he was not a peace officer
or police officer classified under sections
154 and 154-a of the Code of Criminal Procedure, when conducting the search and
seizure, he was acting as an agent of the
city government cloaked with police powers
and participating in the governmental
function of safeguarding a municipal facility. (See, People v. Brown, N.Y. L.J.,
Dec. 15, 1970, p. 19, col. 2.) As a citizen, the Coordinator could arrest for an
offense only if committed in his presence

(Code Crim. Pro., #183). A peace officer
can arrest for an offense committed or
attempted in his presence or, if a police
officer, he has reasonable grounds for
believing that an offense is being committed in his presence (Code Crim. Pro.,
#177). The People admit that none of these
grounds existed prior to the seizure of the
contraband in question.

The philosophy of loco parentis is not
an invitation to a teacher to arrest a student on suspicion alone three blocks from
a school (see Kent v. United States, 383
U.S. 541, 554, 556; One 1958 Plymouth Sedan
v. Pennsylvania, 380 U.S. 693; Matter of
Gregory W., 19 N.Y. 2d 55; Incorporated
Vil. of Laurel Hollow v. Laverne Originals,
17 N.Y. 2d 900; People v. Moore, 11 N.Y.
2d 271). Moreover, the cases relied on by
the majority which appear to justify what
would otherwise be illegal search and seizure
on the basis of the "distinct relationship"
are distinguishable. Moore v. Student Affairs Committee (284 J. Supp. 725) involved
the search of a student's room in a college
dormitory; People v. Overton (20 N.Y. 2d
360) involved the entry into lockers on
high school grounds. Neither involved an
off the premises search, and, of greater
importance, a body search.

The invasion of privacy of a location as
to which the prober has some recognized
dominion or right of access is one thing.
The violation of the sanctity of the person
off the school grounds is quite another.
They ought not be equated.

Overton (supra) is further distinguishable
in that it involved an illegal warrant which
was presented to the school authorities.
The Supreme Court of the United States in
Bumper v. North Carolina (391 U.S. 543)
held that where entry was made by law enforcement officers on the strength of an
unlawful warrant and where a relative of
the defendant who was at the premises told
them to "go ahead," this invitation may
not be distorted into a consent to the
search. "The situation," said the court,
"is instinct with coercion--albeit colorably
lawful coercion. Where there is coercion
there cannot be consent." (P. 550) When
Overton (supra) reached the Supreme Court
of the United States, the judgment was

vacated and the case remanded for further
consideration in the light of Bumper (supra).
On remand, the Court of Appeals held that
its original disposition "was proper when
rendered and is unaltered by the spirit, if
not the language" of Bumper (24 N.Y. 2d 522,
524). It was found by the court that unlike
Bumper, the school authorities in Overton
were acting not under the "lawful coercion"
found objectionable in Bumper but within
the ambit of their duties triggered by
their suspicion that something illegal was
hoarded in the school locker by a student.

Overton defines in general terms the
limits of the relationship between student
and school. But that relationship has no
application to areas beyond the geographical
limits of the school and particularly personal searches in off-premises areas.

Just as the second Overton (supra) in interpreting Bumper (supra) restricted the
latter to the "true meaning of what was
written therein" (p. 524), it too should be
similarly restricted to situations where
school authorities have the right and even
the duty to invade. No such right, no such
duty is present where it involves the body
of the defendant--especially where the
search is not on school premises.

The motion to suppress was properly
granted by the court below and, accordingly,
I dissent and vote to affirm.

A similar case is People v. Stewart, 63 Misc.
2d 602 (N.Y.C. Crim. Ct. 1970).

The other problem--confidential relation-
ships--is somewhat less likely to involve administrators. Teachers, counselors and other personnel may become aware that a student is using
drugs; in fact the student may tell them himself.
From this knowledge three questions may arise:
(1) must I tell the police? (2) may I or must
I keep the information confidential, especially
if the student himself has told me of his drug
use? and (3) can I be sued by the student or his
parents if I tell anyone of his drug use?

The hazards of generalizing are especially
great in the law. Nevertheless it can probably
be said in response to the first question that
there is no legal obligation to report a student's drug use to the police. Mere knowledge

of another's criminal conduct does not make one
an active, wilful participant therein. On the
other hand one who participates in or consciously
facilitates another's crime may find himself subject to criminal liability too.

The question of confidential relationship
must be answered in relation to the questioner's
statue. The idea of privileged communication is
of long-standing in the law. It means that various professionals who receive sensitive information in the course of their work may not reveal
such information without the discloser's permission. Suppose, in the school setting, that
the police or prosecutor demanded that school personnel reveal knowledge about a student's drug
use which knowledge was obtained from the student
himself. To quote again from the State Education
Department Guidelines:

> Statutory protection of confidential
> disclosures relates to such professions as
> physician, clergyman, attorney, certified
> psychologist, and certified school social
> worker. No statutory protection on con-
> fidentiality exists or is created as a
> result of a student's enrollment in the
> public school system. The school physician,
> school nurse, the certified psychologist,
> and the certified school social worker, in
> an appropriate situation may be bound to
> confidence as a result of their professional
> standing and their relationship to a par-
> ticular student; such is not the case,
> however, with the guidance counselor, school
> psychologist (unless also a certified psy-
> chologist), a teacher, the principal, or
> other member of the teaching, supervisory,
> or administrative staff.

Related to confidentiality is the third
question of the consequences of disclosure. Suppose a teacher tells a parent that his son or
daughter is using drugs. A disbelieving parent
is likely to respond with indignation and a de-
famation suit on behalf of the "aggrieved"
youngster. The question is a ticklish one without a complete answer. The "Guidelines" stop
short of being very helpful. In the State Education Department's words:

> Although there is no duty to volunteer
> information, any disclosure should be made

with care, discretion, and tact. School
officials should act from knowledge, not
mere suspicion. When the health and safety
of the school community is concerned, school
officials are faced with a pressing and
serious obligation not only to the individual
student but also to the rest of the student
body and to the community at large.

A partial answer or at least some solace can
be found in a law enacted in 1971. The New York
Education Law now provides:

> §3028-a. Students under twenty-one years
> of age suspected of narcotic addiction.
> Any teacher, school administrator, super-
> visor of attendance, attendance teacher
> or attendance officer having reasonable
> cause to suspect that a secondary or
> elementary student under twenty-one years
> of age is addicted to a narcotic drug or
> under the influence of a dangerous drug,
> who reports such information to the appro-
> priate secondary or elementary school
> officials pursuant to the school's drug
> policy or if the school has no drug policy
> to the school's principal or the parents
> of such student under twenty-one years of
> age shall have immunity from any civil
> liability that might otherwise be incurred
> or imposed as a result of the making of
> such a report.

A careful reading of the language reveals that it
is no complete blanket of immunity. The key
phrases--vital but undefined by the law--are
"reasonable cause to suspect," "addicted to a
narcotic drug" and "under the influence of a
dangerous drug." The last would seem to cover
a good number of situations likely to arise, especially since the term "dangerous drug" probably
bears the same comprehensive meaning as it does
when used in the Penal Law to define drug offenses.

Conclusion:

Drug-abuse today--of whatever substance by
whatever age group--is a complex problem for
which there are no simple solutions. Education
is one avenue which may offer some promise. The
current vogue in drug education programs (excluding alcohol and tobacco) is an effort by experts--
some acknowledged, some such as the writer,

self-proclaimed--to provide adequate factual information to parents, educators and young persons.
These groups must then attempt to structure
realistic programs reflecting their best judgment
or value--laden questions. That is no simple task
and it is complicated by the ever-present commun-
ications barrier raised by The Generation Gap.
Students and school personnel do not always communicate effectively. As one student in a Syracuse high school said recently, "Unfortunately
a lot of teachers will never have a student come
to them with a problem" because they "talk at
you" and not with you or to you. Parents and
children do not always communicate effectively
either. This failure is epitomized by the tragic
case of Linda Fitzpatrick. Unknown to her parents seventeen year old Linda inhabited the drug
world of Greenwich Village in New York City as
well as the affluent world of Greenwich, Conn.
She was involved heavily in the former world and
eventually met her fate there--battered to death
by bricks in the basement of an apartment building. Her parents were incredulous upon discovery
of her lifestyle in the drug world ("The New
York Times," Oct. 16, 1967, p. 1). Her brother's
more resigned reaction was: "It's too late for
the whole thing to do us much good. But maybe
someone else can learn something from it."

Communication, of course, is a two-way process and young persons must listen and learn.
Some at least are doing so, as evidenced by the
astute answers of some students of comparatively
tender years. "The Syracuse Post-Standard" of
January 22, 1972 in its "Young Ideas" column
asked junior high school students: "In your
opinion, what are the reasons for young persons
experimenting with, and in some cases, abusing
drugs?" The responses are illuminating and encouraging to those concerned with drug abuse.

A thirteen year old, eighth-grade girl said:

I think the reasons for young people
experimenting and abusing drugs are to
be in with the crowd or just to be, as
people put it, "cool." Sometimes people
use the excuse that they have a problem
and want to get away from it, but turning
to drugs isn't going to solve the problem.
Some young people say they enjoy taking
drugs, while others say they need the
drugs and still others take drugs for no

reason at all. Foolish reasons, aren't
they?

A fourteen year old, ninth-grade girl said:

   I believe that young people use drugs
because it is a way out of life and reality.
Some people just can't face reality as it
is, and don't try themselves to change it.
Sure, their parents might badger and nag
them, but so do other parents of kids who
don't take drugs. A person has got to be
strong and fight for a good life without
using a crutch of drugs.

The other responses were similar. Perhaps the
real drug experts are those reading and not those
writing drug education handbooks.

NEW YORK STATE DRUG LAWS*

I. OFFENSES

   A. Definitions

      1. New York Penal Law

        #220.00 <u>Dangerous Drug Offenses;</u>
<u>Definitions of Terms</u>

The following definitions are applicable to this article:

1. "Narcotic drug" means any drug, article or substance declared to be "narcotic drugs" in section three thousand three hundred one of the public health law.
2. "Depressant or stimulant drug" means any drug, article or substance declared to be a "depressant or stimulant drug" in section three thousand three hundred seventy-one of the public health law.
3. "Hallucinogenic drug" means any drug, article or substance declared to be "hallucinogenic drugs" in section two hundred twenty-nine of the mental hygiene law.
4. "Dangerous drug" means any narcotic drug, depressant or stimulant drug, or hallucinogenic drug.
5. "Sell" means to sell, exchange, give or dispose of to another, or to offer or agree to do the same.
6. "Unlawfully" means in violation of article thirty-three, article thirty-three-A or article thirty-three-B of the public health law or section two hundred twenty-nine of the mental hygiene law.
7. "Ounce" means an avoirdupois ounce as applied to solids and semisolids, and a fluid ounce as applied to liquids.

      2. New York Public Health Law

---

*These laws are correct as of this printing.

#3301 Definitions

The following words and phrases,
as used in this article, shall have
the following meanings, unless the
context otherwise requires:
    *   *   *   *
38. "Narcotic," "narcotics," or
"narcotic drugs" shall mean opium,
coca leaves, marihuana (cannabis,
sativa and all other substance,
whether synthetic or in plant form,
which contain the active ingredients
of cannabis, sativa or delta-1-
tetrahydro cannabinol, monoterpene
numbering system as used by Mechoulan or delta-3-tetrahydro cannabinol
or delta-6-tetrahydro cannabinol or
delta-8-tetrahydro cannabinol or
delta-9-tetrahydro cannabinol as
numbered by Korte and Isbell or
cannabidiol or cannabinol), pethidine (isonipecaine, meperidine), and
opiates or their compound, manufacture, salt, alkaloid, or derivative, and every substance neither
chemically nor physically distinguishable from them and exempted and ex-
cepted preparations containing such
drugs or their derivatives, by whatever trade name identified and
whether produced directly or indirectly by extraction from substances of vegetable origin, or independently by means of chemical
synthesis or by a combination of
extraction and chemical synthesis,
as the same are designated in the
federal narcotic laws and as specified in the administrative rules
and regulations on narcotic control
as promulgated by the commissioner
pursuant to the authority vested in
him under section thirty-three
hundred two of this article.

3. New York Public Health Law

#3371 Definitions

When used in this article, the following words and phrases shall
have the meanings ascribed to them
in this section:

1. "Depressant or stimulant drug" means:

(a) any drug which contains any quantity of barbituric acid or any of the salts of barbituric acid; or any derivative of barbituric acid which has been designated by the commissioner as habit forming; or
(b) any drug which contains any quantity of amphetamine or any of its optical isomers; any salt of amphetamine or any salt of an optical isomer of amphetamine; or any substance which the commissioner, after investigation, has found to be, and by regulation designated as, habit forming because of its stimulant effect of the central nervous system; or
(c) any drug which contains any quantity of a substance which the commissioner, after investigation, has found to have, and by regulation designates as having, a potential for abuse because of its depressant or stimulant effect on the central nervous system or its hallucinatory effect; except that the commissioner shall not designate under this paragraph or under paragraph (b) hereof any substance that is a narcotic drug as defined in article thirty-three of the public health law.

4. New York Mental Hygiene Law

(429)[1] 229. Hallucinogenic Drugs
  *   *   *   *

For the purpose of this section, the term "hallucinogenic drugs" shall mean and include stramonium, mescaline or peyote, lysergic acid diethylamide and psilocybin, or any salts or derivatives or compounds of any preparations or mixtures thereof.
  *   *   *   *

B. Possession Offenses

(1. Provision renumbered but unchanged.)

255

1. New York Penal Law

    #220.05 Criminal Possession of a
    Dangerous Drug in the Sixth Degree

    A person is guilty of criminal pos-
    session of a dangerous drug in the
    sixth degree when he knowingly and
    unlawfully possesses a dangerous
    drug.

    Criminal possession of a dangerous
    drug in the sixth degree is a class
    A misdemeanor.

2. New York Penal Law

    #220.10 Criminal Possession of a
    Dangerous Drug in the Fifth Degree

    A person is guilty of criminal pos-
    session of a dangerous drug in the
    fifth degree when he knowingly and
    unlawfully possesses a dangerous
    drug with intent to sell the same.

    Criminal possession of a danger-
    ous drug in the fifth degree is
    a class E felony.

3. New York Penal Law

    #220.15 Criminal Possession of a
    Dangerous Drug in the Fourth Degree

    A person is guilty of criminal pos-
    session of a dangerous drug in the
    fourth degree when he knowingly
    and unlawfully possesses a narcotic
    drug:

    1. With intent to see the same; or

    2. Consisting of (a) twenty-five
    or more cigarettes containing can-
    nabis; or (b) one or more prepar-
    ations, compounds, mixtures or
    substances of an aggregate weight
    of (i) one-eighth ounce or more,
    containing any of the respective
    alkaloids or salts of heroin,
    morphine or cocaine, or (ii) one-
    quarter ounce or more, containing

any cannabis, or (iii) one-half
ounce or more, containing raw or
prepared opium, or (iv) one-half
ounce or more, containing one or
more than one of any of the other
narcotic drugs.

Criminal possession of a danger-
our drug in the fourth degree is
a class D felony.

4. New York Penal Law

#220.20 Criminal Possession of a
Dangerous Drug in the Third Degree

A person is guilty of criminal possession of a dangerous drug in the
third degree when he knowingly and
unlawfully possesses a narcotic
drug consisting of (a) one hundred
or more cigarettes containing cannabis; or (b) one or more preparations, compounds, mixtures or substances of an aggregate weight of
(i) one or more ounces containing
any of the respective alkaloids
or salts of heroin, morphine or
cocaine, or (ii) one or more ounces,
containing any cannabis, or (iii)
two or more ounces, containing raw
or prepared opium, or (iv) two or
more ounces, containing one or
more than one of any of the other
narcotic drugs.

Criminal possession of a dangerous
drug in the third degree is a class
C felony.

5. New York Penal Law

#220.22 Criminal Possession of a
Dangerous Drug in the Second Degree

A person is guilty of criminal possession of a dangerous drug in the
second degree when he knowingly and
unlawfully possesses a narcotic
drug consisting of one or more
preparations, compounds, mixtures
or substances of an aggregate weight
of eight ounces or more, containing

any of the respective alkaloids
or salts of heroin, morphine or
cocaine, or containing raw or
prepared opium.

Criminal possession of a dangerous Drug in the second degree is
a class B felony.

6. New York Penal Law

#220.23 Criminal Possession of a
Dangerous Drug in the First Degree

A person is guilty of criminal possession of a dangerous drug in the
first degree when he knowingly and
unlawfully possesses a narcotic
drug consisting of one or more preparations, compounds, mixtures or
substances of an aggregate weight
of sixteen ounces or more containing
any of the respective alkaloids or
salts of heroin, morphine or cocaine, or containing raw or prepared opium.

Criminal possession of a dangerous drug in the first degree is a
class A felony.

C. Sales Offenses

1. New York Penal Law

#220.30 Criminally Selling a Dan-
gerous Drug in the Fourth Degree

A person is guilty of criminally
selling a dangerous drug in the
fourth degree when he knowingly and
unlawfully sells a dangerous drug.

Criminally selling a dangerous
drug in the fourth degree is a
class D felony.

2. New York Penal Law

#220.35 Criminally Selling a Dan-
gerous Drug in the Third Degree

A person is guilty of criminally

selling a dangerous drug in the
third degree when he knowingly and
unlawfully sells a narcotic drug.

Criminally selling a dangerous
drug in the third degree is a class
C felony.

3. New York Penal Law

#220.40 <u>Criminally Selling a Dan-
gerous Drug in the Second Degree</u>

A person is guilty of criminally
selling a dangerous drug in the
second degree when he knowingly and
unlawfully sells a narcotic drug:

1. To a person less than twenty-
one years old; or

2. Consisting of one or more preparations, compounds, mixtures or
substances of an aggregate weight
of eight ounces or more, containing
any of the respective alkaloids or
salts of heroin, morphine or cocaine,
or containing raw or prepared opium.

4. New York Penal Law

#220.44 <u>Criminally Selling a Dan-
gerous Drug in the First Degree</u>

A person is guilty of criminally
selling a dangerous drug in the
first degree when he knowingly and
unlawfully sells a narcotic drug
consisting of one or more preparations, compounds, mixtures or substances of an aggregate weight of
sixteen ounces or more, containing
any of the respective alkaloids or
salts of heroin, morphine or cocaine,
or containing raw or prepared opium.

Criminally selling a dangerous
drug in the first degree is a class
A felony.

II. SENTENCES

Sentencing in drug cases, as in all

criminal cases is a somewhat individual
proceeding. Nevertheless, this chart
below gives some indication of the possible
sentences for drug crimes.

Designation of Crime	Maximum Imprisonment	Minimum
Class A Misdemeanor	1 year	
Class A Felony	Life Imprisonment	15 years
Class B Felony	25 years	8 and 1/3 years
Class C Felony	15 years	5 years
Class D Felony	7 years	2 and 1/3 years
Class E Felony	4 years	1 year

DRUG SURVEY IN SYRACUSE SCHOOLS

1-2 SCHOOL ___RESULTS FOR TOTAL CITY___
 (1-2)

3-4 GRADE ___TOTAL NUMBER 15,140___
 (3-4)

```
_____07
_____08
_____09
_____10
_____11
_____12
```

5. SEX
 (5)
```
_____1. Male          TOTAL
_____2. Female        NUMBER
```

6. Have you ever smoked Marijuana (Pot)?
 (6)

| 87.3 | 1. No | 13,221 |
| 12.1 | 2. Yes | 1,843 |

7. Are you currently smoking Marijuana (Pot)?
 (7)

93.1	1. No	14,100
2.7	2. Yes, once or twice a month	418
1.1	3. Yes, weekends only	179
0.4	4. Yes, once a week	61
1.4	5. Yes, more than once a week but not daily	221
0.6	6. Daily	100
6.5	TOTAL YES	979 15,079

8. Have you ever tried Speed?
 (8)

| 96.5 | 1. No | 14,617 |
| 3.1 | 2. Yes | 480 |

9. Are you currently using Speed?
 (9)

98.4	1. No	14,902
0.4	2. Yes, once or twice a month	75
0.1	3. Yes, weekends only	27
-	4. Yes, once a week	15

0.1	5. Yes, more than once a week, but not daily	23	
0.2	6. Daily	38	
1.2	TOTAL YES	178	15,080

10. Have you ever tried Heroin?
    (10)

98.4	1. No	14,898
1.1	2. Yes	178

11. Are you currently using Heroin?
    (11)

98.8	1. No	14,972
0.2	2. Yes, once or twice a month	35
—	3. Yes, weekends only	10
—	4. Yes, once a week	7
—	5. Yes, more than once a week, but not daily	13
0.1	6. Daily	28
0.6	TOTAL	15,065

12. Have you ever tried Acid?
    (12)

95.4	1. No	14,449
4.0	2. Yes	613

13. Are you currently using Acid?
    (13)

97.2	1. No	14,730	
1.1	2. Yes, once or twice a month	169	
0.3	3. Yes, weekends only	50	
0.1	4. Yes, once a week	26	
0.1	5. Yes, more than once a week, but not daily	24	
0.2	6. Daily	33	
2.0	TOTAL YES	302	15,032

14. If you answered "yes" to the above, have you any flash backs?
    (14)

65.7	1. No	403
34.3	2. Yes	210
		613

15. Have you ever tried Pep Pills?
    (15)

91.7	1. No	13,894
7.2	2. Yes	1,103

16. Are you currently using Pep Pills?
    (16)

97.0	1. No	14,697
1.0	2. Yes, once or twice a month	155
0.2	3. Yes, weekends only	33
0.1	4. Yes, once a week	26
0.2	5. Yes, more than once a week, but not daily	45
0.4	6. Daily	75
2.2	TOTAL YES	15,031

17. Have you ever sniffed Glue or other volatile substances?
    (volatile substances; gasoline, aerosol, paint thinner, etc.)
    (17)

88.2	1. No	13,357
11.0	2. Yes	1,676

18. Are you currently sniffing Glue or other volatiles?
    (18)

97.5	1. No	14,766
1.0	2. Yes, once or twice a month	162
0.2	3. Yes, weekends only	34
0.1	4. Yes, once a week	16
0.2	5. Yes, more than once a week, but not daily	35
0.2	6. Daily	43
1.9	TOTAL YES	290 15,056

19. When did you first try drugs?
    (19)

84.1	1. Never have	2,746
1.3	2. Before age 13	201
1.6	3. 13 years old	244
2.7	4. 14 years old	416
3.2	5. 15 years old	485
3.2	6. 16 years old	487
2.4	7. 17 years old	375
0.4	8. 18 years old	70
-	9. 19 years old and over	407

20. Why did you start using drugs?
    (20)

84.3	1. Never have	12,772
0.8	2. To be part of "the group"	124
1.0	3. To expand the "mind"	154
1.7	4. To escape from "problems"	261
8.5	5. Curious about its effects	1,298
2.6	6. Other	407

21. Who started you using drugs?
    (21)

84.2	1. Never have	12,751
7.7	2. Yourself	713
5.9	3. A friend	905
2.4	4. A group of friends	365
0.5	5. An older brother or sister	89
0.3	6. Parent	46
0.2	7. A stranger	41
0.7	8. Other	109

22. Where do you usually use drugs?
    (22)

85.5	1. Never do	12,952
1.2	2. At school	193
2.4	3. In my own home	364
3.7	4. At parties or social gatherings	562
1.0	5. In cars	166
0.6	6. Parks	99
1.3	7. Friends' houses	210
1.7	8. All of the above 2-7	262
1.1	9. Other	167

23. With whom do you usually use drugs?
    (23)

84.5	1. Never have	12,800
2.2	2. Alone	340
0.3	3. With younger students	58
7.3	4. With students my own age	1,119
0.5	5. With non students my own age	87
0.8	6. With college students	131

264

```
     1.0        7. With older
                   students not
                   in college      162
     0.2        8. With adults      43
     1.3        9. Other           210
```

24. If you have not tried drugs is it because of
    (24)
```
    18.1        1. Legal reasons   2,754
    24.8        2. Moral reasons   3,769
     9.7        3. Fear of having
                   a bad trip or
                   bad experience  1,474
     4.7        4. No opportunity    714
     2.9        5. Parent disap-
                   proval            450
    23.5        6. Other reasons   3,570
```

25. If you have tried drugs and no longer use
    them, is it because of
    (25)
```
     6.2        1. Legal reasons    943
     3.7        2. Moral reasons    565
     1.7        3. Knowing friends
                   who have had bad
                   experiences      262
     1.0        4. Influence of a
                   friend who is a
                   non-user         166
     0.9        5. Bad personal
                   experience with
                   drugs            147
     0.7        6. Parent pressure  121
     2.0        7. Education as to
                   the use of drugs 305
     8.5        8. Other reasons  1,296
```

26. Have you ever sold Marijuana (Pot)?
    (26)
```
    95.5        1. No            14,467
     3.1        2. Yes              477
```

27. Have you ever sold Speed, Acid, or Pep Pills?
    (27)
```
    97.1        1. No            14,714
     1.9        2. Yes              302
```

28. Have you ever sold Heroin?
    (28)
```
    98.3        1. No            14,888
     0.7        2. Yes              118
```

29. Have you ever purchased Marijuana (Pot) on school property?
    (29)
    | 95.4 | 1. No | 14,446 |
    | 3.8 | 2. Yes | 580 |

30. Have you ever purchased Pep Pills on school property?
    (30)
    | 97.2 | 1. No | 14,725 |
    | 1.9 | 2. Yes | 295 |

31. Have you ever purchased Acid on school property?
    (31)
    | 97.4 | 1. No | 14,757 |
    | 1.7 | 2. Yes | 258 |

32. Have you ever purchased Speed on school property?
    (32)
    | 97.9 | 1. No | 14,825 |
    | 1.2 | 2. Yes | 185 |

33. Have you ever accepted for free drugs on school property?
    (33)
    | 94.1 | 1. No | 14,250 |
    | 3.9 | 2. Yes | 605 |

34. How difficult is it to purchase soft drugs?
    (34)
    | 14.7 | 1. They are not available to my knowledge | 2,239 |
    | 1.9 | 2. They are difficult to obtain | 291 |
    | 24.2 | 3. They are easy to obtain | 3,665 |
    | 55.3 | 4. I don't really know | 8,380 |

35. How difficult is it to purchase hard drugs?
    (35)
    | 15.5 | 1. They are not available to my knowledge | 2,359 |
    | 6.6 | 2. They are difficult to obtain | 1,002 |
    | 10.0 | 3. They are easy to obtain | 1,526 |

___64.0___ 4. I don't really
            know   9,691

36. Should Marijuana be legalized?
    (36)
    ___71.9___ 1. No   10,895
    ___24.4___ 2. Yes   3,701

37. If you had an opportunity to try drugs,
    would you try?

    A. (38) Marijuana
    ___88.6___ 1. No   11,715
    ___7.3____ 2. Yes   2,225
    ___2.7____ 3. Currently
               using   827

    B. (39) Speed
    ___93.7___ 1. No   14,191
    ___3.4____ 2. Yes   528
    ___1.1____ 3. Currently
               using   168

    C. (40) Acid
    ___94.1___ 1. No   14,249
    ___2.9____ 2. Yes   448
    ___1.2____ 3. Currently   191
               using

    D. (41) Heroin
    ___95.5___ 1. No   14,462
    ___1.4____ 2. Yes   212
    ___0.4____ 3. Currently   70
               üsing

42. If you were having a problem with drugs, who
    would you turn to first for help in your
    school?
    (42)
    ___22.6___ 1. Guidance
               Counselor   3,428
    ___7.4____ 2. School Nurse-
               teacher   1,131
    ___3.7____ 3. Physical Edu-
               cation Teacher   566
    ___4.0____ 4. Principal or
               Assistant
               Principal   620
    ___3.7____ 5. Science teacher   564
    ___4.6____ 6. Health Education
               Teacher   711
    ___22.2___ 7. Another student   3,367

267

```
   12.8        8. There is no one   1,943
   12.9        9. Other             1,955
```

43. If you were having a problem with drugs,
    who would you turn to first for help
    outside of school?
    (43)

```
   28.2      1. Parents            4,278
    5.5      2. Other adult          836
   24.8      3. Friend             3,767
   10.9      4. Clergyman (Min-
                ister, Priest,
                Rabbi)             1,661
    1.1      5. Law Officer          173
    3.5      6. Community Agency
                (DEN or 1012)        541
   11.6      7. Doctor or
                Hospital           1,765
    4.5      8. There is no one      692
    4.2      9. Other                644
```

44. How well informed are you about drugs?
    (44)

```
   17.8      1. Not very well
                informed           2,708
   26.7      2. Have some
                information        4,044
   38.8      3. Fairly well
                informed           5,887
   14.5      4. Very well
                informed           2,199
```

45. Do you think that the use of certain drugs
    has any effect on the unborn child?
    (45)

```
    6.0      1. No                   913
   76.3      2. Yes               11,556
   15.9      3. Don't know         2,411
```

46. Would you recommend the use of drugs to a
    person who means a lot to you (friends,
    relatives, etc.)?
    (46)

```
   85.6      1. No                12,962
    3.9      2. Yes                  594
    8.6      3. Don't know         1,313
```

47. In my opinion, I would be most willing to
    have information on drugs presented by
    (check one)
    (47)

```
    3.8      1. Priest, Minister
                Rabbi                578
    6.1      2. Police               931
```

56.7	3.	Ex-Addict	8,585
3.9	4.	Classroom teacher	594
3.6	5.	Parent	556
13.8	6.	Medical	2,090
2.6	7.	Pupil Services Personnel (Guidance Counselor, School Nurse-Teacher Psychologist)	396
2.2	8.	Community Specialist	346
4.1	9.	Other	634

48. Which of the following educational techniques would you recommend to give you information about drugs?
(48)

30.8	1.	Small group with discussion leader	4,664
8.1	2.	Large group (assemblies)	1,228
25.4	3.	Films-filmstrips or other audiovisual materials	3,850
20.7	4.	Independent conference with someone knowledgeable about drugs	3,141
4.8	5.	Information resource center in school for independent study	740
6.4	6.	Other	973

49. In which of the following groups would you classify your family income?
(49)

6.3	1.	Up to $5,000 per year (less than $100 per week)	956
27.4	2.	From $5,000 to $10,000 per year (100 to $200 per week)	4,152
20.6	3.	$10,000 to $15,000 per year ($200 to $300 per week)	3,125

| 9.9 | 4. Over $15,000 per year | 1,513 |
| 32.7 | 5. I don't know my family income | 4,952 |

50. Please check one of the following:
(50)

45.1	1. My father or male guardian works	6,830
9.3	2. My mother or female guardian works	1,412
37.6	3. Both parents or guardians work	5,697
4.1	4. Neither parents or guardians work	627

51. What is the highest level of education completed by your father or male guardian? (check one)
(51)

15.0	1. Junior High School	2,279
39.3	2. Senior High School or Equivalency	5,953
2.4	3. Less than 1 year college	370
4.3	4. 1 year college	665
3.8	5. Business school or college	584
1.7	6. Vocational train-	
4.1	7. Junior college or other 2 year college	630
12.1	8. 4 year college	1,845
9.5	9. Education beyond 4 years college	1,439

52. What is the highest level of education completed by your mother or female guardian? (check one)
(52)

13.6	1. Junior High School	2,071
48.7	2. Senior High School	7,375
1.6	3. Less than 1 year college	252
3.2	4. 1 year college	489
7.2	5. Business school or college	1,092

1.6	6.	Vocational training program	261
4.1	7.	Junior college or other 2 year college	630
12.1	8.	4 year college	1,845
9.5	9.	Education beyond 4 years college	1,439

52. What is the highest level of education completed by your mother or female guardian? (check one)
(52)

13.6	1.	Junior High School	2,071
48.7	2.	Senior High School	7,375
1.6	3.	Less than 1 year college	252
3.2	4.	1 year college	489
7.2	5.	Business school or college	1,092
1.6	6.	Vocational training program	252
4.0	7.	Junior college or other 2 year college	609
9.5	8.	4 year college	1,444
4.7	9.	Education beyond 4 years college	714

53. Do you have a brother or sister who is now in college or has graduated from college?
(52)

65.7	1.	No	9,961
31.6	2.	Yes	4,791

54. Are you living with? (check one)
(54)

79.7	1.	Mother & Father	12,081
12.9	2.	Mother only	1,960
2.1	3.	Father only	321
1.5	4.	Male and Female guardian	238
0.1	5.	Male guardian only	25
0.4	6.	Female guardian only	70
0.1	7.	Alone	30
0.2	8.	With a friend or friends	43
0.6	9.	Other	101

55. Which of the following represent your relationship with your father or male guardian?
(55)

    34.7   1. I can talk to him anytime about my problems   5,266

    37.4   2. I can talk to him some of the time   **5,669**

    17.2   3. I can't talk to him at all about my problems   2,604

    6.7   4. I have no father or male guardian   1,021

56. Which of the following represent your relationship with your mother or female guardian?
(56)

    50.5   1. I can talk with her anytime about my problems   7,651

    34.7   2. I can talk with her some of the time   5,265

    9.9   3. I can't talk to her at all about my problems   1,513

    1.4   4. I have no mother or female guardian   217

57. Do you consider yourself to be
(57)

    68.3   1. An average student   10,351

    23.7   2. An above average student   3,598

    4.5   3. A below average student   688

Total N = 15,140